More Praise for

The Many Joys of Sex Toys

"When I first introduced vibrators to feminists in the early seventies, I had to hunt down electric body massagers in the small appliance sections of department stores! Now everyone can take a delightful romp through the ultimate how-to handbook and read about couples and singles happily embracing 'the many joys of sex toys.'"

—BETTY DODSON, PH.D., AUTHOR OF *SEX FOR ONE* AND *ORGASMS FOR TWO*

"Get in the habit. Grab the Rabbit!
For the ultimate touch, Fukuoku does so much.
If you're really hot, go for the G spot.

Anne Semans gives a whole new meaning to 'toys are us'!"

—SUE JOHANSON, HOST OF *TALK SEX WITH SUE JOHANSON*, OXYGEN TV

"Packed with recipes for pleasure, this engaging guide shows exactly how to get sex toys off the shelf and between your sheets where they belong!

Semans dishes up explicit advice and erotic inspiration with her trademark warmth and wit."

—Cathy Winks, coauthor of The Good Vibrations Guide to Sex and Sexy Mamas

"I just read The Many Joys of Sex Toys. I'm kind of a technophobe but some of these sounded great, especially the Audi-Oh. If you don't know what that is, you need to find out! Plus, the descriptions of sex toy play are interspersed with erotic stories, some of which are not only sexy but hilarious. I'll never think of Thanksgiving dinner the same way again."

—Barbara Keesling, author of The Good Girl's Guide to Bad Girl Sex

"The Many Joys of Sex Toys is the best, most comprehensive guide to erotic enhancements ever. And who better to write it than the nation's leading expert, Anne Semans, a noted sex toy pioneer ever since her years at Good Vibrations, the woman-oriented sex shop in San Francisco. This book is chock-full of great information, and friendly, practical suggestions. No matter whether you're a sex toy novice or connoisseur, you'll treasure this guide as much as your favorite vibrator. And I suggest taking off your glasses before reading the ten steamy sex toy tales. If you don't, they'll fog up."

—Michael Castleman, author of Great Sex: A Man's Guide to the Secret Principles of Total-Body Sex

Also by Anne Semans, with Cathy Winks

Sexy Mamas: Keeping Your Sex Life Alive While
   Raising Kids

The Good Vibrations Guide to Sex: The Most
   Complete Sex Manual Ever Written

Sex Toy Tales

The Woman's Guide to Sex on the Web

Anne Semans

BROADWAY BOOKS

NEW YORK

The
Many
Joys
of
Sex
Toys

THE ULTIMATE HOW-TO HANDBOOK

FOR COUPLES AND SINGLES

PRINTED IN THE UNITED STATES OF AMERICA

BROADWAY BOOKS and its logo, a letter B bisected on the diagonal, are trademarks of Random House, Inc.

Visit our website at www.broadwaybooks.com

First edition published 2004

Book design by Caroline Cunningham
Illustrated by Phoebe Gloeckner

Library of Congress Cataloging-in-Publication Data

Semans, Anne.
    The many joys of sex toys : the ultimate how-to handbook for couples and singles / by Anne Semans.
        p. cm.
    Includes bibliographical references.
    (alk. paper)
    1. Sex. 2. Sex customs. 3. Sexual excitement. I. Title.
HQ21.S4444 2004
613.9'6—dc22
                                                            2004045104

ISBN 0-7679-1680-8

10 9 8 7 6 5 4 3 2 1

Contents

Acknowledgments   xi

Introduction   xiii

LEARN

Sex Toy Joys: Why You Should Try a Sex Toy   3

Toys for All Seasons: Basic Sex Toy Styles   10

A Pleasure Primer: Your Body's Hot Spots   26

Maximizing Pleasure: Tips for Sex Toy Success   38

Taking Care of Business: Care and Safety   46

PLAY

The Blissful Buzz: Masturbating with a Clitoral Vibrator   53

Priming the Pump: Masturbating with a Penis Sleeve   61

Steamy Toy Tale: Bus Ride by Colin Ladd   65

G Marks the Spot: The Hunt for the G Spot   74

The Right Tool for the Job: Stimulating Multiple
      Pleasure Points   83

Steamy Toy Tale: Catalog Shopping by Kate Dominic   88

Going for Broke: The Quest for Multiple Orgasms   93
Pump It Up: Get Bigger, Last Longer   100
All Hands on Deck: Hand Jobs Made Simple   105

Steamy Toy Tale: Thanksgiving with the In-laws
by Lauren Mills   112

The Love Muscle: Exercising Your PC Muscle   123
Look, Ma, No Hands: The Art of the Hands-free Dildo Play   127

Steamy Toy Tale: A Girl's Best Friend by Kristina Wright   131

Queen Bee Abuzz: Using a Vibrator in the
   Woman-on-Top Position   140
Missionary Zeal: Spicing Up the Missionary Position with a
   Cock Ring Vibrator   144
Four on the Floor: Doing It Doggie-Style with a
   Hands-free Vibrator   149

Steamy Toy Tale: Secrets by Julia Rebecca   154

Sit Up and Take Notice: Add a Vibrator to the Sitting Position   167
The Slow Simmer: Snuggling Up to a Vibrator in the
   Spoons Position   171
Double Trouble: The Art of Double Penetration   175
Blow Him Away: Give a Blow Job with a Buzz   181

Steamy Toy Tale: Ixchel Does It All by Sage Vivant   188

Ladies' Night: Performing Creative Cunnilingus   192
Bottoms Up: Massaging the Prostate with Anal Beads   199

Steamy Toy Tale: The Meeting by G. Merlin Beck   205

Please Enter from the Rear: Anal Intercourse with a Dildo   216

Baby's Got Back: Masturbating with a Butt Plug   222

Steamy Toy Tale: A String of Pearls by Madeleine Oh   228

The Touch of Love: Erotic Massage for Beginners   236

What's the Buzz? Hot Talk Meets High Tech   243

Steamy Toy Tale: At Home with the Vibrapen
by Joy VanNuys   249

Log On and Get Off: Cybersex with a Sex Toy   252

Wet and Wild: Underwater Sex Adventures   258

Exercising Restraint: Playing with Light Bondage   262

Steamy Toy Tale: Jane's Bonds by Shanna Germain   270

SHOP

Getting the Goods: Where to Shop for Sex Toys   277

The Art of the Deal: Shopping Tips for the Savvy Consumer   285

RESOURCES

Recommended Toy Stores   293

Sex Information Hotlines   294

Favorite Sex Sites   295

Recommended Books   296

Recommended Videos   297

About the Author   299

About the Authors of the Steamy Toy Tales   301

Acknowledgments

Because a picture is worth a thousand words, I owe a debt of gratitude to Phoebe Gloeckner for illustrating all the sexual activities in this book. I also appreciate the ten talented authors whose erotic stories bring sex toys to life in a way that nonfiction can't. Their bios are at the end of this book.

Many thanks to my agent, Amy Rennert, as well as my enthusiastic editor, Kris Puopolo, and her assistant, Beth Haymaker. I appreciate the unique contributions of the individuals who helped with research and ideas: Jenne Holmes, Chris Bridges, Krissy Cababa, Joyce Solano, Adrienne Bennedicks, Carly Milne, M. Christian, Shar Rednour, Jackie Bruckman, Ann Whidden, Caroline Streeter, Genanne Walsh, and Mary Ann Mohanraj.

Much love to my colleague and dear friend, Cathy Winks, for giving me the courage to go it alone. Special thanks to Susie Bright for the well-timed encouragement and for always being a great role model. And thanks to Petra Zebroff, for restoring my faith in the old-school tradition of sex information sharing. All three of these women are pioneers in the sex world.

On the home front, thanks to my babysitters, Jennifer Wong,

Jeffrey Abbott, Shannon Bradley, Trish Chapman, and especially Sheila Semans, who gave up many weekend hours. Without their patience, love, and flexibility, this book would never have seen the light of day. Finally, thanks to Roxanne, a young girl who understands the meaning of "deadline," and to baby Lily, who's always ready with a smile.

Introduction

I was nineteen when I took my first spin with a vibrator. I spent the summer with a friend who kept her beloved electric vibrator lying by her bed. One day while she was out my curiosity got the better of me and, after giving the toy a quick sponge bath, I turned it on and pressed it against my clitoris. Nothing could have prepared me for the delicious and totally unexpected sensations that traveled through my body, not to mention the powerful orgasm that rippled clear through to my toes. Needless to say, I made up a lot of excuses to stay indoors that summer, and enjoyed some of the best orgasms of my life.

I tell that story because it illustrates how simple erotic exploration can lead to a richer sexuality. In the twenty years since my maiden voyage I've encouraged thousands of people to "just try sex toys, you'll like them." In my conversations I've encountered all kinds of stereotypes about sex toys, but I discovered they're usually a smoke screen masking feelings of embarrassment, fear, or discomfort. Trying anything new involves risk, but when pleasure is at stake, success becomes its own reward. A sex toy can open up new vistas of pleasure—who needs a better incentive to try one than that?

Perhaps one of the most tenacious myths about sex toys is that they're okay to use alone, but they're off limits once you're in a relationship. By tossing your toys back into the closet (or burying them, as did a friend of mine), you miss out on an exciting opportunity for erotic discovery *with* your partner. Sex toys create new possibilities: for better orgasms, for new positions, for finding erogenous zones, and for improved communication. All that will become obvious to you as you read—or play—your way through *The Many Joys of Sex Toys*.

I want to draw your attention to the heart of this book, the twenty-five sexual activities described in the Play section. They represent the most popular types of sex play—from masturbation to oral sex to anal penetration—but each is given an exotic new twist by the addition of a sex toy. Rather than overwhelm you with exhaustive lists of sex toys and all the body parts they can arouse (as sex toy catalogs often do), I focus on a specific activity, and recommend one toy that will get the job done in style. And because I don't think one technique will work for everyone, I also suggest variations on the activity so you can adapt it to your tastes. Although the activities are written for heterosexual couples, you'll find that most can be enjoyed—or easily adapted—for couples of any sexual orientation.

I've found that between figuring out what they want to do sexually, and finding a toy to do it, people often give up in exasperation. *The Many Joys of Sex Toys* is designed to make sex toy play simple, fun, and exciting. Much as you'd choose a recipe from a cookbook, I invite you to browse through these activities and try any or all that intrigue you. Whether it's locating your G spot, adding a sex toy to your favorite position, or learning to give a better hand job, you'll find step-by-step instructions, clear illustrations, and a recommended toy. You'll also find tips for partnered as well as solo play, plus suggested variations on each activity, so your fun is limited only by your imagination.

If that's not enough to make you want to drop this book and pick up a toy, the ten erotic stories interspersed throughout the Play section will do just that. Designed to ignite your imagination while also showing you the toys "in action," these steamy toy tales—of a daring bus ride, an unusual corporate meeting, a special anniversary gift—will prime the pump of your own fantasy life while also teaching you a thing or two.

After reading these inspiring tales and techniques, your thoughts will probably turn to purchasing a sex toy. If the large product selections in catalogs, sex toy shops, or websites dazzle you to the point of inaction, don't despair. The truth is, there are only a dozen or so different types of sex toys—everything else is just a variation on these basic styles. You don't have to own a sex toy for every day of the month (though you certainly can if you want to). You can get away with a few toys that will satisfy a variety of sexual needs. In the Learn section, you'll find an overview of these basic styles along with suggestions for getting the most out of your toy experience. And whether you're a sex toy novice or are adding to your toy chest, you'll appreciate the Shop section, with its savvy consumer tips about where and how to buy sex toys.

Sex toys can change your life. Ask anyone who learned to have an orgasm thanks to a vibrator. And there's no denying that sex toys have changed my own life. I've had a lifelong love affair with sex toys, both personally and professionally. I moved on from the little plug-in (to a bigger one, the Hitachi Magic Wand), and I managed to parlay my enthusiasm into a career in sex education. I've worked for three upscale sex toy shops, written several sex books and online columns, and answered thousands of questions about sex. Without the many people who have shared their experiences, stories, and questions with me over the years, this book would not have been possible. I hope you will learn from our experiences, pick up a sex toy, and go out and make some stories of your own.

ANNE SEMANS
OCTOBER 2004

Learn

SEX TOY JOYS: Why You Should Try a Sex Toy

A reporter once asked me for an analogy that would illustrate why someone would want to use a vibrator. I replied, "Using a vibrator to get off if you're used to your hand is a lot like driving a car with an automatic transmission after you've practiced on a stick shift. It's a lot less work, so you can just sit back and enjoy the ride." Of course, if you've never driven a stick, that analogy does nothing for you, so you'll just have to read the rest of this chapter. Here, in a nutshell, are five great reasons why you should try a sex toy.

Sex Toys Make Some Things Easier

It's easier for many women to have an orgasm with a vibrator; it's easier for women to get clitoral stimulation during intercourse with a vibrator; it's easier to reach the G spot and the prostate with a sex toy; it's easier to prolong an erection with a sex toy—the list could go on and on. The beauty of making things easier during sex, as in the car analogy above, is that you can sit back and enjoy the ride. Instead of worrying about whether you're going to come or if you're going to come too soon, you can relax and focus solely on the pleasure at hand.

Sex Toys Help You Break Out of a Routine

Do you require a certain stroke to masturbate, a particular position to orgasm, or a just-so lick during oral sex? Sex toys can expand your range, offering certain types of stimulation that hands or tongues can't. A penis sleeve might tickle your fancy, a strap-on vibrator might free you up to try different intercourse positions, or a small vibrator might add a delightful extra buzz to your next blow job. Think of sex toys as adding more entrées to an ever-expanding sexual buffet. And if you enjoy the food as sex metaphor, bear in mind that food itself works well as a sex toy. If you have any doubts, read the sexy and hilarious erotic story, "Thanksgiving with the In-laws."

Sex Toys Inspire Sexual Confidence

By picking up a sex toy and pressing it to your genitals, you are taking responsibility for your sexual needs and desires. In a culture where we learn very little about sexual pleasure, this act alone is impressive. Rather than waiting passively for someone to fulfill all your sexual needs, you take matters into your own hands. As a result, you learn more about your sexuality, you gain greater self-confidence and expertise, and you're more likely to have satisfying sexual encounters in the future.

Sex Toys Spice Up Partner Sex

As I mentioned in the introduction, despite their reputation as singles' playthings, sex toys actually enhance partner sex play by en-
abling you to do certain things you might not otherwise be able
to—whether it's a vibrator adding just the right clitoral stimulation
during intercourse or a butt plug that makes coming from prostate
stimulation possible. Over the years I've heard from hundreds of
couples who describe toy experiences that changed their lives—
whether they discovered a new erogenous zone, learned to climax
together for the first time, or enjoyed a renewed passion because of
a sex toy.

Sex Toys Make the Mood

You'll discover that certain types of sex play beg for some sex toy accessories. That back caress may feel even better when it's given with
a warming oil, that kiss may resonate even more deeply if your
hands are tied to the bedposts, and that cyber fling might short-
circuit your computer if you're wearing a vibrator. Adding sex toys
can incite your imagination and lend just the right spark of adventure to your love life.

COMMON MYTHS ABOUT SEX TOYS

Even with all these great reasons to try sex toys, most people still
harbor a few reservations about trying them. I've found that a little
information and encouragement go along way toward relieving

those anxieties, freeing people to explore this new realm of erotic pleasure.

Sex Toys Are Only for People Whose Sex Lives Need Help

The fact that sex toys have been referred to as "marital aids" and "sexual aids" for so long has done much to further this myth. The word "aid" implies that you should use one of these toys only if you need to fix something that's broken. But a woman who finds that a vibrator helps her have an orgasm more easily is not broken, nor is a man who discovers that a cock ring helps his erection last longer. Individual sexual response falls on a vast continuum, and it fluctuates over one's lifetime. If we measured sexual performance against one single ideal, we'd all end up broken at some time in our lives, and who needs to walk around under that cloud? I've always been a fan of the term "sex toy" because it reminds me not to take sex too seriously—it's hard not to smile when there's a butterfly vibrating one's clitoris. Sex is unpredictable, exciting, elusive, messy, and playful, and sex toys make a natural addition to this wonderful mix.

Sex Toys Are Unnatural

This stems from the belief that proper sex should involve only the equipment that you were born with. If you're strict about this, sex is bound to get a little boring. Forget the sexy lingerie, the romantic movie, the candlelight, the satin sheets, or the massage oil. All these things contribute to our experience of sex and are no more "natural" than sex toys, yet most folks don't have a problem with them. If you want something organic, take a tip from our ancestors, who fashioned dildos out of stone or wood. Or just lighten up! I'm not suggesting you play with bioengineered corn, for heaven's sake.

Guys Don't Use Sex Toys

In general, when it comes to sex toys, men tend to fall into two camps: those who think (1) toys are an insult to my manhood, or (2) I like 'em, but I'll never admit it. To illustrate, let me tell you about my first boyfriend, who falls squarely into camp number one. When I went to my twentieth high school reunion and told him that I sold sex toys for a living, he replied, "I don't need those things, I'm huge." Of course my reply was the time-honored "It's not what you have, but what you do with it that matters, and sex toys let you do a whole lot more with it." But what he said reflects the attitude of many men: in the bedroom you shouldn't need anything more than what you were born with, otherwise it's a sign of failure, inadequacy, or downright wimpiness. Which is just a load of bull, especially when you stop to consider that men's other "toys"—fast cars and power tools—are often viewed as signs of virility. So take a chance on a toy and show the world what a sexually adventurous guy you really are.

If I Use a _____, People Will Think I'm a _____

"If I use a butt plug, people will think I'm gay." "If I like dildos, then I must be a lesbian." "If I want to tie my partner up, I must be a dominatrix." These are just sexual stereotypes that will only hinder your sexual curiosity and growth. One thing I learned working at a sex toy store is that all kinds of people have all kinds of sexual tastes, and they absolutely cannot be neatly compartmentalized based on sexual orientation. Sure, lots of lesbians like dildos, but so does the woman who wants to have a dildo in her vagina while her husband anally penetrates her. Not all gay men like anal sex, just as not all heterosexual women like giving blow jobs. Your desire to try out a pair of wrist restraints doesn't mean you're headed for a career in SM, it just means you have a healthy sexual inquisitiveness! Your sexual identity defines who you are, not your sexual practices. So quit worrying what the Joneses might think, and just do what feels good.

Sex Toys Are for Losers, Loners, or Geeks

If you've paid any attention to pop culture recently, you'll know this stereotype is on its way out. Vibrators, which seldom appeared in TV or movies, and then only as fetish objects or punch lines for jokes about lonely women, are finally gaining some respect. Witness the popularity of shows like *Sex and the City,* and the way its female characters rhapsodized about their toys (sending sales of two popular vibrators, the Hitachi and the Rabbit, sky high). One day while reading *Vibe* magazine I ran across a quote from rapper Ice T about how he likes to use his favorite vibrator (the Pocket Rocket) on the ladies. Who'd have thought that sex toys would one day rise above their ignoble past to become positively hip! But you needn't be a trendsetter to enjoy sex toys, just open-minded. Chances are, if you buy one today, you'll have something in common with your favorite celebrity, the parent at the PTA meeting, or the girl, like me, who discovered their sweet charms one lazy summer.

▨ ▨ ▨

If you started this chapter with any reservations about using sex toys, I hope they are now banished from your mind. Enjoying great sex requires letting go of sexual insecurities and just focusing on what brings you pleasure. And sex toys are just waiting to expand your potential for pleasure.

TOYS FOR ALL SEASONS: Basic Sex Toy Styles

Does the term "sex toy" conjure up images of flesh-colored plastic dongs? If it does, it's because these were the standard-issue sex toys for decades. But within the last twenty years, changes in toy material and technology, as well as in consumer's tastes, have resulted in a dazzling array of toys. You can buy a dildo that looks like it's made of marble, a vibrator shaped like a bunny, a harness that could double as sexy thong underwear, or a butt plug that looks like a flower. True to the adage, "find a need and fill it," the adult industry has come up with a device that'll stimulate, prod, soothe, or tingle any sexual itch you might have.

Navigating this sea of sex toys can be rather overwhelming until you realize there really are only a dozen or so basic styles of sex toys. Once you understand what the toy is designed to do, you can look for variations that will suit your particular position, aesthetic, or whim. In this chapter I'll describe various styles of toys, explain their purpose, and offer tips on choosing between similar models. But don't worry about retaining it all, because in the Play section, I recommend a specific toy to use for each activity. In some cases, I've chosen a brand name (see sidebar, page 15), but in other cases I refer to one of the generic toy styles below, since any of the models within that style will do. Of course, you are free to experiment with any toy you desire, and I encourage you to do just that. You'll also find tips in the Shop section that can help with selection, especially if you're looking for quality toys.

VIBRATORS

Vibrators come in all shapes and sizes—some look like handheld mixers, some like fake penises, some like eggs, and some like animals. Some are waterproof, some glow in the dark, some talk back. They are powered either by batteries or electricity, and deliver more intense stimulation to the genital area than a hand, a penis, or a mouth.

Vibrators have long been recommended to women learning to have orgasms, but they are by no means exclusively a woman's toy. Men enjoy the feel of vibrations on their genitals, and couples use them to enliven partner sex. Vibrator orgasms—which can be more intense and easier to achieve—are so enthralling that they soon become a regular part of a person's sexual repertoire.

Most people think of vibrators as long, penis-shaped toys, because that's what they looked like for so long. Unfortunately, this misleading vibrator shape has created endless confusion and resulted in disappointing toy experiences for thousands of women. The phallic-shaped toy suggests vaginal insertion, but since most women orgasm from direct clitoral stimulation, a dildo-style vibrator can prove disappointing unless it's pressed against the clitoris. Fortunately, there are plenty of styles on the market today, so whether you have orgasms from clitoral or vaginal stimulation, or a combination of the two, you can find the right toy for the job.

Basic Vibrator Styles

Clitoral Vibrators

Any vibrator can stimulate the clitoris, but some accomplish this much better than others. Perhaps the most well-known is the Hitachi Magic Wand, a massager with a phenomenal word-of-mouth reputation. It packs a very powerful vibration and is often recommended to preorgasmic women, but it's loud and large, which intimidates some first-timers. (It's not intended for insertion, so don't let the tennis ball–size head scare you off.) Coil-operated vibrators are a quieter, smaller alternative (Wahl makes a popular model); they look more like handheld mixers than anything remotely sexual. Both toys run on electricity and provide direct, focused vibration to the clitoris. Battery-powered clit vibrators come in all shapes and styles, but some of the more popular models (see illustrations) are

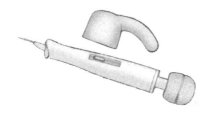  

Hitachi Magic Wand (with G Spot Attachment)   Wahl 7-in-1 Personal Massager   Bullet

the Bullet, the Pocket Rocket, Natural Contours, and the Fukuoku 9000—a vibrator that slips over the fingertip!

Pocket Rocket   Natural Contours Ultime   Fukuoku

Vaginal (Insertable) and G Spot Vibrators

These are the most traditional-looking dildo-type vibrators; they appeal to women who want a vibrator that can be used both vaginally and clitorally. Some resemble a penis while others are smooth, but you'll find many variations in texture, color (including glow-in-the-dark), and subtle features (nubs or ridges). Vibrators with a bend toward the tip are designed specifically for G spot stimulation, the most popular of which is a somewhat generic adult toy that goes by many names (Classic G, Nubby G, Crystal G). It's made of clear jelly rubber, curves near the tip, and features a ring of jelly fingers around the base designed to stimulate the vaginal opening (see illustration).

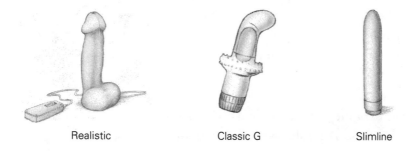

Realistic   Classic G   Slimline

Dual-Style Vibrators

The Japanese improved on the dildo-type vibrator by inventing an insertable toy that also sports a clitoral branch, so you can enjoy

both vaginal and clitoral (or vaginal and anal) stimulation at the same time. Since realistic sex toys are banned in Japan, these toys are crafted in the likeness of animals and sea creatures, with the Rabbit Pearl and its cousin, the Rabbit Habit, being the most famous. There are many knockoffs of this style, but the Japanese-made toys tend to be a higher quality than those made elsewhere.

Rabbit Pearl

Hands-free Vibrators

Imagine vibrating underwear and you get the basic concept behind hands-free vibrators. A clitoral vibrator is attached to a G string or thong-style panty, with the vibrator positioned right over the clitoris. The vibrator is often shaped like a butterfly, sea creature, or some other tiny critter. This is also a great toy when you want a little extra clitoral stimulation during intercourse. Remote-controlled versions make this toy especially fun for adventurous partner sex.

Butterfly Vibrator

Vibes in Disguise

These are vibrators that masquerade as something else—a pen, a lipstick case, or a paperweight, for example. They're popular as novelties, traveling vibes, or gifts for the sex toy novice.

Men's Vibrators

Most of the penis sleeves and cock rings described in the men's section (below) are also available in vibrating models.

Anal Vibes

Most of the anal toys mentioned below are available (or can be adapted) as vibrators.

Choosing a Vibrator

First decide where you want to use the vibrator (clitoris, anus, G spot, penis, etc.) and choose a toy made for that purpose. If you want a strong, reliable vibrator, look for the electric toys made by name-brand manufacturers. If you want to experiment inexpensively or need a toy that travels well, choose a smaller battery toy. If you want something more adventurous, try one of the high-tech toys like a remote-controlled toy or one that responds to sound (like the Audio-Oh). In general, most people base their choices on intensity, sound, and aesthetics. Fortunately many websites are beginning to rate vibrators based on the first two factors.

Name-Brand Toys

Hitachi Magic Wand

Wahl 7-in-1

Rabbit Pearl

Natural Contours

Fukuoku 9000

Pocket Rocket

Audi-Oh

Nexus

Terra Firma

Fleshlight

Toys with recognizable brand names are good bets because:

- they've earned a reputation as a quality toy
- they're not likely to go off the market anytime soon
- they're easy to locate by name, making it easier to compare prices, reviews, etc.

DILDOS AND HARNESSES

A dildo, typically thought of as a penis substitute, is designed for vaginal or anal insertion. In general, dildos don't vibrate, although many penis-shaped vibrators can be used as dildos. Some dildos have handles, some have suction-cup bases, some are double-ended, and some curve toward the top to provide G spot stimulation. Some metal dildos are used for Kegel exercises and have been nicknamed "vaginal barbells" since they strengthen the PC muscle (see the "Love Muscle" activity). Glass and acrylic dildos are curvaceous, sensuous works of art that also make great G spot toys.

Dildos have been used throughout history—I saw one beautiful stone phallus unearthed from a four-thousand-year-old burial mound in Ireland—a testament to their age-old pleasure potential. Today's dildos are available in a magnificent array of sizes, styles, colors, and textures: sleek glass wands, marblized silicone, fetishy black rubber, or jewel-toned jelly rubber.

A dildo can be used by itself or in a harness to enable hands-free penetration of a partner. The latter is often referred to as "strap-on sex" and is a common practice among straights and gays alike because it feels great to be anally or vaginally penetrated by a lover wearing a dildo. Many men also don strap-ons to experiment with double penetration on their lovers or to prolong intercourse after an erection has subsided.

Choosing a Dildo

If you'll be using your dildo in a harness, make sure it has a flared base, as this holds it in place. (If you'll be using the dildo anally, the flared base is also necessary to keep it from slipping into the rectum.) Beyond that, your decision boils down to four considerations: material, size, function, and aesthetic. Rubber and plastic can be an inexpensive way to test the waters, but the undisputed ideal material for dildos is silicone, as it is easy to clean, warms quickly, and lasts longer than other materials. As for aesthetics, you can choose between dildos that are realistic, abstract, or whimsical.

Size is simply a matter of getting the right fit. Dildo sizes usually refer to length and width. If you're planning to use a dildo in a harness, you need to add about half an inch to the length to accommodate the space between bodies. A good-size length is about seven inches. The width usually refers to the diameter of the dildo—the measurement across the toy if you were to cut it in half. If you're not sure about the diameter, choose something slightly smaller than what you think you'll need. Here's a tip if you want to get really precise: buy a fat cucumber, peel it, and then warm it in the microwave. Try inserting it. If it doesn't fit comfortably, keep paring it down till you've found the right size. Then cut it in half and measure the diameter across your cuke. Voilà! It's not as easy as figuring out your shoe size, but it works.

Function refers to how you plan to use your dildo. Will you use it alone or with a partner? What body part do you want to stimulate? When you're all suited up in your harness, what position are you partial to? A dildo with a suction cup is great for solo masturbation, and one that has a handle can be easily gripped by a partner. A dildo that curves up will stimulate the prostate or G spot in the missionary position, whereas a straight (or less curved) dildo affords more range of motion for those who want to try different positions. Women who want to wear a dildo while penetrating their partners give rave reviews to the double dildo known as the Nexus.

Emperor   Mistress Silicone Dildo   Crystal Wand

Choosing a Harness

Comfort and a good fit are essential in a harness. If you hate thong underwear because you can't tolerate a thin string between your butt cheeks, stay away from the single-strap harnesses (called

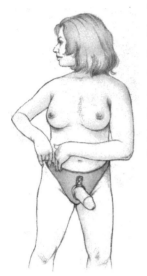

"thong" or "G-string" style). Try a two-strap harness (also known as "jock" harnesses), which have two leg straps connected to a waist strap. Also, men prefer this style because it leaves their testicles unrestricted. For maximum comfort, look for a harness that is fully adjustable, has a flap behind the hole to prevent the dildo from chafing pubic hair or skin, and features a removable ring that enables you to accommodate much larger or smaller dildos (the Terra Firma is a popular leather model). Most harnesses are listed with dimensions and will fit a wide range of body types, but you should check to make sure the leg and waist straps are adjustable.

Harness with dildo

Finally, you will have to choose between leather and fabric. Both are durable, but leather tends to be more supple and sexy, while fabric is more economical. Additional variations on the harness theme include a double harness, which allows the wearer to insert a dildo, or the thigh harness, which lends itself to some interesting positions.

ANAL TOYS

Anal toys are designed for insertion into the anus and have a flared base to prevent them from slipping into the rectum. Some anal toys vibrate. The anus is an erogenous zone for both men and women, and anal toys take pleasurable advantage of that. You may want to stimulate the sensitive anal opening, massage your prostate, or engage in anal intercourse. Anal toys are particularly effective at stimulating the prostate in men, which is analogous to the G spot in women. Most men find prostate stimulation is a source of sexual pleasure; some find it enhances other types of sex play while others can orgasm purely from prostate stimulation.

Basic Anal Toys

Butt Plugs

Designed to be inserted and left in place, these are short, stout toys with a bulge in the middle and a narrow neck toward the base. After insertion, your sphincter muscle contracts around the neck of the toy so that it stays firmly in place. Some plugs bend slightly to one side to apply pressure to the prostate when inserted.

Essential Plug

Anal Dildos

These are smooth dildos (that is, there's no bulge) designed to penetrate the anus using an in-and-out motion.

Anal Beads

A series of marble-size beads strung together on a cord with a loop at one end, anal beads feel good when inserted into the anus one at a time. The beads are available in different sizes, and sometimes they are mounted on a thin dildo rather than on a string.

Anal Vibes

Anal toys that vibrate.

Anal Beads

Choosing an Anal Toy

The most important thing to look for in an anal toy is a flared base. Beyond that, you must choose based on material, size, function, and aesthetics. As with dildos, you can find rubber and plastic anal toys, but silicone makes the very best material for an anal toy because it is so easy to clean. Size is a matter of personal preference, but if you're new to anal play you might want to start with a finger-width toy.

What you plan to do with your anal toy will determine the style. If you want to move the toy in and out, you want a smooth toy like a dildo. If you want to leave the toy in place, you want a butt plug. They come in all different widths, so start small and work your way up. Some people enjoy anal vibrations; any vibrator can be pressed against the anal opening, but choose a vibrating anal plug or dildo with a flared base for insertion.

PENIS SLEEVES

Great masturbation toys, penis sleeves are intended to replicate the feeling of penis-in-vagina, which they do with varying degrees of

Fleshlight

success. Some look like tubes, while others take the form of blow-up dolls. The sleeve's texture has a lot to do with how well it gets the job done—something many guys learn the hard way thanks to plastic Sally's scratchy seams. Fortunately, a new material called Cyberskin, which looks and feels a lot like real skin, has revolutionized men's sleeves. One sleeve in particular, the Fleshlight, has earned rave reviews from men who've used the product.

Choosing a Penis Sleeve

Comfort is the key to a good penis sleeve, which can usually be achieved by adding lots of lubricant. Finding a sleeve that is snug yet elastic enough for easy removal is also important, as is choosing a material that is easy to keep clean. Vibrations are another option.

COCK RINGS (PENIS RINGS)

These are rings designed to fit around the base of the penis and the scrotum, restricting blood flow out of the penis. The resulting pressure can be very pleasurable and can heighten sensation in the penis and testicles. Some men find that wearing cock rings prolongs the erection or even makes the erection firmer, a side effect that can enhance intercourse for both parties. Vibrating cock rings are great for partner sex—a bullet vibrator attached to the cock ring is positioned so that it will rub up against the woman's clitoris during intercourse (while also vibrating his penis). This is great for women who need a little more stimulation during penetration. Alternately, you can flip this toy upside down so the vibrator is underneath the

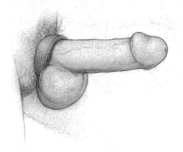

Cock Ring

Cock Ring Vibrator

penis and facing inward. This stimulates the testicles during partner sex or solo play.

Choosing a Cock Ring

If you're new to cock rings, choose one that is easy to remove and can be adjusted to fit various sizes. If you're looking for the couple's toy (the cock ring with clitoral stimulator), try one that has a self-contained battery pack.

PENIS PUMPS

Penis pumps temporarily enlarge the penis by drawing blood to the surface. The cylinder slips over the length of the penis and creates a seal against the skin, while the pump (usually hand operated) creates a vacuum inside the cylinder. Many men enjoy the feeling of pressure on the penis while pumping.

Choosing a Penis Pump

Novelty pumps are pretty similar in terms of quality, but the pricier pumps offer stronger suction and more bells and whistles (attachments, controls, etc.).

SM TOYS

Many people think of SM as a deviant sexual practice involving pain. SM is shorthand for the term "sadomasochism," but there is a difference in the terms. People who enjoy others' suffering (bullies, for example) are often referred to as sadists, while those who seek humiliation are called masochists. But in contrast, SM is a consensual exchange of power that can be highly erotic for the participants. Although the media tends to fetishize SM play with depictions of leather-clad, stiletto-heeled dominatrices, many people dabble in SM play without the fashion trimmings or hard-core edge. If you've ever tied your lover's wrists with a scarf or donned a blindfold, you've experienced the thrill of erotic power exchange. Consult a book or website for an extensive discussion of SM technique and gear, but these basic toys make a nice introduction to power play.

Basic SM Accessories

Restraints

Many people engage in bondage of some sort during sex because it can be nice to escape the egalitarian roles we've been taught to assume in the bedroom. Just let yourself "do" or be "done to"—submitting to a partner's ministrations is an incredibly intimate gesture that resonates quite powerfully in the bedroom. You can fashion your own restraints out of stockings, backpack webbing, or clothesline, or purchase leather or fur-lined wrist

Bondage Restraints

or ankle restraints with easy-to-release clasps and tethers that will secure them to bedposts.

Blindfolds

Sight deprivation is a time-honored way of increasing your enjoyment of your other senses. With a blindfold on, you're tuned in to the sounds of breathing, words, and bodies, the feel of skin on skin, the smell of the candles burning, or the images floating through your mind. In addition, you can manipulate exquisite sexual tension through this game of anticipation and release.

Whips, Paddles, Floggers

Sexual excitement increases one's tolerance for pain, often transforming it into something erotic, which is why spanking, slapping, or whipping can feel especially good during the heat of passion. Some folks refer to this not as pain, but as an altered state of heightened sensation. If this sounds intriguing but you're a novice to flagellation, it's worth doing some research into the types of devices available, as the difference in the sting or bite between them is enormous. Whether you crave a light spanking from a paddle or a thrashing from a cat-o'-nine-tails will determine your toy of choice.

Clamps

Clamps are designed to simulate pinching, and many people like to experiment with them on nipples and genitals. While everyday items like clothespins can be employed as makeshift clamps, I'd suggest investing in something designed specifically as a nipple clip, which allows you to adjust the pressure and can accommodate a variety of nipple sizes.

Choosing SM Toys

With restraints and clamps, choose toys that are adjustable and easy to remove. What type of whip or paddle you use depends on how much sting you desire, so read up on the different types before purchasing.

SENSUAL TOYS

A lot has been written about the importance of expanding our definition of sex beyond intercourse. After all, one's sexuality encompasses so much more than just this particular act. What we see, feel, hear, taste, and touch can all be part of our sexual experience. Toys designed to take erotic advantage of our five senses—things like massage oil, feathers, edible gels, erotica, and food—all fall into this category.

Now you know a lot about sex toys. Don't worry, there won't be a quiz, but you are encouraged to come back time and again to this chapter if you need clarification or help choosing a toy. Hopefully, a few of these styles sparked your imagination and you're eager to try one . . . or two . . . or more!

A PLEASURE PRIMER: Your Body's Hot Spots

I have long attributed my quest for sex information to the moment in the eighth grade when the nun teaching my religion class instructed us to "think of a hamburger when your thoughts stray to the impure, as this will distract you." My body was undergoing the ravages of puberty, my thoughts were definitely straying, and I wanted answers—not guilt or hamburgers.

It's a crime, really, that sex education classes don't offer much in the way of instruction on sexual anatomy and sexual response. Teachers would be surprised by the perfect attendance, and students would sit in rapt attention because they'd be learning about things that were happening to their bodies at that very moment. Instead, kids get dry lessons on reproductive biology, with little or no mention of sexuality. Left to their own devices, kids end up graduating with more sexual experience than sex education, which is doing them a disservice. Statistics reveal that most teens do have intercourse by the time they graduate from high school.

Consequently, we enter adulthood, and sexual maturity, without knowing very much about our bodies. We arrive at the magical age where it's legal for us to vote, to drive, to drink, and to have sex, but we've learned way more about civics, road rage, and alcoholism than sexuality. And yet we're expected to fall in love, to magically please ourselves and our partners, and to live sexually fulfilled lives without letting on that we haven't a clue what we're doing.

So it's up to each of us to fill in the gaps in our sexual education. Being proactive about your sex education has many benefits. By learning about your own sexual anatomy and responses, you become a more sexually aware and confident person. Rather than spending lonely, frustrated nights waiting for some mythical lover to sweep you off your feet, you can discover dozens of different ways to please yourself. This will only increase your chances for sexual fulfillment when you do have a partner. And if you've done your homework on the opposite sex, you're well on your way to being a thoughtful, attentive, and soon-to-be expert lover.

> ## Toy Testimonials
>
> "I had my first orgasm at 58 thanks to a vibrator my granddaughter gave me."

This book is all about discovering new erogenous zones and spicing up your sex routine by playing with sex toys. But without a basic grasp of anatomy and sexual response, you might as well be pressing the vibrator to your bedroom wall for all the good it might do you. What follows is a brief overview, but if you're in need of further information, check Resources for great books, videos, and websites.

FEMALE GENITALIA

Vulva

The outwardly visible female genitals are referred to as the vulva, and include the labia, the clitoris, the urethral opening, and the vaginal opening. The internal parts include the vaginal canal, the urethral sponge, the cervix, and the pubic bone.

Labia

The vulva consists of two sets of lips—the labia minora (inner lips) and the labia majora (outer lips). Most women's inner labia don't come in a matched pair, which many women find troubling, though this is quite normal. Women's labia are a lot like snowflakes in that no two are alike. In particular, the inner lips vary a great deal in terms of size, shape, and the way they fold over each other. If you want a firsthand look at a magnificent variety of women's genitals, take a peek at the color photographs of women's vulvas in the tasteful book *Femalia*.

Clitoris

Look for the clitoris at the top of the vulva, where the labia meet. The clitoris, packed with thousands of nerve endings, is the most sensitive spot on a woman's genitals. If you take a finger and press down gently over the clitoral hood, you'll feel a little bump under the skin—that's the clitoris. You can pull back the hood to reveal the clitoral glans, but most women find direct contact with the glans irritating and prefer stimulation through the hood. Women's cli-

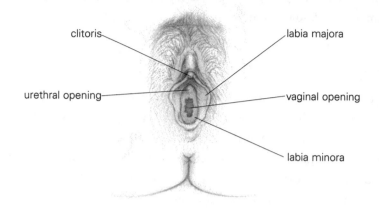

clitoris

labia majora

urethral opening

vaginal opening

labia minora

Female Genitalia—External View

torises can vary in size—most aren't much bigger than a pebble—but size has nothing to do with their orgasmic capacity. The clitoris is made up of erectile tissue that swells and fills with blood when aroused, just as a penis becomes erect. What you see is only a portion of the clitoris—it has legs that extend into the body and around the vaginal opening, so it can receive indirect stimulation from different parts of a woman's anatomy. The clitoris bears the notable distinction of being the only organ in the human body that exists solely for sexual pleasure.

Urethra

If you part your inner labia and look just beneath the clitoris, you should see the urethral opening, which is where your urine exits the body. It too is surrounded by nerve endings, which some women find pleasant to touch and others find irritating. It extends into the body and is surrounded by the urethral sponge, a soft spongy tissue that can be stimulated through the vaginal wall, via an area that has come to be known as the G spot (more on this below).

Vagina

The vagina is a muscular tube capable of expanding to much larger proportions during arousal. At the back wall of the vagina is the cervix. Located in the cervix is the opening to the uterus, called the os, which leads to your reproductive organs. This opening is tiny so you needn't worry about any toys getting through. Some women find that pressure on the cervix from a penis, toy, or fist is pleasurable; others find it irritating. The vaginal opening and the first couple of inches within the vagina are more textured and sensitive than the deeper regions. Lighter stimulation, such as licking, finger play, or vibrations, can be felt much better around the entrance to the vagina, whereas pressure and firm strokes feel better with deeper penetration.

G Spot

Named after the doctor (Granfenberg) who first identified it, G spot refers to the small area on the upper vaginal wall through which it is possible to stimulate the sensitive urethral sponge. All women have a G spot, though not all women know how to touch it, or like having it touched when they do. Many women, however, find that G spot stimulation, either on its own or in conjunction with clitoral stimulation, can lead to potent orgasms.

The G spot is about the size of a quarter, and its bumpy texture feels noticeably different than the smoother walls around it. Since it gets bigger when you're aroused, it's easier to try to locate it when you're turned on. To find it, insert a finger into your vagina and press and pull firmly using a "come hither" motion. With proper stimulation you may feel the urge to pee, which is an indication that you're doing the right thing. If you give in to the feeling, you may ejaculate a clear fluid. Female ejaculate has often been mistaken for pee but is chemically different from urine, and is perfectly normal. For more on the G spot, see the "G Marks the Spot" activity in the Play section.

MALE GENITALIA

The external male genitals consist of the penis and the scrotum, while the primary internal components include the epididymis, the vas deferens, and the prostate gland.

Penis

The penis is made up of spongy erectile tissue, which fills with blood during arousal and becomes erect. Despite euphemisms for male erection like "boner," there are no bones in the penis. Penises come in all sizes, but a flaccid penis is typically four inches long, while an erect penis can be anywhere from four to eight inches long, with six inches being about average. The average circumference (that's around—not across) of an erect penis is four to six inches. Despite men's preoccupation with penis size, size has little impact on sexual enjoyment since the vagina is not terribly sensitive (and long penises can painfully bump the cervix during intercourse). Women's vaginas are wonderfully elastic, so they expand and contract to fit a variety of sizes.

The head of the penis, where the urethral opening is located, is

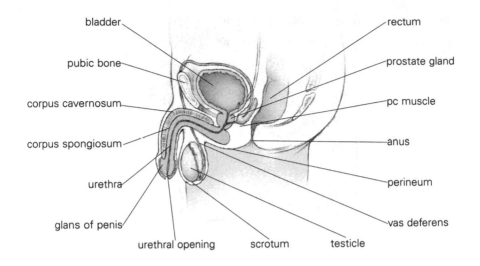

bladder

rectum

pubic bone

prostate gland

corpus cavernosum

pc muscle

corpus spongiosum

anus

urethra

perineum

glans of penis

vas deferens

urethral opening   scrotum   testicle

Male Genitalia—Cross Section

called the glans. The glans is a highly sensitive area, particularly the frenulum, an indentation on the underside of the penis where the glans meets the shaft. Extending down from this spot is the raphe, a vertical strip running along the underside of the penis down to the middle of the scrotum, which is also very sensitive. All men are born with a foreskin, a bit of protective skin that covers the glans when the penis is flaccid. When the penis is erect, the foreskin retracts to just below the head. Men who are circumcised have had their foreskins removed, so the glans is exposed at all times.

Scrotum and Testicles

The scrotum is the loose pouch of skin containing the testicles (or "balls"), which produce sperm and testosterone. Because the testicles are extremely sensitive to pain, the scrotum acts as both protection and insulation, keeping the testicles at a comfortable temperature. The epididymis is a coiled tube within the testicles where sperm mature until they travel through the vas deferens before they are ejaculated during sexual arousal. Men have two testicles; it is not uncommon for one to hang lower than the other. A lot of men enjoy stimulation of the testicles, which can involve licking, tugging, or simply cradling the scrotum in your hand.

Prostate Gland

The prostate gland produces ejaculatory fluid and is located close to the root of the penis and below the bladder. Because of its close proximity to the rectum, many men enjoy prostate stimulation provided by inserting a finger or toy into the rectum and stroking toward the front of the body. Some men can have an orgasm from prostate stimulation alone, while others find it enhances other types of sexual activity.

THE PERINEUM AND THE ANUS

Two potential erogenous zones shared by men and women are the perineum and the anus. On women, the perineum is the space between the vaginal opening and the anus. During sexual arousal, the blood vessels in the underlying perineal sponge become engorged, making the area sensitive. On men, the perineum lies between the anus and the testicles; massaging the perineum using a firm stroke or direct pressure can stimulate the sensitive root of the penis.

The anus is rich in nerve endings and can respond sexually when stimulated with fingers, tongues, or toys. The anus is about an inch long and leads to the rectum, which is between five and nine inches long. Entrance to the anus is regulated by two sphincter muscles that you can learn to relax, so you can enjoy anal intercourse, butt play, or prostate stimulation. Just make sure anything you put in the anus is well lubricated and has a flared base. Unlike the vagina, the rectum is not sealed at one end, so anything inserted without a flared base could potentially be pulled up into the colon.

PC MUSCLE

The pubic bone is surrounded by the pubococcygeus muscles (otherwise known as the PC muscle), which play a vital part in your sexual health. Locate the PC muscle by stopping a stream of urine and then letting it go again. You can exercise your PC muscle by doing Kegels, described later in the "Love Muscle" activity. A well-toned PC muscle can enhance sex—a woman can better squeeze or grip a penis or toy during intercourse, intensify her orgasms, and even learn to ejaculate. It helps men learn ejaculatory control and can lead to stronger erections.

ORGASM

Ask someone to define orgasm and you'll get anything from rhapsodic waxings about waves crashing or embers igniting to technical descriptions of involuntary muscle contractions. To the person who's never had one, these aren't terribly helpful, though the poetic musings certainly give one reason to keep trying.

Sexual Response

In fact, orgasm is just one phase in what sex therapists Masters and Johnson identified as four phases in the human sexual response cycle: excitement, plateau, orgasm, and resolution. Each phase is marked by changes in one's physiology, so if you're paying attention, you can usually identify them in yourself or a partner. The excitement phase is characterized by elevated heart rate, increased flow of blood to the genitals, breasts, and lips, and flushed skin color. Women often experience vaginal lubrication, a swelling clit, and vaginal expansion, while men's penises become erect and their testicles pull up into the body. The plateau phase is a continuation of these occurrences with full engorgement in both sexes, an elevated uterus in the woman, and pre-come emitted by the penis. The sexual tension that builds during these first two phases is released during orgasm—involuntary muscle contractions (anywhere from a few to several) throughout the pelvic regions in both men and women—that typically result in ejaculation for men (and sometimes for women). The resolution phase describes your body's return to its unaroused state, with blood flow, heart rate, and skin color all returning to normal.

Getting to Orgasm

Most women have orgasms through clitoral stimulation or a combination of vaginal and clitoral stimulation. Sadly, this still comes as big news to many women (and their partners), who mistakenly believe that vaginal penetration is the fastest route to orgasmic bliss. The sex toy industry contributed to this confusion for years by churning out thousands of phallic-shaped vibrators, and women today still purchase them in the hopes that the added vibration will trigger the elusive vaginal O. Sure, some women can have an orgasm from vaginal penetration alone, but the vast majority of women need direct stimulation of the clitoris. If you're a woman learning this for the first time, I suggest you try the "Blissful Buzz" activity. If you're a man who's surprised to learn about the clitoris's pleasure potential, make sure you know where it is (let her give you a good look), and then show her you know what it can do by trying the oral tips in the "Ladies' Night" activity.

Men learn to have orgasms because they start masturbating fairly early on—the penis invites exploration. Most men come from penile stimulation—with each preferring his own combination of strokes on the shaft and glans—but some men enjoy testicular stimulation as well. As you learned from the prostate discussion, plenty of men have discovered this pleasure zone as another pathway to orgasm. If you want to bring your partner to orgasm, check out the "All Hands on Deck" activity. If you're intrigued by the prostate's potential, start experimenting with the techniques in "Bottom's Up," or if you want a new masturbation technique, see "Priming the Pump."

Multiple Orgasms

Women are capable of having more than one orgasm in a succession; very often all that's needed is continued stimulation and the desire to give it another go. Men experience what is called a "refractory" period after ejaculation, where they are usually unable to begin the cycle again until a period of time has passed (the length of time depends in part on age). However, by learning some ejaculatory control techniques, men can separate ejaculation from orgasm, and they too can become multiply orgasmic (see the "Going for Broke" activity).

It's good to remember that each person's experience of orgasm is subjective, and any one person can have lots of different kinds of orgasms. Some folks describe full-body orgasms, whereas others experience orgasms primarily in and around the genitals. Deep breathing, tantric exercises, and strong PC muscles are among the many things that can affect your experience of orgasm, as can the type of stimulation (vibrators, tongues, toys, body parts), your arousal level, and your emotional state at the time. Your expectations and your perspective will also play an important part in your enjoyment of your orgasmic quest. Some nights you might want a little orgasm to put you to sleep, and other times you might anticipate a night of mutually explosive orgasms for the two of you. Finally, learning to enjoy sex without orgasms is a powerful step in your sex education—you can forgo performance anxiety and discover the pleasures of a suspended state of full-body arousal.

MAXIMIZING PLEASURE: Tips for Sex Toy Success

Successful sex toy adventures, like delicious meals, require the proper ingredients. But unlike your grandma's secret recipes, the requirements for sex toy play are no great mystery. Besides needing the sex toy itself, you'll want to add these to the mix: masturbation, imagination, communication, and lubrication.

MASTURBATION: YOUR PATH TO PLEASURE

This is where I invite you to give yourself a hand, literally. I promise you there will be no hairy palms, no blindness, no insanity. On the contrary, you might find that masturbation relieves stress, helps you sleep, fights yeast infections, relieves menstrual cramps, burns up calories, and reduces the risk of prostate cancer. Oh, and it feels pretty darn good too.

But perhaps the single biggest reason to masturbate is that it helps you learn what you like sexually. Sure, you can wait for a partner to help you discover this, but why pin all your hopes on one person—who may or may not deliver the goods—and deprive yourself of hours of sexual bliss in the meantime? By yourself, you are free to take your time, make noise, and try different things, without worrying about performance anxiety or pleasing anyone but yourself. And the bonus—once you know what feels good, you'll be able to show a partner later on.

If you already masturbate, this might not be news to you. But if you feel anything less than satisfied with your masturbation habits, you might still be buying into some of the societal taboos around masturbation. For example, most of us know that masturbation isn't really bad for us, we just think of it as lesser sex somehow: something to keep us sexual until we're partnered, when we shouldn't need it any more. In fact, masturbation lends an erotic—and educational—edge to partner sex play. Masturbating in front of your partner requires you to get in touch with your exhibitionist side, which can be incredibly sexy, but it's also a great way to show him or her how you like to be pleasured.

Masturbation will teach you things about your sexual response that will help you determine what kind of sex toys you want to play with. For example, a woman who likes rubbing her clitoris while also being penetrated might choose a toy that vibrates her clit while also filling her vagina. A man who likes masturbating into pillows might select a penis sleeve. Obviously, once the toy arrives you'll be masturbating with it, but even if you're planning on using it with a partner, it's good to play with it alone first. This may take some of the element of surprise away, but it also might help you discover what you want it to do so you'll be better able to show a partner.

IMAGINATION: ANYTHING IS POSSIBLE

Think back to your high school English class when the teacher introduced the concept called "suspension of disbelief." This was the fancy way of saying "anything is possible, so just sit back and enjoy what you are about to read, rather than worrying that it's too fantastic, improbable, or unrealistic." Believe it or not, this concept comes in very handy with your sex life as well.

When you take an "anything is possible" approach to your sex life, you begin to jettison the cultural stereotypes and sex negativity you may have picked up during your journey to sexual adulthood. Simply let yourself consider the possibilities. Maybe you'd like to have sex with the lights on (do good girls do that?); maybe you're intrigued by anal sex (does that mean I'm gay?); maybe you want to tie your girlfriend up (will she think I'm kinky?). Imagine a world where you just experience pleasure for pleasure's sake and all those bubble-thoughts become irrelevant. Sex toys are liberating because they don't care about your sexual orientation or your personal proclivities; they're equal-opportunity pleasers.

So forget your preconceptions about sex toys and just pick one up and play with it. Suspend any anxieties you have about the different sexual activities described in this book, and just imagine yourself enjoying them as you read along. If you can visualize sexual bliss, you're that much closer to attaining it.

And remember, just because you imagine enjoying a certain type of sex doesn't mean you want to act on it. The fantasy component of your sex life can be as powerful as anything you do in real life. You can boost your excitement level by silently fantasizing about a hot sexual encounter, by talking dirty to a partner, or by reading or watching explicit erotica. The more you flex your erotic imagination, the more variety you will have in your lovemaking.

COMMUNICATION: INTRODUCING TOYS TO YOUR PARTNER

Say you've gotten comfortable with masturbation and you've fantasized about using a sex toy on your partner. How to make that a reality? That's where communication comes in. As you've probably noticed in your own experience, sexual communication can make all the difference between a great sexual encounter and a disastrous one. If your partner is doing something that causes you pain, you can keep mum and have a lousy time, you can criticize your partner's technique and throw a damper on the activity, or you can politely suggest an alternative and revive the thrill for both of you. That example illustrates the difference between no communication, poor communication, and good communication.

Good communication takes work, particularly because sex is such a loaded subject for most of us. We're not used to being so explicit, we're afraid of hurting a partner's feelings, or we don't want to appear vulnerable. But your conversations don't always need to be focused on your sex life. Practice talking about sex when you're *not* in the heat of passion, and you'll get more comfortable with the language of sex. There are lots of ways to do this: ask your partner questions about his or her sexual upbringing, watch a racy TV show or movie together, write an erotic e-mail or sexy letter to your partner, or discuss some news article or study about sex. Not only will this help put you at ease with sex as a subject matter, it will give you a better understanding of your partner's concerns or opinions about a variety of sexual matters.

Knowing how your partner feels about different sexual practices will help you gauge whether he or she will be receptive to playing with a toy. If you sense resistance, share a fantasy of yours involving a toy or browse a catalog of sex toys together, and let him or her know you're curious about sex toy play. Reassure your partner that the toy is not intended as a substitute, but as a way for you both to experiment and have fun. In general, it's unwise to surprise a lover by whipping out a toy during the heat of passion unless you're absolutely sure it'll go over well. You can do more damage than good this way—feelings of inadequacy, jealousy, or sadness can come out, so head these off at the pass by talking about toys beforehand.

When introducing your partner to the idea of sex toys, always frame your suggestions in a positive or nonthreatening way, such as "Honey, I read about this sensitive spot inside my vagina and I'd love it if you'd help me find it with a G spot toy," rather than "Honey, if you ever expect me to orgasm during intercourse you better buy me a toy!" Share whatever you've learned, any anxieties you might have, and any questions you've come up with, and approach your toy experience as a joint venture. Partners, even if you're taken off guard by the suggestion, try to respond with an open mind. Do a little homework yourself if you need more information, then talk about what you've learned.

Once you've opened your new package and are ready to strap on that cock ring or rev up that vibrator, your communication skills will be tested further. Once you've masturbated with the toy, you'll want to describe for your partner where and how to use it. If you're not comfortable with such explicit language, try practicing alone first. It can be awkward to hear yourself using words like "vagina" or "cunt" at first, but with practice your verbal skills can add an erotic thrill to your sex play. If you're a fan of nonverbal feedback, like moaning, try to make your intent clear—a moan of displeasure can sometimes be mistaken for a moan of ecstasy.

Whenever you talk about sex with a partner, remember these basic tips:

- **Avoid the negative.** Nothing stings like criticism.
- **Be generous.** Nothing tastes as sweet as a compliment.
- **Be specific.** If you want direct contact with your clitoris, ask for that, don't say "more rubbing."
- **Make requests.** Don't demand action, remember your manners and ask politely.
- **Use "I" statements.** "I come more easily when you lick my balls" will get you more action than "You always ignore my balls during oral sex."
- **Compromise.** If you can't each get your way, come up with creative compromises ("I'll go down on you once a week, if you let me masturbate in the shower").

LUBRICATION: KEEP THINGS GOING SMOOTHLY

Just as communication helps keep the sex play going, lubrication helps keep your bodies flowing. It ensures a slippery smooth encounter, so that your pleasure isn't marred by irritation or chafing, especially during penetration. Mother Nature's lubricant (in the form of pre-come, vaginal lubrication, or saliva) isn't always adequate, so keep a bottle of artificial lubricant on hand.

You'll notice that, in most of the activities described in this book, lubricant is recommended along with the sex toy. That's because sex toy materials can absorb your natural lubrication quickly, leaving you high and dry. With a bottle of lube on hand, even the Energizer Bunny won't outlast you. Lubricant livens up masturbation, it can make vaginal penetration more comfortable, and it's essential for anal penetration, since the anus doesn't produce its own lubrication.

In general, water-based lubricants (such as Astroglide, KY, Slippery Stuff) are recommended for most types of sex play. This is because they're safe to use with condoms, they wash out of the body easily, and they won't irritate or cause yeast infections in most women. Thicker water-based lubricants, often sold as gels, are recommended for anal play. The biggest complaint about water-based lubes is that they dry up quickly, a problem that can be easily rectified by applying a little water or saliva to reactivate the lube.

Silicone-based lubricants are fairly new to the market and are popular because they don't evaporate as quickly as water-based lubes, so you don't need to reapply as often. They also won't wash off in water, so they're great for underwater sex. They are compatible with condoms and can be used externally for genital massage. On the down side, they're more expensive, are not always compatible with silicone toys, and are harder to clean up (soap and water will do the trick externally, but vaginal cleanup is more problematic).

Oil-based lubricants like Vaseline will deteriorate the latex in condoms or diaphragms, plus they're hard to wash out of the vagina. They're okay to use anally or externally for hand jobs (unless you're having safer sex with condoms or dams).

Choosing a lubricant comes down to a matter of personal preference. Most water-based lubes claim to be taste and odor-free, but sensitive taste buds often detect a soapy aftertaste. Some people like stringier lubes, others prefer creamy or gellike textures. If you're very sensitive, or prone to yeast infections, choose a glycerin-free lube. Many vendors now sell packets of lube samples, which can be a great way to try a variety.

Now that you've got the main ingredients for an exotic sex toy adventure, go play!

TAKING CARE OF BUSINESS:
Care and Safety

If you're tempted to skip this chapter because sex toys pose little threat to your sexual health, please don't! Sure, when you enjoy sex toys alone, you can't give or get a sexually transmitted disease, but if you are using toys with a partner, you'll want to know how they can be shared safely. And because sex toys are often incorporated into other types of sex play, it's helpful to review basic safer sex guidelines.

WHAT IS SAFER SEX?

Let's just start with a brief primer. Safer sex is intended to prevent the transmission of sexually transmitted diseases (STDs). There are more than fifty known STDs, the most fearsome of which is HIV, the virus that causes AIDS, a life-threatening illness. STDs are either bacterial (chlamydia, syphilis, gonorrhea), which can be treated and often cured with antibiotics, or viral (herpes, HIV, genital warts), which can be treated but aren't always curable. Safer sex practices minimize the exchange of bodily fluids like semen, blood, and saliva, as these provide the conduit for viruses and bacterial infections to pass through. Activities like dry humping, dry kissing, and massage are considered absolutely safe, but other sexual

> **Toy Testimonial**
>
> "My safer sex ice-breaker?
>
> Colored condoms!"

activities, usually variations of oral, anal, and vaginal sex, require some kind of latex barrier (condoms, gloves) for them to be considered safer sex. (It's called "safer" because even with a barrier, you're still at risk of it possibly failing.)

ARE YOU AT RISK FOR AN STD?

Basically, if you're sexually active you are at risk for contracting an STD. Currently, one in five people has an STD, so your odds of hooking up with someone who has one are pretty good. Given that a lot of folk have STDs and don't always know it because some symptoms aren't detectable (chlamydia and genital warts, for example), practicing safer sex just makes good sense, as does getting tested once a year. If you're in a monogamous relationship and you've both tested negatively recently, your risk is negligible. If you are taking an HIV test after unprotected sex, bear in mind that HIV can live in the body for up to six months without being detected, so for definitive results the test should be taken after this period.

BREAK OUT THE CONDOMS

You may not have realized it before, but one of the key components to safer sex is a well-known, if little appreciated, sex toy: the condom. How many other sex accessories do you know that can prevent pregnancy and disease transmission, while also coming in a splendid array of sizes, colors, textures, and flavors? Condoms are the star players in a lineup of safer sex accessories that also includes dental dams (used for oral sex), latex gloves (used for anal finger penetration), or finger cots (used externally, if you have cuts on your fingers). But for a lot of people, condoms still feel like a necessary evil. Most of us are familiar with the old wearing-condoms-is-like-taking-a-shower-with-a-raincoat analogy, but isn't it really all about attitude? Consider the man for whom condoms elicit an erotic thrill because they remind him of his youth, when carrying condoms in his pocket meant he might be getting laid soon!

So give condoms a break, and give them a chance. If you want more sensation on your penis, try a thin one (Kimono) or one with a pouchy tip (Pleasure Plus or Inspiral). If you're allergic to latex, try one made of polyurethane (Avanti). If you want more friction, get an unlubed condom, and if you want more glide, add extra lube to your condom. If you hate the taste of latex, get a fruit- or mint-flavored condom, or add your own flavor. If you're a woman and you want to take control, try a female condom (Reality). Finally, make sure you know how to put the condom on correctly. Always unroll it the right way, put a dab of lube in the tip, and, before you start unrolling it down the shaft, squeeze the air out of the tip. Hold on to the base when you're done, so the condom doesn't slip off.

SEX TOYS AND SAFE SEX

If you're using your sex toys alone, just remember not to insert a dildo into your vagina after it has already been in your anus, as this can transmit bacteria. Toys made of rubber, cyberskin, or other porous materials are best used with condoms over them, as dirt and bacteria can be difficult to scrub out of the material. Toys made of nonporous materials like silicone, plastic, latex, and acrylic can be cleaned with hot soapy water and left to air dry. If you have any questions about the toy material or cleanup requirements, contact the company where you bought it.

If you're planning on sharing a toy like a dildo, put a fresh condom on it each time you use it. Or consider investing in two toys—one for each of you. Keep in mind that while sex toy play is a pretty safe activity, it becomes unsafe if you are engaging in other forms of unprotected sex. For example, if you like wearing a butt plug during intercourse, you still need a condom over that penis if you intend to practice safer sex.

SAFE SEX IS SMART SEX

Safe sex is smart sex because you're taking responsibility for your own and your partner's sexual health. This is a sign of respect, self-confidence, and sexual agency. It's too easy to let passion overwhelm your common sense, so make a commitment to yourself beforehand to practice safer sex. If you need some practice asserting your desires, there are some good websites and books to help you role-play.

I've given you only the most basic facts about STDs and safer sex here. If you want more information, contact the Centers for Disease Control or a sex information hotline (see Resources). Smart sex also involves advance planning about birth control, so please take some time to research your contraceptive options.

Play

THE BLISSFUL BUZZ: Masturbating with a Clitoral Vibrator

Toy(s) you will need: Wahl 7-in-1 or Pocket Rocket
(or any clitoral vibrator)

Type of play: Solo

The vibrator, an amazingly versatile instrument of pleasure, has single-handedly introduced thousands of women to orgasmic bliss. If you think that sounds like an adult bookstore's marketing hype, visit a women's sexuality website, read some erotica, or ask a sex therapist—you'll see that the vibrator plays a pivotal role in women's experience of sex. During the years I worked in a sex shop, I had countless people—married, singles, old and young—come back after buying their first vibrator and blushingly utter two words to me: "Thank you." If you can remember what it was like to orgasm for the very first time, you know what an incredibly powerful awakening this is.

When you think about what and how women learn about sex, it's no surprise the vibrator sweeps us off of our feet. Unlike men, whose genitalia, being external, make erotic exploration unavoidable, women have to search for their clits and vaginas. And few do, thanks to cultural messages we receive about being dirty "down there" and "saving" ourselves till marriage. All this does is set women up for frustration once they finally find themselves in a sexual situation. How many of us have spent nights hoping a lover's penis or tongue would get us off, only to be teased or disappointed!

Enter the vibrator, a small device that does two things: first, it requires women to masturbate, a necessary part of sexual self-discovery. Second, vibrators help women achieve orgasm. Whether it helps you climax for the first time or makes it easier for you to come, a vibrator can fill in where Mother Nature comes up short. For years I masturbated manually, only to have my hand cramp up seconds before I came. Now I'm never more than a pair of batteries away from reliable stimulation.

If you're trying vibrator stimulation for the first time, choosing the right toy is key (see the "Toys for All Seasons" chapter). Many women futilely thrust phallic-shaped vibrators in and out of their vaginas, assuming this simulated intercourse will lead to thigh-clenching orgasms. In fact, according to the Kinsey Report, about 80 percent of women orgasm primarily from clitoral stimulation and 20 percent from vaginal penetration. Given those statistics, the following advice is geared primarily toward clitoral stimulation, but you are most certainly welcome to add vaginal stimulation to this activity as well. For more on vaginal orgasms, see the "G Marks the Spot" activity.

If You've Never Had an Orgasm . . .

The two vibrators recommended for this activity are particularly well suited for first-timers. Any vibrator will do, but I chose these for the intensity of their vibrations and their nonthreatening appearance. The Wahl is an electric vibrator available in most drugstores and looks like a handheld mixer or small appliance. It delivers strong, focused vibrations and is the quietest vibrator I've encountered (great if you have nosy housemates or kids). If you want something that's not quite so appliance-like, consider the Pocket Rocket, a smaller toy with surprisingly strong vibrations. It runs on batteries, which makes it a great travel vibe, plus it's easy to stash in bedside tables or purses.

Wahl 7-in-1
Personal Massager

Pocket
Rocket

- **Relax.** The key to your enjoyment is your ability to relax and stay in the moment, so check your anxieties or frustrations at the door. Stop thinking about work, the kids, or the dirty laundry. Take a warm bath or get a massage beforehand.
- **Turn yourself on.** Think about what things have turned you on in the past and focus on them now to jump-start your arousal. Fantasize about a steamy sexual encounter, replay a scene from a sexy movie, or imagine yourself naked with your favorite celebrity. If you enjoy additional stimulation, put on some sexy music or read some erotica.
- **Have a look.** If you've never really looked at your genitals before, take out a mirror and hold it with one hand while you use the other hand to locate the parts of your genitalia. Look for the clitoris under its protective hood at the top of your vulva;

identify your labia, vagina, and anus. It might help to have an anatomical diagram next to you if you're having trouble figuring out what's what.

- **Let your fingers do the walking.** Use your fingertips to explore all the parts of your genital anatomy. Notice the smoothness of the labial folds, and the hardness of the clitoris. Peel back the clitoral hood and touch the glans so you are familiar with its sensitivity. Insert a finger into your vagina and notice the different textures as it moves in slightly. As you explore, pay attention to the parts of your vulva that feel especially good when stimulated.

- **Play with yourself.** Put the mirror down, lie on your back, and touch yourself all over. Begin by running your hands all over your skin, lingering on the spots that feel particularly sensitive—including the breasts and the insides of your thighs. Try a variety of movements on your labia and clitoris, pulling, pinching, and rubbing along the smooth skin. Focus on the clitoris, paying attention to any erotic sensations that certain moves generate. Some women like to use two fingers to rub over the clitoral hood in a circular motion; others place a fingertip on either side of the clitoris and move from side to side.

- **Feel the buzz.** Turn your vibrator on and explore in much the same way that you did with your hands. Try running the toy over different parts of your body, including your genitals, but saving your clit for last. Lightly place the tip of the vibrator on your clitoral hood. If the vibration is too intense, place a washcloth or piece of clothing between your body and the toy.

- **Add your Kegels.** Slowly rock your hips back and forth, contracting your PC muscles (what you squeeze when you want to stop a stream of urine) in time to the motion.

- **Mix it up.** Vary the speed on your vibrator or apply pressure to get a stronger vibration on your clitoris. If you're moving the toy around, try changing the direction of the motion. As your arousal builds, try stopping and starting the vibration. By "teasing" your clit you coax it along—when you withhold the stimulation, your body jumps back after it when it's resumed. If you have a hard time getting over the top, stop the toy for longer periods and relax your muscles. Try using the vibrator in a different position—squeeze it between your legs or lie on top of it.

- **Breathe deeply.** Resist the urge to hold your breath; instead, take long, deep breaths. With practice, you can coordinate the rhythm of your breathing to your mounting arousal. When you feel yourself close to orgasm, inhale, then time your exhale with the onset of the orgasm, and you'll feel the sexual contraction flow through your body to your toes.

- **Stay with it.** One of the frustrating and magical things about orgasm is that it can feel very elusive up until you're actually seconds away from having one. Once you hit the point of no return, your orgasm will sweep over you in a matter of seconds, and your body will be wracked by several contractions.

- **Go for multiples.** Vibrators are tireless—they can keep going and going long after hands or penises tire out. After your first orgasm, remove the vibrator if your clit is too sensitive, but return after a few seconds to try for another orgasm. You might be surprised at how easy it is to go for more than one, or two, or three . . .

- **Try and try again.** Don't worry if you don't make it on your first go-round. Just pick up the toy again later and give it another try. Sometimes it can take several weeks before your body becomes accustomed to the stimulation. Try to learn from each attempt, paying close attention to which types of stimulation feel best and building on those.

If You've Had Orgasms but Never with a Vibrator . . .

I've had a few people ask, "Why would I use a vibrator when I can come just fine without one?" to which I often reply, "Why hand wash when you've got a machine?" At their most basic, vibrators are labor-saving devices—they last longer than our (or our lover's) hands—getting a job done efficiently and expertly. But they've had a bigger impact than that. Just as the industrial age freed up time to pursue leisurely activities, vibrators free our minds (no more anxieties about whether we're coming), free our hands (to explore other pleasure spots), and free our sexual appetites. When sexual pleasure is easily attained, our self-confidence grows and we're likely to want more sex. Put simply, good sex leads to better sex, which leads to more sex.

On top of that, vibrators can add something new to your routine. Many women claim that vibrator-induced orgasms are more intense than those they get through manual stimulation. Many women become multiply orgasmic thanks to the vibrator's unfailing dedication to their clits. And plenty of couples in search of simultaneous orgasms find that vibrators offer women the necessary stimulation to reach this end. Here are some things to keep in mind if you're an old pro at orgasms, but you're new to vibrators:

> ### Toy Testimonials
>
> "My husband uses the Wahl body massager with the small rounded tip on my clit with some KY warming lotion, and I'm off in ninety seconds, over and over again."

- **Go with what you know.** Since you know what kind of stimulation already feels good to you, select a vibrator that offers something similar. Decide where you want to use the vibrator (vaginally, clitorally, anally, etc.) and then narrow down the selection based on what type of stimulation (strong, light, diffuse, focused) meets your requirements.

- **Masturbate with your toy.** Even if you're buying a toy to use with a partner, masturbate with it first so you get to know what feels best and can later show your partner. Follow the steps above, paying particular attention to breathing and experimenting with the toy on different parts of your body.

- **Add or subtract.** Once you've come with your vibrator, try changing your style. Most people feel dependent on one method of stimulation for their orgasms, but if you've successfully used your vibrator, you now have at least two ways. Capitalize on your success by adding other toys to the mix (a vaginal or anal toy perhaps) or by trying it in a new position. Experiment with breathing and fantasy.

Stimulating multiple pleasure points with a vibrator and a dildo

Variations

- If you like the feeling of your hand on your genitals, try masturbating with the fingertip vibe known as the Fukuoku.
- If you're able to get off from a spray of water in the shower or tub, try using a waterproof vibe on your clit during your next soak in the tub.
- If you want to free your hands to play with your breasts or to add vibration during intercourse, try a hands-free clit vibe.
- If you like to masturbate by lying on top of an object, try

putting a wand-style vibrator (like the Hitachi) underneath you or slipping a Natural Contours vibrator into your underwear and pressing against an object.

- Add an insertable vibrator for G spot stimulation or a butt plug for anal stimulation.

PRIMING THE PUMP: Masturbating with a Penis Sleeve

Toy(s) you will need: Fleshlight (or other penis sleeve)
                                Lubricant
Type of play: Solo or partnered

I must admit, before writing my first book, *The Good Vibrations Guide to Sex*, I just figured all men masturbated with their hands. Sure, that is a time-honored masturbation method, but over the years I've heard from countless men who've employed everything from couch cushions to knotholes in the floor to get off. Today, you don't need to worry about stains or splinters, because there are plenty of sex toys around to help you get the job done more safely, from sleeves and cock rings to penis pumps and vibrators.

In this activity, you'll have fun masturbating with something called a sleeve. Intended to re-create the feeling of a penis in a vagina, sleeves are simply tubes into which your penis is inserted. The most popular sleeve on the market today is the Fleshlight. It's made out of a special material (commonly referred to as cyberskin) that feels an awful lot like real skin. It's shaped like a large flashlight, with an outer casing made of plastic and an inner removable lining. The Fleshlight was invented by a former police officer at a time when sex with his wife was off-limits (she was having a high-risk pregnancy). He recognized the potential marketability of his toy, but wanted something that would appeal to men and convey a sense of humor—and so the flashlight design was born. It's a great story that illustrates one man's attempt to bridge the gap between boys and their sex toys.

- **Prep.** Take the cap off the Fleshlight and keep some water-based lubricant handy. It's important to use water-based lube rather than oil-based (like Vaseline). Some men like to cut their lube with water (in equal parts), as this prevents it from getting tacky faster and makes the lubricant really slippery.

Fleshlight

- **Get the toy hot.** Take the gel insert out of the plastic casing and run it under hot tap water until it's nice and warm. Shake it a bit to remove the excess water and place it back inside the casing.
- **Get yourself hot.** Do what you do to get yourself in the mood—watch an adult video, fantasize, touch yourself.
- **Lube it up.** Apply lube to your penis when it's firm enough to penetrate the toy. If you're uncircumcised, pull the foreskin down and lubricate the head of your penis in addition to the outside area. This will give you double the friction. Squirt a bit

of lube inside the sleeve and around the entrance.

- **Dive in.** Put your penis into the opening of the sleeve and experiment with movement. Hold your penis still and move the sleeve up and down on top of it or hold the sleeve still and thrust into it. You can adjust the tightness of the end cap, which will create a bit of suction many find pleasurable. Go slow at first, don't force things. You can also remove the end cap and insert a Bullet vibrator if you want to add vibrations to your play. You may find that it takes a few sessions with the Fleshlight to appreciate it.
- **Clean up.** Remove the insert from the plastic case and rinse it out with warm water. Air dry it, then dust it with cornstarch, which will minimize the tackiness.

Toy Testimonials

"When I close my eyes I imagine my girlfriend going down on me—my dick in the Fleshlight feels a lot like getting a blow job, but I don't have to worry about her teeth!"

Variations

- **Free your hands.** Sandwich the Fleshlight between mattresses or clamp it into a desk.
- **Try other toys.** There are plenty of other sleeve-type toys on the market; some vibrate, and some are open on both sides. Open-ended sleeves can be turned into vibrators by inserting a bullet in one side.
- **Add extra stimulation.** Increase the thrill by masturbating with a butt plug or a cock ring as well. Nipple clamps are also great for men with sensitive nipples.

- **Do it together.** You can play with the sleeve together, which can come in handy during times when the woman is not comfortable with sex (after childbirth or an operation, or if she's got vaginismus). She can hold the Fleshlight between her legs and he can enter her from behind in the spoons position.

Bus Ride

by Colin Ladd

Chloe strolled over barefoot and took his wineglass from him, taking a sip.

"Hey, that's mine," Steve protested feebly.

She nodded, taking another. "Well, don't you think it's a good idea?" She rubbed her knee against his thigh as she stood over his reclining form on the sofa. Reaching out, he massaged her inner thigh just below the hem of her nightgown.

"Sure, baby," he murmured. The wine and the late hour were clouding his brain. He heard her laugh softly as she straddled him and sat down on his legs.

She put the wineglass down unsteadily on the nearby coffee table, turned, and placed her palms on his chest.

"You have no idea what we were talking about, do you?"

He laughed as he held her lightly by her hips. "No," he admitted as he watched her unbuckle his belt. "But I'm guessing I might like the idea."

She glanced, a flash of green under her lashes, then smiled a little as she reached for his zipper. "You might. I'll have to remind you in the morning."

"Oh." He tried not to sound disappointed and wracked his brain for whatever they were talking about before the wine took hold. The feeling wore off as he lifted her nightgown to slide his hands underneath.

She slowly unbuttoned his shirt and bent to kiss his chest.

As he let his hand play across the curve of her spine he murmured, "Give me a clue?"

After nipping his chest and kissing it better she stood to pull down his pants. "A clue, mmmm."

She was tantalizingly out of reach again as she exposed him and made approving sounds as she examined his excitement. Her fingers trailed lazily around his erection. "Mmm, a clue." Idly she massaged him as she sat astride his legs again. She let him lift the nightgown over her head as she squeezed his balls gently, watching him wriggle under her.

Bending forward, she kissed him. It was several minutes before she breathed, "The butterfly," between kisses.

Steve knew it was the clue but he didn't really take it in right then.

■ ■ ■

The following morning Chloe padded into the bedroom quietly after making some coffee. She put some down on Steve's side of the bed then walked around and sat on the white sheet. Sunlight filtered through the trees outside and fell across the bed, settling on her nakedness. With her feet she kicked the covers off his firm body and snuggled closer, draping her calf over his hip, feeling the warmth from his sleeping form.

Slowly she let the sole of her foot press up and down against his inner thighs, feeling him stir a little. She turned the TV on, the sound low, waiting for him to surface.

It was several minutes before he did, then one more while he panicked then remembered he was off work that day. He smiled as he felt Chloe's hands squeezing his upper arm and tangling in his hair.

"Good morning." She followed the words into his ear with her tongue, making him laugh and turn to taste her kiss. She tasted of coffee and toothpaste, soap and shampoo; she was always up early. Turning over, he reached for her.

"Uh-uh," she said, sliding a little away to reach for her coffee. He sat up and stretched. "Come on you slug, lying in bed till all hours." He looked at the TV news.

"All hours? It's 8 A.M."

She nodded, "Yes, I know. It's late and we have things to do."

He looked confused. Chloe had a plan, he could see it in her eyes. Mind you, at the moment her eyes weren't his top priority; he let his gaze take in her curves as she sat against the light. She smiled impishly as she eyed his early morning excitement but teasingly did nothing to relieve it.

He gave up on his memory. "Okay, what is it that we're doing that means I can't molest you this morning?"

She shuffled forward comically on her knees and leaned against Steve, putting her arms around him.

"Today we're going for a bus ride," she said simply.

Nodding, he said, "That's nice," none the wiser. "Why are we doing that?"

"Useless object." She tickled him and he grabbed at her. "Well, last night you thought it was a very wicked idea."

"Good, we'll do it then," he said.

She giggled. "Are you going to regret that when you remember?"

"I doubt it," he said, gazing down at her short brown hair.

"I'll get my butterfly, that might remind you." Leaving him to his coffee, she wandered away.

Butterfly? The only butterfly he recalled—something stirred in his memory to make him smile. On her return she was wearing her red leather miniskirt—*just* her red leather skirt, or so it seemed. It showed off her legs very nicely. He cleared his throat.

"I see you like the skirt," she said, sitting on the edge of the bed and letting her eyes take in his twitching erection. Leaning back on her arms, away from him, she parted her legs and beckoned him to come closer. He slid a hand up the inside of her soft thigh. Covering his hand, Chloe guided him slowly higher. He was only half surprised at the feel of soft plastic and latex covering her pussy.

He smiled. *"That* butterfly."

She nodded. They had bought the toy recently but hadn't used it yet.

"Remember what it said on the instructions?"

He smiled, trying to think.

"'Can be used with remote control for discreet pleasure all day,'" she quoted.

"So you would like a discreet pleasuring?" he asked hopefully.

"Very much so. And, I believe, we agreed on a nice bus drive, so neither of us had to concentrate on the road while we—well, road test it."

"Mmmmm, now, that is a fine idea," he said, sliding his mouth over her breast and lapping her nipple. She held him there for several moments feeling his morning stubble tantalizingly graze her soft skin. "Now we just need the remote. And a few more clothes." She sighed as he paid close attention to her breasts. Slowly she tore herself away and rummaged in a drawer, pulling out the little handset that controlled the speed of the toy. Lying on his side, Steve said, "Can I have a demonstration?"

She looked over her shoulder and lifted a quizzical eyebrow. "Who's to say I don't have it turned on now?"

"Mmmm . . . your voice is remarkably steady. I seem to recall a little more cracking when—"

"Okay, okay." She blushed and grinned. Sitting on the bed, she turned the control and shuddered a little. "God," she said.

"Your voice cracked." He chuckled. Quickly she turned it down. But not off.

"So do I get the remote? I seem to remember reading that men normally look after them," he said, swallowing a smirk.

She leaned over and smacked his ass. "Not this one you don't. Get ready. We've got a bus to catch."

■ ■ ■

Chloe slipped on a bra and white blouse, carefully secreting the remote in her purse, resisting the temptation to turn the toy back on. Later, she thought, feeling the wetness between her legs. Her anticipation increased while she waited for Steve to dress after his shower. On the short walk down from their apartment they had to pause in the hallway to make some adjustments to the toy. Giggling, they huddled in a doorway while Chloe made herself more comfortable.

"You can walk now?" Steve grinned.

She sashayed off, swinging her hips. With a glance back she said, "What do you think?" He slung his jacket over his shoulder, caught up quickly, and fondled her ass through the leather.

They started out hand in hand, but by the time they reached the bus stop they were standing close, sharing their secret vice in murmurs.

"You're a very bad girl, you know." Steve kissed the end of her nose.

"Am I?"

"Yes. Terrible. You're going to get excited in public. Very excited."

Nodding. "Maybe I shouldn't do it then," she teased.

"Did I say that? I like you bad."

Leaning in, Chloe nibbled his earlobe. She whispered, "You're going to watch me come, aren't you? Going to see me climax on the bus. I think that excites you too." She quickly brushed a hand over the bulge at the front of his faded blue jeans before kissing him deeply.

They would never have made successful criminals, Steve thought when the bus arrived. They both looked guilty climbing aboard; change went everywhere as they tried to act normal. The bus driver shook her head as they slunk off to a seat, giggling like teenagers.

The bus set off, slowly heading downtown, with few passengers. Steve put his hand on her knee; they both blushed.

"Sooo," he said. "Here we are then. Now what can we do?"

She swallowed, suddenly nervous for a second before putting her purse on her lap. She slipped her fingers inside; Steve squeezed her knee, feeling her tense up. He leaned close, whispering in her ear, "You turned it on didn't you, you bad girl?"

"Yes," she said softly, setting the purse between them, clasping his hand on her leg with her thighs squeezed together.

He looked at her; she licked her suddenly dry lips, dropping her eyes. "I'm going to watch closely," he said, turning a little away from the window to study her. She rocked forward a little and bit her upper lip.

Leaning close, he whispered, "Do you think you'll be able to keep still soon? Maybe people will notice?"

She tried to sit still, wiping her hand on the seat, looking over to him as the bus rolled to a halt at another stop.

"These two women are getting on, they're going to walk right by you as you sit there getting more and more excited," he whispered.

She stretched out one leg under the seat in front of them, trying to look casual as the new passengers made their way down the bus. Her sandal fell off and she shifted in her seat. Steve massaged her inner thigh as he watched her trying not to writhe.

"You're very excited right now, aren't you?" He spoke the words and glanced out of the window as if he were describing something outside. "Wet, I expect?"

She let out a long moan, then tried to stifle it with a cough. She looked at him, nodding, unable to trust her voice not to give her away.

He leaned in and pecked her on the cheek, whispering, "You're going to come for me soon, aren't you?"

She stretched out both legs under the seat, her hips moved as she leaned back then into his side. "Now, now," she moaned in his ear; he tried to hold her but she had to sit up in the seat and clutch his hand on her leg. She was panting and breathed to him, "Turn it off, please."

Reaching in her bag, he pulled out the controls and switched it to zero. Chloe slumped against his arm, her breathing settling a little.

He smiled. "Well, that was the first," he said. "And now I've got the remote."

She sat up and pinched his thigh. "You want more?" she asked, straightening her hair. He nodded.

"Well, the next one is going to be mutual," she said.

"Mut—ahhhhh . . ." He blushed and she chuckled evilly.

"Scared?"

"No," he said, flustered.

She leaned in. "You can cover yourself up with your jacket. No one will know. Well, maybe not." She kissed his cheek. "You'd do that for me, wouldn't you? Mmmm? With a little help?"

He looked at her, a question on his face. She rummaged in her purse and pulled out the bullet vibrator they'd bought with the butterfly.

He swallowed. "I see." He took the toy and covered it with his palm.

As they kissed she stole back the controls to her butterfly and giggled. "You know how excited I just made you," she urged. "You know you want to do it for me."

He looked out of the window with pretended calm. "Yes, I do," he said.

"Good." Chloe adjusted the jacket in his lap and slipped his right hand under it. She watched him move in his seat as he fumbled with his zipper. She slid her hand under the jacket to feel his fingers surrounding his stiff cock and felt his other hand slide the bullet over his balls. Its soft vibrations ran through their hands as she held him. She patted them and withdrew, taking the controls to her toy.

"Next notch up, I think, this time," she whispered.

The bus was moving slowly through the downtown traffic.

Writhing a little in her seat, she turned to him, putting her head on his shoulder. "You know what this is doing to me, don't you, baby? You know how it's pulsing on my pussy and clit, inside me too? Does that make you hard?"

She watched as he moved his hips, holding the jacket over his exposed cock. "Tell me what you're doing," she said huskily.

"F . . . feeling myself," he groaned. "Holding my cock for you. Using the toy . . ." His voice faded as he began to pant, trying to control his motions, wondering what people behind their seat were thinking.

"It's nice and big, isn't it?" she groaned against his neck. "It would like to be where my toy is right now, wouldn't it? You seem to be moving f . . . faster," she grunted and her hips rose and fell as she again increased the speed of the vibrations. He looked at her as if he was trying to look through the leather of the skirt to see how damp the soft curls at the top of her legs were, to see how the toy penetrated and aroused her.

She reached over and kneaded his arm with her nails, then leaning close, she growled, "Show me."

"No." The word was louder than he meant as he felt himself getting close to his climax.

"Yes," she said. "No one will see," she whispered, her mouth hot next to his ear. She moved closer, her body tight against his, lifting the jacket just enough for her to see, exposing him to her eyes as he massaged his cock, as his fingers pressed the bullet to his balls. She moaned, getting close to him, running her hand over the front of her skirt in order to push the toy closer. She needed to feel the toy deeper, pressed between her soft lips, as she approached orgasm. She struggled to maintain composure, though no one on the half-empty bus seemed to notice them.

He rubbed his hardness for her, then groaned and leaned forward.

"Yes, baby," she breathed. "Show me. Right here. Do it for me." Chloe wrapped her ankles around his as she watched him touch himself, making her shudder and thrust, stifling her moans as she was again engulfed by her climax.

Steve moaned, helpless under her gaze, and clutched at his cock while running the bullet around his balls. She knew without him saying how close he was. Moments later his seed spurted onto his jacket and his pants, and she watched his Adam's apple bob as he tried to silently climax. Another spurt followed onto the floor before his coming subsided into streams down his cock, fingers, and balls.

For long moments they sat together, kissing and feeling their racing hearts slow, before she reached in her purse for tissues. "Messy man." She smiled. "That jacket will need dry cleaning."

G MARKS THE SPOT: The Hunt for the G Spot

Toy(s) you will need:	Classic G vibrator or Crystal Wand dildo (or any G spot toy)
	Lubricant
Type of play:	Solo or partnered

Like so many women, I was completely mystified by the G spot when I first heard about it. Mystified and more than a little perturbed. I mean, after years of having orgasmless intercourse, I had finally discovered that the clitoris was the key to my climax. Then here comes news of this mysterious spot inside the vagina that could also lead to orgasm *and* (big blush) result in ejaculation! I was convinced I didn't have one or I would have felt it by now. Then I calmly reminded myself that I'd thought my clitoris was broken until I eventually hit the big O while masturbating. So I started looking for it. Those early G spot expeditions felt a lot like a game of pin the tail on the donkey. I couldn't see what I was doing, I felt around blindly for the right spot, and I was not entirely convinced I wasn't making an ass out of myself (with my hand stuck up my vagina at a very unnatural angle). But persistence paid off and I discovered a unique erotic sensation. In my case, a dildo rubbing the G spot and a vibrator on my clit will be rewarded by a pretty wonderful orgasm (and a little messy ejaculate too).

The G spot is an area of spongy tissue on the front wall of the vagina. It was named after the doctor who noticed his patients responded to stimulation of the area. Keep in mind that while every woman has a G spot, not everyone responds to it in the same way. I've heard from women whose experiences run the gamut—some get off quickly with G spot stimulation, some find it complements other forms of sex, some notice a slight change in their responsiveness, and others don't feel a thing. Some women ejaculate, and others do not. There's absolutely nothing wrong with you if you never find your G spot, but I encourage you to at least look for it. You might not find a buried treasure, but you may discover some other new path to pleasure.

Some women are reluctant to experiment with G spot play because they're embarrassed about possibly ejaculating (which happens for some women). Having put up with it from men for years, I'm not sure why we all aren't shouting "Hey, bub, it's my turn," but if you're worried about it, you might be reassured to know that ejaculate is not urine, despite decades of doctors and scientists insisting it is. It does come through the same glands as urine (much the same way men's ejaculate does), but it has a different chemical composition. If you need to convince yourself, pee beforehand and if you still ejaculate you'll know it wasn't because you had to go. And rest assured that you are in good company—female ejaculate has been revered in other cultures for centuries; it's believed to have healing, rejuvenative, and aphrodisiacal powers. Men can also help alleviate concerns about ejaculation. Whether you tell her it's hot, funny, or just doesn't matter, make her feel as comfortable as possible, so she's free to fully pursue her desires. Once she's able to let go of this anxiety and allow herself to orgasm and/or ejaculate, you may both come to see it as a turn-on.

The toys suggested for this activity are two of the most popular G spot toys available today. I've given you a choice here because some women prefer the rock-hard texture of a toy like the Crystal Wand, which is shaped like an *S* and made out of acrylic, while others like more pliant toys like the Classic G vibrator. (This vibrator goes by many different names—Crystal G, Nubby G—so it's best to look for it based on its description. It is made of translucent rubber, bends gently midway up the shaft, and sports a band of bumps near the base that are designed to stimulate the vaginal opening during insertion.) Every woman is unique, so by all means experiment with different toys to discover exactly what pleases you. If your curiosity is piqued, now's the time to start exploring! If you're new to G spot play, practice alone first so you're free to look funny, get messy, and take as long as you wish. Once you've gotten familiar with the particular sensitivities of your own G spot, you'll be well equipped to show your partner.

Going Solo

- **Prep.** Get naked, have your toys and lube handy, and put a towel under yourself in case you ejaculate.
- **Get hot.** Since the spongy area around the G spot gets engorged with blood when you're sexually aroused, it'll definitely help your responsiveness if you're turned on. Read some erot-

ica, watch a sexy movie, have your partner give you a massage, tease your nipples or your clit, but don't come.

- **Start the hunt.** Try to locate your G spot with your fingers first, so you know where to put your toy later. It might be difficult to reach it if you're lying on your back, unless you can pull your knees up to your chest. Try squatting, lying on your stomach, or propping yourself up slightly on hands and knees. Place your palm facedown on your vulva and slowly insert a finger inside your vagina (use lube if you're feeling a little dry), crooking it forward. When you're up to about the second knuckle you should feel a slightly bumpy or ridged area on the upper wall of your vagina; the texture feels noticeably different from the typically smooth walls of the vagina. When you're aroused it can expand from the size of a pea to about the size of a quarter, so feel it at different times during your arousal to get familiar with its contours and sensitivity.

- **Time for the toy.** Some expeditions were made for toys, and the G spot quest is one of them. Because it can be rather awkward to stimulate the G by hand, a vibrator or dildo can get the job done more effectively. Lie on your back, apply a little lube to your toy, and insert it with the tip pointing up toward the top wall of your vagina. Work it in slowly, far enough (a couple of inches) so the tip is pressing against your G spot. If you're using the vibrator, don't turn it on yet, but use it first as a dildo so you can get used to the feeling of the toy against your G spot.

- **Squeeze your PC muscle.** A well-toned PC muscle (the muscle you use to stop a flow of urine in midstream) will help increase your vaginal sensitivity and your ability to ejaculate. Feel the muscles bearing down on your finger, paying attention to any tingly sensations as you do so.

- **Tickle your G.** Apply pressure to the toy so that you can

Masturbation with a G spot vibrator

experiment with the amount of friction you prefer against your
G spot. The G spot responds to firm pressure, so there's no need
to tread lightly. In the beginning, use your toy as if you were trying to scratch an itch—don't pull the toy all the way out, but use
short strokes—pressing and pulling it firmly against the G spot.
Try a variety of movements to see which feels the best to you: a
circular or back-and-forth motion may be necessary to get you
started, but you might soon graduate to a more vigorous thrusting. If you've got a vibrator, try playing with the vibrations both
on and off to see which you like better. Some women love internal vibrations; others find them too distracting.

- **Bring in the clit.** You'll know you're hitting the spot as you
feel tingly sensations, the urge to pee, and an overall elevation
in your arousal. When you feel the urge to come, stimulate your
clitoris using your favorite method. A lot of women find clit
stimulation is necessary to take them over the top, so keep
stroking your G spot while you use your hand or a vibrator on
your clitoris.

- **Give in and let go.** With continued stimulation, you'll eventually feel a sensation much like having to urinate. This can be quite disconcerting at first and has probably led plenty of women to abandon the process, but if you stick with it you'll be in for a pleasant surprise. If you give in to the feeling you may feel the release of orgasm and ejaculation simultaneously, which can be a potent combination. The force of your orgasm will cause your vaginal muscles to expel the toy, along with the ejaculate. So loosen your grip on the toy and let nature take its course!

- **Try, try again.** If you don't make it, try again later. It can take several practice sessions before you notice any change in your responsiveness. Try varying your position, using a different toy (see below), experimenting with breathing and Kegel exercises (to strengthen your PC muscle), or having a partner help you. Because the G spot is most responsive when aroused, you might try stimulating it immediately after you've come.

Getting Your Partner in on the Action

G spot play is a natural for couples. Helping a woman discover her G spot, using your body to bring her to orgasm, and watching her ejaculate are a few of the things you can look forward to together.

- **Awaken the G spot together.** If you've already explored your G spot alone, you can describe for your partner where and how you like to be touched. If you haven't, follow the same steps described above, but let your partner find your G spot with his fingers or using your toy before you try it with his penis. Give him plenty of verbal cues and feedback while he tries a variety of strokes on your G spot.
- **Hand over the toy.** Putting your partner in charge of the

toys means you can relax and simply enjoy the sensations that flow through your body. He might hold one in your vagina and one on your clitoris, or you can each hold one. Experiment with lying on your back or stomach and having him penetrate you with different toys (use plenty of lube). If your ultimate goal is to orgasm from intercourse, this is a good midway step. When using a dildo or a toy on you, your partner gets a close-up look at your expressions and reactions as he manipulates the toy. He pays attention to the subtle changes in motion and how you react to them, so when he replaces the toy with his penis, he can try to duplicate the movement.

- **Try the tongue.** For a particularly potent combination of pleasures, have your partner massage your G spot with a dildo or vibrator while he's tonguing your clit. Start first with the toy until you're feeling aroused, then have him begin oral sex, focusing on wide, long licks rather than fast flicks. Rock your hips gently, giving him feedback on rhythm and pressure.

- **Get that penis in on the action.** Some intercourse positions are better for G spot stimulation than others. Woman on top is great, as the woman stays in control of the positioning and can move her body slightly (usually bending backward) to focus his penis on the front wall of her vagina. It's also easy to incorporate clitoral stimulation into this position using her hand or another toy. Rear entry is also popular, affording deep penetration at an angle well aligned with the G spot. You can modify this position by standing up and bending over slightly, with your arms braced against the wall, as this puts more pressure on your G spot and it's easy to push the penis out when you need to. When you want to add a little clitoral stimulation, either of you can use your hand or you can strap on a vibrator if you want your hands free. If you want to try to reach the G spot in the missionary position, a pillow under your hips will tip your pelvis up, allowing the penis to enter at a better angle during penetration.

- **Stand clear!** Partners should pay attention to the woman's arousal, as her powerful pelvic muscles might shoot out whatever's inside her during orgasm. If you want to see her ejaculate, arrange a signal—a word, squeeze, or noise—that lets you know she's about ready to come, then stand aside.

Variations

Toys designed specifically for G spot play proliferate on the market today, so here are a few things to consider when choosing:

- If you like the fullness, but not the vibration, choose a dildo. Look for dildos with a slight bend toward the tip. Some dildos come with a flexible spine so you can bend them to your desired angle. Other G spot toys feature a ball shape at the tip, designed so the bulbous part offers firmer pressure when rubbed over the G spot. If you want a hands-free experience, experiment with the dildos that suction onto surfaces. Texture also plays an important part in G spot stimulation. Many women report that firmer toys work better than soft rubber ones. Look for toys made of silicone, hard plastic, and acrylic.
- Some dildos can be turned into vibrators by inserting Bullet vibrators into their hollow cores. For solid dildos, especially those made of silicone, hold a strong clitoral vibrator such as

the Hitachi to the base when the dildo is inside you and you'll feel the vibrations.

- If you want simultaneous clit and vaginal vibration, try a combo vibe. The Hitachi with G spot attachment gives you strong vibrations both internally and externally. The insertable part is small, though, so if you want a bigger dildo, try one of the dual vibes.
- If you want to go for broke, consider adding butt or nipple stimulation too. Either you or your partner can don butt plugs for this activity, and the addition of nipple clamps can elevate your arousal even further.

THE RIGHT TOOL FOR THE JOB:

Stimulating Multiple Pleasure Points

Toy(s) you will need: Rabbit Pearl

                            Lubricant

Type of play: Solo

As you're quickly learning from the activities in this book, there's a toy out there that will take care of any sexual itch you might have. But what happens when you want to scratch more than one itch at a time? You wouldn't be the first, which is why you don't have to look far for toys designed to stimulate several of your hot spots at one time. I once encountered a toy called the Octopus, with eight attachments that could be used in various combinations to vibrate nearly every nook and cranny of your genital area. Granted, most people aren't fond of sexual encounters that resemble a scene from the movie *Alien,* but almost everyone has wished for a toy that would do at least two things at once.

For example, a man might like a vibrator that stimulates the penis and the testicles simultaneously, a woman wearing a strap-on dildo might choose one that vibrates her clitoris as well as the dildo, or either sex might enjoy anal vibration at the same time as they're experiencing clitoral, vaginal, or penile stimulation. I can't illuminate every toy possibility here, so I chose one toy with a lot to offer. It's often called a "dual" vibrator because it combines vaginal penetration with clitoral stimulation. Women insert the vibrating dildo vaginally and the external branch is positioned to stimulate the clitoris. This type of toy has been around for years because this dual stimulation is very popular with those who try it.

Rabbit Pearl

This particular model, the Rabbit Pearl, is a sexy battery vibrator imported from Japan, where it is illegal to make toys that look like human genitals. As a result, Japanese toymakers turn out some of the most artistic, whimsical toys you can imagine. The dildo is carved to look like a geisha; the branch is a little bunny whose ears flick vigorously when the toy is turned on. This toy has one other special appeal— small plastic balls are housed in the midsection of the dildo, so when the vibrator is turned on these balls tumble around inside you. Compared to the rather industrial look of the Hitachi or the cat-dragged-in look of typical realistic vibrators, the Rabbit Pearl just oozes sex appeal. I often refer to it as the Marilyn Monroe of vibrators.

Another version of the Rabbit Pearl is known as the Rabbit Habit; its controls are contained in the base of the toy rather than in the attached battery pack. You may of course substitute any similar dual-action vibrator for the Rabbit Pearl, but it's worth noting that the Japanese-made battery toys are a much better quality than those made elsewhere. You can also use two separate toys—a vibrating dildo and a clitoral vibrator like the Bullet or Pocket Rocket—to achieve almost the same effect. You can play with this toy alone (and I hope you do), or you may take turns using it with a partner. Just make sure to clean it thoroughly between uses, or invest in his-and-hers Rabbits!

- **Prep.** Put batteries in your toy and keep it within arm's reach. Turn yourself on. You want to be good and aroused before inserting the dildo part of this vibrator into your vagina.
- **Position.** Try using this toy in whatever position you use to masturbate normally. Flat on your back with legs propped gives you easy entry, plus the battery pack will be within easy reach.
- **Rev it up.** Turn the toy on and experiment with the controls so you can see how they interact with one another. One control will let you adjust the swivel of the dildo, while the other will affect the vibration of the shaft and the rabbit. Notice that if you bend the shaft slightly, you will increase the arc of the dildo. Make sure you remember which control turns the rotating pearls on and off as these can be pleasant or irritating.
- **Hop to it.** Run the vibrator over different parts of your body, getting a feel for the intensity of the vibrations. When you're ready, apply lots of lubricant to the shaft and a dab to the rabbit (the branch coming off the shaft). Run the shaft along your genitals to tease yourself before inserting the toy.
- **Invite the geisha in.** With the rotating pearls and the vibrator turned off, add lube to your toy and insert the shaft

Toy Testimonials

"I have a dildo that I lube up and put in my pussy. Then I get out the Hitachi with the Gee Whiz attachment. This I ease inside, in front of the dildo so that it is up against my wall, really filling me. Then I add the clit buzzer and *yow!*"

gently into the vagina. Position the toy so that the rabbit vibrates against the clitoris. Now you've got the toy right where
you want it, and your next move is up to you. You can focus on
each pleasure point in turn, so you can isolate which settings on
the vibrator feel the best, or you can turn them all on and see
what happens. Here are some settings you'll want to try:

- *The swiveling dildo.* If you hold the dildo by the base, you'll
  feel the swivel internally. If you let it rest inside you unas-
  sisted, the force of your vaginal muscles will grip the toy so
  hard, the only part swiveling will be the base as it protrudes
  from your body. You might also find that at one angle,
  the dildo feels great against your G spot, so you turn off
  the swivel function and use the toy primarily as a dildo.
- *The vibrating dildo.* Turn off the swivel function and the
  dildo will vibrate along with the bunny ears.
- *The dildo with the rotating balls.* Some folks adore this sensation; others find it unexciting or downright annoying. The
  rotating balls make a snap, crackle, and pop noise as your
  muscles bear down on them, but the resulting stimulation
  can feel quite heavenly.

- **Rabbit ears to the rescue.** Experiment with moving the
  bunny ears slightly to the left and right of your clitoris, or up
  and down. If you need more intensity, press down with your
  hand against the bunny and the vibrations will feel stronger
  against your clit. (You might also prefer to lie on your stomach
  so the vibrator presses against your clit, freeing one hand to
  hold the shaft in place while the other operates the controls.)

Variations

- If you're a woman using the Rabbit Pearl vaginally, turn the rabbit around so it vibrates against your perineum and anus. Then you can hold a second vibrator over your clitoris, so you can stimulate four sensitive spots at once (clit, vagina, perineum, anus)!

- If you find the clitoral vibrations offered by the rabbit ears aren't strong enough for you, you can achieve the same effect with two toys instead of one. Use a clitoral vibrator paired with a G spot vibrator or dildo. Some women prefer this combination to the all-in-one stimulation, because they can control the dildo thrusting without interrupting the stimulation on the clitoris.

- Nipples are another great erogenous zone. Use nipple clamps or vibrating nipple clips while you're playing with other toys.

- Women and men can also use this toy for anal penetration, with the bunny ears turned to vibrate against the perineum.

Catalog Shopping

by Kate Dominic

If I lived in Texas or Alabama, I'd be breaking the law. I own more than five dildos—excuse me, "representational" sex toys. In other words, I have a sizable collection (all puns intended) of penis-shaped fake rubber/plastic/silicone dicks that look like the real thing. When, how, or even *if* I may (or may not) actually *use* these toys is privileged information. I'm a porn writer—I don't write nonfiction about my own sex life. But dildos are toys, adult toys, and writing about them isn't the same as writing about my own personal, private sex life. I'm writing about the toys, you know?

So, that's why lusting over sex toy catalogs isn't sexual behavior. It's shopping. And with selections like my favorite store has, I've been known to shop for hours. They ship overnight, direct from San Francisco, which means I could be playing with my toys in less than twenty-four hours. The only way I could get them faster would be if I walked in there myself! I wet my lips and open the book, which in this issue features the Silver Pearl.

This baby has everything! Representational look—long (six inches), thick (1¾-inch diameter) and pink, with a beautifully peeled back foreskin nestled beneath a smooth and shapely glans. Jelly rubber for comfort. Silver pearls on the rotating shaft for extra stimulation. A strong clitoral vibe that definitely looks like it represents (hell, is!) a good vibrator. And for the technophile in all of us, a lighted LED display for in-the-dark adjustments. The same page has Fun Fur Cuffs (strongly recommended). Soooo, I'm slipping in my first clear sticky note to mark my place.

Sparkling Curve (moving on a few pages) is another cutie. Again, pink jelly rubber, and from this angle, it looks like a thick foreskin is staying snuggled up right below where the glans has peeked out. Even the frenulum connection looks real. So many dildos are circumcised. Granted, circumcised cocks are standard fare for those of us of a certain age. And from a nonowner's point of view, it doesn't make a difference to me, erect penises looking largely the same when they're, well, raring to go. But it's nice to see some variety in the toy world. The spice of life, something for everyone, and all that.

The only drawback to Sparkling Curve is the same as for Hard Candy (on the same page)—no base, which means no ass play. Granted, Hard Candy and its translucent red hard plastic has a specific raison d'être—reaching the often elusive and pressure-loving vaginally located G spot. Reaching it with vigorous, mind-blowing, orgasm-inducing, won't-bend-out-of-place-until-you-squirt vibes. It's easy to imagine kneeling between a woman's widespread legs and parting her warm, slippery folds with your gloved fingers. You slide the translucent candy red dildo head back and forth, teasing whorls in her slick and curly pussy hair. You tell her to bend her knees and pull them back. She does. When her cunt is open, you slide your hands up her thighs and spread her hot, slippery labia with your fingertips. You diddle her pussy for a while, just for the fun of it. And when she's moaning, you slide the highly representational hard red plastic head slowly, oh so tantalizingly, into her moist, musky pussy. She groans as the clear red shaft disappears into her glistening pink flesh. You can feel her heat, smell her fresh, sweet cunt scent as you fuck your see-through red cock into her soft and slippery dark pink folds. You fuck it slowly in and out, in and out, until you settle deep and start rubbing upward, hunting for that elusive but oh, just-so-right spot. When she gasps and stiffens, you freeze.

"Show me what you like," you purr, slowly turning on the vibe.

She moans, softly, or maybe loudly, trembling as the vibrations hum her, into That Spot, her pussy resonating with the buzz of electricity that you gradually increase as you keep the pressure right there, right on That Special Spot, and slowly start to rub.

"Come for me, babe," you whisper, sliding your other hand quietly over her mons. You stop with your thumb resting just above her clit, dip the end of your thumb onto her labia, getting it wet and slick. "I'm going to rub your pretty clitty now." You slowly slide your thumb down, until you're gently rubbing the hood back and forth over the erect nub quivering beneath. She's panting loudly now, pulling back tightly on her legs. Her chest is flushed a lovely glowing red and her whole body is trembling.

"Please," she begs. You nod.

"I'm going to make your clit feel so good. I promise you, sweetheart. But right now, I want you to pay all your attention to that special girly place in your cunt that I'm rubbing. You're going to squirt for me when you come, love. I'm going to rub your clit and your honey spot until you feel so good you shoot your pretty girly cunt juice all over my face."

You slide your hand down her labia and turn the vibrator all the way up, pressing it deep into The Spot. And in the same motion, you start rubbing two slippery fingers over her clit in the relentless, erotic, tormenting circles that can find relief only with an orgasm. You press up deep into The Spot.

Her cry makes your own crotch quiver, makes you wish you had a thick 6¼- × -2¼-inch Randy representational dildo (two pages farther) buried deep inside yourself or that you were fucking yourself wildly over a semirealistic jelly rubber Tidal Waves (same page) with raised rings on the shaft and the on knob below the pearl-blue testicles turned all the way up. You grind against the bed and whisper, "Fuck, oh, *fuck,* yes!"

She starts bucking, and you keep the pressure steady. Your fingers are a merciless blur over that hard little nub in her folds as she yanks her legs farther back, arches her cunt up to you, and you rub, just there, *there!* And her whole body starts to twitch and with a screech, she bucks up hard and a flood of flowery slick juice squirts onto your hand and your chest and you grin and wish that fuck, oh, fuck, you were sitting on a thick, fat, filling Randy. As she falls back onto the bed, her legs falling down onto you, you rock against the mattress and turn off the vibrator. She moans contentedly when you pull the sopping toy free and lay it on the bed, leaning over to kiss her still-trembling knee.

"You are so hot," you whisper, smiling at her and rubbing your own horny legs together. She lifts her arm from her face, half opens her wasted eyes, and laughs.

"Go wash the dishes, babe. As soon as I can breathe again, it's your turn."

You leave her lying on the bed with her legs spread and tiptoe into the bathroom to wash the toy. Later on, when you're resting contentedly beside her, you slip your catalog back out and peruse the rest of the pages. There's always the new Pearl Jelly Dildo with siliconelike firmness that's specifically designed for harness compatibility and low budgets. You've been thinking about trying a harness, and budgets are a consideration, even when you don't live in a dildo-illegal state. So, you flag the page. After all, when you have toys on hand, there are so many wonderful possibilities.

GOING FOR BROKE: The Quest for Multiple Orgasms

Toy(s) you will need: Firm dildo or vaginal barbell
(women)
Clitoral vibrator (women)
Butt plug (optional for men)
Lubricant (men and women)

Type of play: Solo or partnered

During my career the one question I've heard almost as much as "How can I find my G spot?" is "How can I have multiple orgasms?" The funny thing is, that question used to be asked primarily by women, and now I hear it most often from men. The quest for multiple orgasms—the ability to have several orgasms in a row without much time elapsing between each one—has been a popular sex goal for years. While women's ability to have multiple orgasms has long been recognized, men (at least in Western culture) have only

Toy Testimonials

"One of the surest ways for me to have intense multiple orgasms involves a vibrator, a dildo, and a finger. I begin lying in bed on my side, using a Pocket Rocket or an egg-shape vibrator to stimulate my clit. As I relax and get more turned on, I slip a long, clear acrylic dildo inside. Because of its length, I am able to curl my legs up underneath me and use them to guide the dildo in and out of myself. As my pleasure begins to peak, I add a lubed finger from behind into my anus. Depending on the placement of the vibrator,

recently become aware of some techniques that can help them rack up orgasms of their own.

Why would someone want to be multiply orgasmic? The main reason has to do with pure physical enjoyment. After all, if one orgasm feels great, several can feel utterly fantastic. Since many people experience their orgasms differently, having multiple orgasms in one session can add a richness or level of unpredictability to your sexual encounter. Plus, learning to have multiple orgasms requires you to be in tune with your sexual responses, so you can exercise more control over not just the quantity but the quality of your orgasms. Strengthening your PC muscle (see the "Love Muscle" activity) can help women with G spot orgasms and ejaculation and men with ejaculation control so they can learn to orgasm without losing their erection. And men who maintain erections for longer periods of time are more able to satisfy partners who want to orgasm once, or more often, during partner sex.

Given all those great reasons to "go for broke" in the orgasm department, remember to keep your expectations in check. Too often people get hung up on the pursuit of a sex position, a technique, or even a pill, in the hopes that it will magically revive a flagging sex life. The quest takes on an exaggerated importance, putting more pressure on you or a partner, and robbing you both of what should be a fun experiment. Multiple orgasms can be the ice cream on the cake, but they aren't necessary for you to have an absolutely delicious sex life.

Both men and women can learn to be multiply orgasmic by tuning in to their sexual arousal, strengthening their PC muscles, and learning to control their breathing. Women most often just need to push past the first orgasm and continue with stimulation in order to achieve a second one. Men, however, will need to learn to separate orgasm from ejaculation, as the refractory period that occurs for most men after ejaculation is what prevents them from having another orgasm.

Because multiple orgasms require a certain amount of focus, it's best to try these techniques alone first. Especially because learning to separate ejaculation and orgasm requires practice and patience, men may prefer masturbation rather than partner sex at first. When you do want to pursue multiple orgasms with your partner, you'll find that the woman-on-top position gives him more ejaculatory control, and the rear-entry position gives her more direct G spot stimulation.

I can sometimes free up my other hand to touch my breasts or slip a finger into my mouth. The combination allows me to imagine I am being touched all over and penetrated by my lover (and another partner). The result is always an intense, pulsating orgasm that leaves me so turned on I do it all again.

"Sure, it's a lot of work to bring this all together, but I spend most of the day anticipating my night of indulgence, planning out every detail and getting turned on in the process."

- **Fuel your fantasies.** Think about what things have turned you on in the past and focus on them now to jump-start your arousal. Fantasize about a steamy sexual encounter, replay a scene from a sexy movie, or imagine yourself naked with your favorite celebrity. If you enjoy additional stimulation, put on some sexy music or read some erotica.

- **The masturbation tease.** If you normally masturbate to orgasm, use your favorite techniques to build toward an orgasm. Make sure you get plenty of clitoral stimulation. Have your first orgasm using hand stimulation (unless you need a vibe to come), and use the vibrator on subsequent orgasms to relish the contrast. Tease yourself by getting close to an orgasm, then backing off so your arousal diminishes a bit. By doing this several times you'll be in a pretty high state of arousal, so it'll be easier to have a second orgasm. When you just can't take it any more, let yourself come.

- **Round two.** Instead of stopping now, continue on with the stimulation. Your clit might be really sensitive at first, but if you persist, you'll start building up toward another orgasm. You can also take a short rest between orgasms, but no longer than a minute so you don't lose your momentum. Use the vibrator on your clitoris now, as the extra intensity might give you just the boost to get to the next orgasm.

- **Squeeze and breathe.** Insert a dildo or vaginal barbell, then squeeze your PC muscle at regular intervals. Don't hold your breath—instead take long deep breaths. Notice how you can push your arousal forward by breathing deeply and contracting your PC muscle. With practice, you can coordinate the rhythm of your breathing to your mounting arousal. When you feel yourself close to orgasm, inhale, then try to time your exhale with the onset of the orgasm, and you'll feel the sexual charge flow through your body to your toes.

- **Come again.** Let yourself come again. Consider using a vibrator on your clitoris if you need an extra push over the top. You can come as often as you like! Keep in mind that some women find their multiple orgasms are more intense than the first, and others are just the opposite. Keep practicing and you'll uncover all the ways you like to come again and again.

MULTIPLE ORGASMS FOR MEN

Because orgasm and ejaculation often occur simultaneously for men, many people don't realize that by separating the two men can learn to have multiple orgasms. You don't need to ejaculate to orgasm, so by learning to suppress the urge to ejaculate you can still enjoy the orgasm—in all its glory—and have more than one at a time.

- **Fuel your fantasies.** Think about what things have turned you on in the past and focus on them now to jump-start your arousal. Fantasize about a steamy sexual encounter, replay a scene from a sexy movie, or imagine yourself naked with your favorite celebrity. If you enjoy additional stimulation, put on some sexy music or read some erotica.
- **The masturbation tease.** Use your favorite technique to masturbate, using lots of lube to keep things slippery. This time, instead of coming, pay attention to your arousal and about ten

seconds before you come, stop masturbating. What you're trying to do is isolate the point at which your orgasm is imminent, and stop just before.

- **Squeeze and breathe.** Since the PC muscle surrounds the prostate, which is where ejaculate passes on its way out, tightening your PC muscle around it will help you stop before you ejaculate. Taking long, deep breaths will help you relax more quickly, allowing you to drop down into your first orgasm.

- **Curb ejaculation.** There are a few tricks that can help stop you from ejaculating, so experiment with any or all of these:
  - squeeze the tip of the penis, at the base of the glans
  - press against the base of your penis
  - use your thumb and forefinger to form a ring around your testicles and pull them away from your body
  - press your thumb against your perineum, the spot between your balls and your anus

- **Have an orgasm without the ejaculate.** As you learn to back off once you feel the urge to come, you will feel what the authors of *The Multi-Orgasmic Man* call "contractile phase orgasms." They may not feel very strong at first, but as you become more focused on the sensation, you should feel several contractions. Don't worry if you don't feel them at first or if they're disappointing. Just keep practicing bringing yourself to the brink of orgasm and then backing off, paying attention to your sexual responses as you do, and eventually these new orgasms will feel just like the ejaculatory ones you are used to. You may notice that your orgasms can be felt as contractions around the prostate. Try this exercise while wearing a butt plug and your contractions may feel more intense.

- **Know when to quit.** After you've had several nonejaculatory orgasms, take a moment to just relax and enjoy how you feel. The Taoists, early proponents of this technique, believed that the ejaculate that was formerly expelled from the body is now redirected internally, infusing the body with more sexual energy. Many men claim that they feel rejuvenated and that orgasm is felt more throughout the body rather than just the genitals.

Variations

- Men who want to pursue multiple orgasms during partner sex can try several things to stop ejaculation: switch positions, pull out of her vagina, or squeeze the base of the penis.
- Strap a cock ring onto your penis to maintain an erection even longer.
- To keep your arousal level high, stimulate other body parts such as breasts, thighs, anus, and perineum.

PUMP IT UP: Get Bigger, Last Longer

Toy(s) you will need:	Penis pump
	Cock ring
	Lubricant
Type of play:	Solo or partnered

Have you seen the infomercials for products that enlarge the penis? I watch them with a mixture of fascination and horror as beefy guys who look like former football players chat with inarticulate aging porn stars about penis size. I'm fascinated by the fact that penis size is no longer a private obsession but one fit for prime time (yup, these shows air during the family hour). But what's tragic about them is the way they exploit men's biggest sexual insecurity: penis size.

Whether you're looking at e-mail spam, men's health magazines, or TV talk shows, it's apparent that men are obsessed with penis size. Most men want to be bigger, no matter how many times women reassure them that size doesn't matter or they read statistics confirming their size is "normal" (according to Kinsey, five to seven inches long, four to six inches in circumference when erect). One interesting theory suggests that since a man looks down at his own penis, he gets a skewed view of its size. If his only comparison is the guy in the locker room who's giving him a full frontal, he's bound to come up short. (My personal theory, based on the principle of karmic returns, has to do with men being saddled with this anxiety in exchange for their cultural obsession with large breasts!)

Let me set the record straight—the penis enlargement creams and drugs are pure hype. Nothing will permanently enlarge your penis except surgery. The one comment the porn star on the infomercial made that rang true was that men with bigger penises have more self-confidence, and that self-confidence makes them better lovers. Ah, if we could only bottle confidence and sell it! Sexual confidence is necessary for good sex, but you aren't likely to find it in a bottle or a pill, because it comes from within. If you want to be a good lover, study up and practice. If you want to feel sexy in your body, act sexy, strut your stuff, and show off for your partner.

With that said, there are some toys on the market that can help you be a bigger man. It can be fun to experiment with temporary size enlargement and the sensations this creates. Approach this

Toy Testimonials

"One time I gave my boyfriend a penis pump because I got tired of hearing him wish he had a bigger cock. I called him on the phone and asked if he'd tried it yet. He answered with a slow 'Yes . . .' and when I prodded further to see how he liked it, he said, 'Wait a minute and I'll tell you.' Turned out he was using it while we were on the phone!"

play with the same spirit of fun and adventure as you would any other sex toy or new technique. You can enlarge the penis temporarily, which you might find arousing, amusing, or merely functional; either way, it helps to keep your expectations in check so you won't be disappointed. Anyone who wants to experience new sensations on his penis will enjoy this activity, as will those who have difficulty with erections or premature ejaculation.

This activity employs two time-honored men's toys: the penis pump and the cock ring. The penis pump will temporarily enlarge the penis, and the cock ring will keep it hard long enough for a good masturbation session or roll in the hay. The penis pump creates a vacuum around the penis that causes it to swell to a larger size. It's a temporary enlargement; when the pump is removed, the penis will gradually resume its original size. Cock rings are designed to restrict the flow of blood back out of the penis, so their purpose is to help you maintain the sizable erection. If you're new to cock rings, look for single-strap rings that are easy to adjust and remove. You might want to play with your toys alone first, so you can take your time experimenting. One final note: if you bleed easily, are diabetic, or suffer from heart conditions, don't use cock rings. Consult your doctor if you are unsure.

- **Prep.** Although it's not necessary, some men like to shave the area around the base of the penis to ensure a tight seal with the pump's cylinder. Apply a very thick lubricant or oil-based jelly to the base of the pump (Vaseline works well if you've got a lot of hair). Apply lube to your penis and the inside of the tube, as this will prevent your skin from sticking to the tube.
- **Get the fit.** In a reclining or standing position, slide the cylinder over your penis until it rests at the base. Slowly begin squeezing the pump handle, and you'll notice a feeling of pres-

sure on your penis as the vacuum occurs. Press the cylinder against your body and pull down on your testicles, to avoid having your balls pulled into the vacuum.

- **Pump it up.** Pump gently until you find the most comfortable level of suction, but never past that point, or you could bruise the penis. Just leave the pump on and enjoy the sensations while you engage in other erotic activities. In the beginning, don't use the pump for more than fifteen minutes each session. Some men find heat increases their enjoyment, so you can try pumping in the bath or shower (assuming your pump is not electric).

- **Get it off so you're ready to get off.** Most pumps have a release valve to help you remove the pump when you're ready. You or your partner can stroke your penis and just enjoy the change in texture, size, and sensation. Some men find their penis is more sensitive since more blood has been pulled to the surface.

- **Wrap it up with a cock ring.** If necessary, apply more lube to the penis and balls to avoid pinching any pubic hair. Fasten the cock ring around the base of the penis and tuck it under the scrotum (if you don't like this, just try it around the base of the penis). You want a snug fit, but not one that is too tight. Some men find that the cock ring cre-

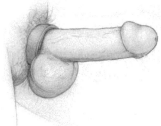

Cock Ring

ates a pleasurable feeling of tightness and pressure. Wear the cock ring for only as long as it's comfortable. In the beginning this may be for only a few minutes, but as you gain experience you can go for about half an hour (but don't wear it longer than this).

- **Playing alone.** If you're alone, stroke your penis and engage in your favorite type of masturbation, noticing the subtle differences the cock ring makes. You may find that your orgasm is more intense when it occurs, thanks to the pressure that builds up while you're wearing a cock ring.

- **Playing with a partner.** Get up and let your partner admire your cock ring. You worked for it, so strut your stuff! Indulge your exhibitionist side and show off your erection while she plays the voyeur. Now you're free to engage in your favorite kinds of sex play—she can explore with her hands and her mouth so you can appreciate the feelings coursing through your pumped-up penis. When you're ready, apply more lubricant, and experiment with your favorite positions.

Variations

- If you're looking for another way to add girth using a sex toy, try a penis extender—a sleeve that slips over your own penis to add length and width.
- Some pumps also offer vibration, which some men find pleasurable and others find distracting.
- Try using a vibrating cock ring with a clitoral attachment (see the "Missionary Zeal" activity), as this will give you both a buzz during intercourse.
- Go for broke and try an anal plug while you're pumping.

ALL HANDS ON DECK: Hand Jobs Made Simple

Toy(s) you will need: Fukuoku finger vibrator
                           Lubricant
Type of play: Partnered

If the hand job isn't already part of your sexual repertoire, it's time to let your fingers do the walking. An underrated but highly valued sexual activity, a hand job is simply the act of masturbating your partner. Most people think of hand jobs as something teenagers furtively give each other in the backseats of cars, but anyone who masters his or her partner's favorite masturbation technique will be forever adored. By discovering the key to your partner's turn-on, you unlock the door to all kinds of sex play, because most sex acts build on the basic pleasures we learn through masturbation. And a hand job in itself is a simple, sexy act that can be performed anywhere, anytime. It lends itself well to spontaneous sexual trysts, it can bridge a gap between couples with varying sexual needs, and it's safe and sensual.

To give a good hand job you must first and foremost be a good student. Not everyone responds to the same rhythm or motion, so don't expect that what worked on your last partner will do the trick now. It's up to you to discover exactly how your partner likes to be touched. You can start with some of the basic strokes I suggest here, but watch your partner's reactions and be prepared to modify your technique to suit his or her needs.

Another way to learn is through a bit of show-and-tell. Watch closely as your partner shows you how he or she likes to be touched. Ask questions so you get a sense of just how hard, how fast, and how consistent you need to be. You can always place your hand on top of your partner's during masturbation, which is an intimate and exciting way to learn.

Adding vibration to your hand job can help if you're having difficulty bringing your partner to climax, or if you want to introduce an exotic new element to the masturbation routine. Oftentimes we get so used to our own masturbation rituals that it takes the creative contribution of a partner to help us break out of a rut and try something new.

Keep in mind a few simple guidelines when practicing the techniques below. Use consistent, confident, and smooth strokes. Don't be afraid to apply pressure; he or she will let you know if it's too much. While you may want to try several of the suggested techniques, it's often preferable to choose one or two and stick

Toy Testimonials

"I love it when my boyfriend uses a vibrator inside my vagina while pressing the Fukuoku on my clit. The Fukuoku is small enough that it doesn't get in the way, but is strong enough that, when teamed with a dildo vibrator, it's enough to send me over the edge very quickly."

with them. When you hit the right combination of movements on a woman, she'll want you to repeat them until she comes. Vary your moves only if you're trying to prolong her buildup or if your hand gets tired, but resume them when you can. With men, it's not so much about "jerking" or "whacking," as the euphemisms imply, but applying a firm grip and a steady hand.

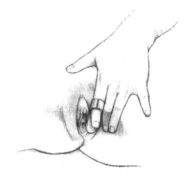

Add the Fukuoku finger vibrator
to your hand job

GIVING HER A HAND

Most women like to be stimulated in this order: vulva, clitoris, vagina/G spot (or a combination of clitoris and G spot through climax).

- **Prep.** Put batteries in your toy, and keep some lube and a towel nearby.
- **Position.** Find a comfortable position that won't strain body parts or tire you out easily. Lie alongside her so your hand reaches over at about the same angle her own would. If you'll be using both hands on her, sit between her legs.
- **Add lube.** Strap the finger vibe over your index finger. Pour some water-based lube into both hands and warm it up a bit before touching her.
- **Massage the vulva.** Place your well-lubed, nonvibrating hand palm-side down over her vulva with your fingers pointing between her legs. Slowly slide your hand up toward her navel. Now alternate hands, performing the same moves, so she can

feel the vibrator on her vulva. After a few minutes, use your fingers to explore the inner and outer lips of the labia. Try a combination of tugging, stroking, and gently rubbing the lips between your fingers, working your way up one side and down the other. Use the vibrating pad on your finger to trace circles along the labia, starting at the perineum and working your way around the clitoris in a clockwise motion. Pay attention to her breathing and body movements and move on to the clitoris when she's pretty aroused.

- **Tickle the clit.** Apply the vibrator first to the inner lips and then bring it up and around the clitoris in a fluid motion. Repeat this slowly and consistently if she appears to enjoy it. Try not to draw back the clitoral hood and touch the glans of the clitoris directly, as this is too intense for most women. Now focus your movements primarily on the clitoris, experimenting with a side-to-side motion, a circular pattern, or an up-and-down movement. Alternate with your nonvibrating hand or keep the vibration steady, depending on which she prefers.

- **Explore the vagina.** Using your vibrating finger, periodically circle around the edge of the vagina, then insert a finger about an inch inside. Hold still for a moment so she can enjoy the sensation, then explore the vaginal walls by alternating pressure with rubbing. Continue stroking her clit with your other hand, or switch hands so that the vibrator is on her clit.

- **Tease the anus and perineum.** Stroke the area between the anus and the vagina (called the perineum), then lightly circle the anus, stopping periodically over the anus to apply pressure with the vibration.

- **Don't stop.** Once she starts to climax, keep going until she tells you to stop or moves your hand away. Congratulate yourself on a hand job well done!

GIVING HIM A HAND

Most men like a combination of strokes on the penis and the balls. Most women handle penises too gently—so ladies, don't be afraid to put some muscle into it!

- **Prep.** Put batteries in your toy, and keep some lube and a towel nearby. If you won't be having intercourse later, consider using something thicker than water-based lube. Vaseline works, as does a great product called Men's Cream, which is designed specifically for masturbation.
- **Position.** He's lying on his back, so you can sit beside him or kneel between his legs, whichever is more comfortable.
- **Lube it up.** Strap the finger vibe over your index finger and turn it on. Pour some lube into both hands and warm it up a bit before touching him.
- **Massage his genitals.** Begin with a stroke that presses his penis against his stomach. Place your well-lubed palm over the penis with your fingers pointing toward the anus and slightly cupping his scrotum. Slowly glide your hand up toward his navel, pressing his penis against his body. Alternate hands, so he experiences the vibrations intermittently on his genitals. Monitor his reactions, as he might find the vibrator annoying at first, in which case you can turn it off till he's more aroused. Move on to another technique: form a ring with your thumb and vibrating forefinger, encircle his scrotum, and gently pull away from the body as you stroke his penis.
- **Stroke the shaft.** Encircle the base of his penis with your thumb and vibrating forefinger and stroke upward along the shaft. As you get near the top, palm the glans with a twisting

motion, while your other hand begins the same stroke from below. Or you can perform this move with just your vibrating hand, while your other hand cups his testicles or tickles his anus. Try changing directions or slipping the vibe onto your thumb.

- **Vibrate the frenulum.** The sensitive area on the underside of the penis, where the glans meets the shaft, is known as the frenulum. Slip the vibrator over your thumb and clasp the penis between your hands, interlocking your fingers on one side so your thumbs meet on the same side as the frenulum. Start at the base and slowly glide your hands up the penis, using your thumbs to provide pressure, vibrations, and massage.

- **Juice the glans.** Stimulate the sensitive top part of the penis known as the glans using a juicing motion. Grasp the penis around the middle with your vibrating hand, while you place the palm of your other hand on top of the glans and move it as if you were juicing a lemon. Or wrap your nonvibrating hand around the penis, place the palm of your other hand on the glans, then twist your fingers as if you were unscrewing a lid off a jar. With one finger vibrating, this gives the glans a pleasant buzz. On an uncircumcised penis, roll the foreskin over the head and lightly massage it with your vibrating finger or thumb. Work the skin back down and, when he's fully erect, lightly vibrate or palm the exposed glans.

- **Tickle the testicles.** Try gently cupping (don't squeeze) his testicles with your vibrating hand while you stroke his shaft with the other. You can also use your vibrating finger to trace circles or give a light massage to his testicles.

- **Tease the anus and perineum.** Stroke the area between the anus and the scrotum (called the perineum), then lightly circle the anus, stopping periodically over the anus to apply pressure with the vibration. Applying vibration to the perineum as he approaches orgasm can be extremely pleasurable, as this indirectly stimulates the prostate.

Variations

- To turn your entire hand into a vibrator, try the Fukuoku Glove, which positions a vibrator over each finger. There are also vibrating "rings" (a vibrator worn on the finger like a ring) that provide similar hand-to-skin contact.
- Any small vibrator can be incorporated into a hand job. The Pocket Rocket or any egg-type vibrator can be nestled in the labial folds. They also fit easily into the palm of your hands, so you can stroke his shaft with it.
- To add to her excitement, consider slipping a dildo or G spot vibrator inside her vagina during your hand job and working both at the same time.
- Men and women may also enjoy anal penetration. Use your free hand to massage the anus, or have your partner wear a butt plug.
- Keep both hands busy. While one hand is working on your partner's genitals, use the other to explore sensitive body parts. The fingertip vibrator also feels great on nipples, lips, inner thighs, etc.

Thanksgiving with the In-laws

by Lauren Mills

I don't remember exactly when Thanksgiving with my in-laws went from the most stressful day of the year to the most anticipated. It must have been about five years ago. I love my husband dearly, but I just can't stand Beatrice, his mother. Unfortunately, the feeling is mutual, so we limit our time together to one day: Thanksgiving.

You see, when Brian and I started our own family, we began our own traditions. I prepare the food the way we like it. I make the pies differently than Beatrice does. I add nuts to my stuffing. And, in what would be my greatest sin against Beatrice, I don't serve Jell-O. The nasty stuff wiggles and I don't like it. She can eat her damn Jell-O 364 days of the year, but not at my house. So, every Thanksgiving Day, we sit around the dinner table, she laments about what foods are missing, what she would have served instead, and why whatever I cook isn't up to her rigorous standards. Every year, according to

Beatrice, there's always something missing from the perfect holiday meal.

Several years ago, I remember saying to Brian, "Honey, if she brings up her carrot casserole one more time, I'm going to tell her where she can shove her carrots!" Brian chuckled and a dangerous glint lit his eyes. It was the start of a new Thanksgiving tradition—one that changed my whole outlook on the holiday and on time spent with my mother-in-law.

■ ■ ■

"Mom, I'm starved! When are the Gs and the rest of the family getting here?" asked my fifteen-year-old human garbage disposal. "Gs" was his term for the grandparental units.

"Bill, I thought I asked you to dress for dinner." My son stood before me in the same tattered jeans he'd had on this morning and a T-shirt announcing the 2003 concert tour for Creed. His dark hair with its blond tips stood up in spikes that only expensive gel can sustain.

"I did," he said with an engaging smile. "I changed my earring from the steel stud to the diamond."

"Not enough. Go change into a shirt that has buttons and pants without denim. Then I'll find you some cheese and crackers to tide you over."

He grumbled, but left the kitchen to go change. Just then the love of my life breezed through the door.

"Whoa! Honey—that dress is made for the bedroom, not the kitchen! You look sexy as hell!" said Brian.

I must say I felt sexy in it. The top was a skintight black lace turtleneck that accentuated my overdeveloped breasts and my slender bare arms. The skirt was also black lace and it skimmed the tops of my knees and twirled out as I spun around. It was designed to be loose and free—requirements for our new Thanksgiving tradition.

"Want to see the best part?" I presented my backside and quickly lifted the skirt off my bare bottom. Yep, naked as a jaybird. Then, turning to give him the frontal view, I flashed him again. Bald as an eagle. My legs were encased in sheer black thigh-high stockings, making the overall package even more alluring.

"Holy shit, Annie! You shaved!" His grin said it all, not to mention the growing bulge in his pants. I pulled down my skirt and turned back to the sweet potato casserole I was making. He came up behind me and wrapped his arms around me, nestling his shaft against my butt. "I'm going to have a boner all through dinner!"

"You always have a boner all through Thanksgiving dinner. Did you hide the basket?"

Kissing my neck, he mumbled as he nibbled. "Of course I hid the basket. Best damn part of dinner! Thank God we discovered how to endure this holiday years ago."

"Jeez, guys, get a room," Cassie declared as she strolled into the kitchen and plucked a piece of celery from the veggie tray. Cassie was fourteen going on twenty. Her makeup came straight from *YM* magazine—shiny hot pink lips, gold lamé eye shadow, and dark eyeliner. Her long blond hair had been pulled up into a messy bun. "Everyone's late. I'm starving."

Bill sauntered in dressed to make his mother proud. "Well, if you ate more than celery, you wouldn't be, dimwit."

Well, so much for making his mother proud. "Billy, lay off your sister for one day. Please. It's Thanksgiving."

"Mom, Dad, the Addams Family is pulling into the driveway," Cameron called from the living room where he'd been perched by the window waiting for everyone's arrival. As the youngest, Cameron, who's nine, struggles to compete for attention with his older siblings. I must say he does quite well.

We all walked to the front door to greet them as Brian playfully swatted Cameron's butt. "Don't call your grandparents and my sister's family the Addams Family. They're just esoteric."

"Huh?" rang three puzzled voices, glancing up at their dad.

We opened the door with smiles and hugs, and escorted Brian's relatives into the family room, where I'd laid out a veggie tray, some cheese and crackers, and a chicken liver pâté. In truth, the Addams Family wasn't far off—Beatrice always did remind me of Morticia— she was tall and thin with black hair. She still wore it long and straight, a desperate attempt to recapture her lost youth. Her husband, George, was as charming as could be—like Gomez—but this was such a stark contrast to Beatrice's personality that I never understood how they'd become a couple. Brian's sister, Audrey, her husband, Tom, and their two teens, Justin and Emily, were quirky but in a lovable sort of way. And they had the same battles with Beatrice that we did. One Thanksgiving when Tom and I were fed up, we stole out to the back porch, rolled a joint, got high, and trashed Beatrice. Like Letterman, we had a Top 10: "Accidents" for Beatrice. Number one on my list was suffocating in a bathtub full of Jell-O.

As Beatrice breezed by, an air kiss hanging in the wind, she said brightly, "I've brought my famous pecan logs!"

"I've seen better logs floating in the toilet," Bill whispered to Justin.

"Bet they'd taste better too," Justin replied.

The kids all went to the basement to play foosball, leaving the adults to self-medicate.

As I served drinks, Beatrice didn't disappoint me. Always one for the first sting, she commented, "Well, Annie, I see that you got an early start on the holiday weight gain this year. Must be the stress of working full time and trying to be an adequate mother." She smiled sweetly and I willed the olive in her martini to lodge in her throat. Alas, Satan was protecting her again.

"Mother." Brian stepped in. "Could we try for *mildly* pleasant this year?"

"What? What did I say?" she asked, looking around at the faces of those silently plotting her death.

Brian put a calming hand on my knee and started stroking, reminding me that he found me plenty attractive.

And so it began. I drank three Cosmopolitans in forty-five minutes. Pleasantly toasted and aching to move the evening along, I declared dinner. I gave Brian a lingering gaze that spoke volumes and asked him to rally the troops downstairs.

We have a beautiful dining room table that seats ten perfectly. Unfortunately, we number eleven. But over time, Brian and I realized this was a godsend. He and I could sit next to each other at the end of the table, as close as could be, while everyone else spread out comfortably. Of course, I was about to spread out and become wickedly *uncomfortable.* I have a lovely ivory linen tablecloth that hangs low enough to cover our laps from prying eyes.

After everyone was seated and grace had been said, we began passing the food. I strategically placed my hand high on my husband's thigh and scratched my long nails softly. "Let her bitching begin," I whispered.

I started to squirm in my seat knowing what was ahead. Beatrice would begin her slow diatribe about how she would have prepared the meals or what dish was missing. I couldn't wait. I looked at Brian expectantly and wet my lower lip with my tongue. His pupils grew dark.

Food was passed and conversations continued quite pleasantly. I kept waiting for Beatrice to make the first comment. She was eating everything and engaged with Cameron about his soccer team— almost like a real grandmother. I looked at Brian with near panic in my eyes. This couldn't be happening. He had the basket in his lap waiting! My skirt was up; I was open and wanting. I'd been without underwear for two hours, for God's sake.

Bless her heart, Cassie came to the rescue without even knowing it. "Grandma, what do you think of Mom's new sweet potato recipe?"

Yes! I cried inside and looked at Beatrice expectantly. I could feel my husband's hand gripping my thigh.

"Welllllll, of course, it's just fine, Cassie." She gave me a weak smile.

What? "This can't be happening," I whispered to Brian.

"Maybe Dad finally grew some nuts and told her to behave," he grumbled. He was no happier than I.

"Of course . . ."

"Yes?" Brian and I turned to her at once as if she were the pope about to announce the end of priests' celibacy.

"It would be better if it had marshmallows on top like I used to make it."

There is a God! I nearly cried with relief.

Brian reached into the basket. A handful of soft fluffy marshmallows were now being massaged all over my mound, each little round pillow like a velvet button. Without pubic hair to tangle in, they glided sensuously around my smooth skin. I sighed and smiled ever so sweetly at Beatrice.

"Beatrice, please, tell me what else you'd do differently."

Audrey and Tom gazed at me in disbelief.

"Well, dear, since you mention it, I don't know why you

don't take the time to make fresh cranberry sauce. Canned sauce just isn't the same without the full round berries you get in homemade."

Those full round berries replaced the soft marshmallows in my Thanksgiving massage. Brian cupped as many as he could in his palm and rubbed them against me. They were hard and smooth; the friction was delicious. They rolled against my heated flesh, soon coated with moisture. Then he slowly pushed several inside me. I purred softly. "This is the only way to consume cranberries, darling," I whispered, holding my wineglass in front of my lips so no one else could see or hear.

I heard the cranberries drop back into the basket and wondered what was next. The children began their side conversations, not paying attention as Beatrice droned on and I smiled happily.

"Did I ever tell you how we used to crack walnuts before dinner? We'd buy the biggest ones we could find, then crack and fry them in butter and sugar for a treat. Really, Annie, would it hurt you so much to buy some walnuts for the kids to crack?"

Oh, it was hurting me a lot as Brian pushed the fifth large shell inside me. I was chock full o' nuts! I can't begin to tell you how erotic and naughty it felt. I was stuffed. I squirmed on the chair, the nuts caressing me, tantalizing the inner walls of my sex.

"Mom, can I have some more milk please?" Bill asked.

I brought myself back to the present and gazed back at him.

"Mom! Dude! Your eyes look like you've been doing weed. They're all glassy."

"Oh, nonsense," I said, "I just have tears in my eyes because I'm so happy to have the family all together."

Emily leaned over to Cassie and stated the obvious. "Man, your mom is whacked."

I passed the pitcher of milk while Brian slowly removed the

walnuts and cranberries from my cavity. His fingers teased and stroked as he pushed the crunchy globes around. Leaning close, his voice hoarse, he said, "Your shaved bush is driving me crazy! It's so smooth and slick with your wetness." Then he paused for a second and chuckled. "Hey, it's not a bush anymore! I don't even know what to call it!"

Conversation had taken a turn away from Beatrice, and after several minutes I couldn't take it anymore. I was waiting for the last course.

"Beatrice, dear, what was that casserole you've mentioned before that your mother used to make?"

I tensed, waiting for the answer. My thighs trembled.

"Oh, you mean the one with . . ." She snapped her fingers like she was trying to remember.

"Carrots?" Tom asked incredulously, not understanding why I would possibly encourage her.

"Yes, carrots!" she said brightly.

"Yes, *carrots!*" I shouted as Brian surprised me by ramming a large one deep inside, instead of slowly embedding it like he usually did.

I glared at him through my sexual haze, but the grin on his face told me he wasn't sorry in the least. But he did slow his rhythm to an agonizing pace.

All heads turned to me. Billy was certain I was high. All the others just looked concerned.

My sweet old father-in-law George finally said, "Annie, are you all right tonight? You're acting awfully strange."

I was feeling awfully strange too. Strange like a ravenous bunny in heat: Give me the carrot . . . give me the carrot.

"I'm fine, really." I playfully slapped my husband's shoulder. "Brian, don't pinch me like that again!"

"Sorry, folks, just having a little fun. Guess I pinched her a little hard."

Tom and Audrey weren't buying it. Audrey had now spotted my flushed skin.

Never one to let the conversation stray far from her, Beatrice announced, "I know what's missing from this dinner!"

Brian and I held our breath. Every now and then, something new would get added to the basket.

"What?" I asked with bated breath.

"Cucumber salad!"

A flood of moisture bathed my thighs as I clenched my inner muscles. Two years earlier, we'd thought to protect the seats of the chairs with towels, and I was thankful that one was beneath me now.

"It's simple, really, you slice them, sprinkle them with a little sugar and vinegar, and eat them! Even *you* could do that, Annie!"

And she thought she was being such a bitch! I wanted to hug her with gratitude! Next year there'd be cucumber in the basket!

Smiling wickedly at me before turning to Cassie, Brian said, "Cassie, I believe we have cucumbers in the kitchen. Would you please bring two of them with some vinegar and the sugar bowl? Mother, I'd be delighted to serve you.

"And you, darling," he mumbled to me.

Beatrice was beaming, surprised by her son's goodwill gesture.

Cassie returned with two large, fat cucumbers.

"Give one to your grandmother and bring one to me, honey. Thanks. It looks like most of you kids have finished eating, so if you'd like to clear your plates, you may be excused."

In case things got out of hand, he didn't want the children to see their mother in the throes of orgasm.

They needed no further encouragement and disappeared in a rush of teen babble. Beatrice began slicing her cucumber, and carried on a conversation for the next five minutes about the health benefits of cucumbers while Audrey, Tom, and George fought to keep from nodding off.

No one noticed where Brian's cucumber went except me. After the slender carrot, the contrast was staggering. Brian pushed gently but he still stretched me nearly to the point of pain.

"It's too big!" I whispered frantically.

"No, it's not. Relax, they're about to sing. You know what that means."

I groaned softly as Brian continued to rock the cucumber gently, pushing a fraction deeper each time. It took him nearly five minutes to fill me with the glorious vegetable! It was cool and hard against my warm wet flesh. I was having a hard time concentrating on the conversation—I was stretched to capacity, filled to the brim, and each movement jolted my throbbing clit.

"Okay, everybody, let's close up this Thanksgiving dinner in the traditional way," Beatrice said brightly. Tom and Audrey groaned. George smiled indulgently, and I began shaking like a NASA rocket at countdown.

They broke out in song to the tune of "Frère Jacques" . . .

"Next Thanksgiving, next Thanksgiving,
Don't eat bread! Don't eat bread!
Shove it up a turkey, Shove it up a turkey,
Eat the bird! Eat the bird!"

Brian was shoving it up my turkey with practiced finesse. I gripped the arms of the chair and choked down a strangled cry as the thrusting cucumber sent me launching into space.

They all stood up, dinner officially over, as I collapsed in my chair.

Brian leaned over and gave me a kiss. "Happy Thanksgiving, honey."

As they all started clearing the dishes and moving to the kitchen, Audrey glanced at us and smiled. "Next year I'm having whatever you're having."

THE LOVE MUSCLE: Exercising Your PC Muscle

Toy(s) you will need: Firm dildo or vaginal barbell
(women)
Butt plug (optional for men)
Lubricant

Type of play: Solo or partnered

You already know that regular exercise improves the quality of your life. Well, the same is true when it comes to sex. By performing a simple exercise called Kegels, you can enhance your orgasms. Named after the doctor who first prescribed them to women, Kegels exercise your pubococcygeus muscles (PC muscles for short), a set of muscles that surrounds your pelvic area. Both men and women have a PC muscle that can be located by stopping a stream of urine in midflow. A strong PC muscle can lead to more intense orgasms or to multiple orgasms for both women and men. It can also help women who want to ejaculate and men who want ejaculatory control or stronger erections.

The beauty of the Kegel exercise is that it doesn't involve trips to the gym, regular jogging, or even breaking a sweat. It's an exercise that you can do anywhere, whether you're sitting on the couch, waiting in line at the market, or driving a car. You can practice Kegels without a resistive device, but in women especially a toy will help speed up the process. Ideal objects for practicing are vaginal barbells (heavy metal dildos with different size balls you practice on) or firm dildos (glass or silicone are best). For men who want to try Kegels while wearing a butt plug, choose a toy with a flared base, a wide middle, and a tapered neck.

- **Locate your PC muscle.** The next time you pee, practice stopping and starting the flow of urine. That is your PC muscle.
- **Prep.** Unless you plan on using a resistive device like a dildo or plug, you can do these exercises wherever you like. First, empty your bladder.
- **Build up.** Clench your muscle and hold it for three seconds, then release for three. If you're new to Kegels, do this about five times, and repeat it three times a day. As it gets easier, you can add more repetitions to your sitting. Ultimately you want to work up to one hundred repetitions in one session, and do this a couple times a day. You can alternate sets where you do rapid-fire clench and release with sets where you squeeze for a longer period and then push out with your PC muscle.
- **Women, with fingers or dildo.** Place two fingers or a dildo in the outer third of the vagina. Try tightening or clenching your PC muscles, which can also feel like you're trying to suck them in. When you push out, it feels like you're trying to force out the fingers or dildo. Count the reps as you would

in the first exercise and repeat. If you're using a vaginal barbell with balls that graduate in size, work your way from the largest ball to the smallest ball.

- **Men, with a butt plug.** Because the PC muscle contracts around the prostate, having a resistive device in your anus can help strengthen the muscle and feel great at the same time. If you're just learning how to separate ejaculation from orgasm, I would hold off on using a plug until you've been able to accomplish this first goal, then play around with the sensations caused by the plug.
- **Women, on a penis.** The next time his penis is inside you, grip down repeatedly on it using your PC muscle. Men love the sensation and it'll motivate you to keep up your exercise regime.
- **Men, in a vagina.** You can flex your PC muscle during penetration, and your penis might flick and bob a bit inside her vagina. Don't be surprised if this doesn't send her into rhapsodic orgasms, as the vagina isn't that sensitive, but you can always withdraw and show her your latest party trick.
- **Measuring up.** Find out whether your exercises are paying off by investing in a Perineometer. You slide it into the vagina and squeeze; it calculates PC strength and charts your progress.

> **Toy Testimonials**
>
> "I'm kind of a gym buff so I take my Kegel exercises pretty seriously. I actually squeeze my PC muscle as part of my workout routine (it's easiest when I'm on the bike). My boyfriend took it to the next step and bought me a vaginal barbell with the graduated balls, and he gets turned on watching me lift those weights!"

Variations

- **Breathe.** Many people find that their orgasms can be felt more deeply when they coordinate their breathing with PC muscle contractions during masturbation or intercourse. As you inhale, contract your muscle; as you exhale, release the muscle.
- During masturbation (stimulating your clit or penis), do some Kegels to see how they change or enhance your arousal.

LOOK, MA, NO HANDS: The Art of Hands-free Dildo Play

Toy(s) you will need: Dildo with suction cup base
                               Lubricant
Type of play: Solo

Ever wonder why the fifties sitcom housewife was always suspected of fooling around with the milkman? Well, inside joke or no, women can be overcome by sexual cravings and will make do with whatever's close at hand. If supermarkets hadn't made milkmen obsolete, the dildo surely would have. Thanks to the handy penis substitute known as the dildo, women can now pleasure themselves whenever and wherever they see fit—without worrying about the milk spoiling.

And while I'd like to remind you that most women have an orgasm through clitoral stimulation, plenty of women also like to masturbate or have partner sex with a penis or dildo inside of them.

Women enjoy many aspects of penetration: the feeling of fullness a dildo or penis provides, the physical thrill of vigorous thrusting, and the stimulation of the G spot and vagina. It's harder to do this with just your fingers, so if you've got a hankering for penetration and you don't have an accommodating penis nearby, you'll love this activity.

Some of the oldest depictions of hands-free dildo play appear in vintage Japanese erotica, where women are shown with dildos strapped to their feet. Today, dildos have become such an indispensable part of the sex toy chest that for many women it's not a question of whether they own one, but how many they own! Depending on your mood, you might want a curved one for G spot play, a pudgy one for anal play, a double one for partner play, or a vibrating one for multiple stimulation. And then there's the question of aesthetics, since dildos come in different textures and colors, including glitter, swirl, and even camouflage patterns. But there's one dildo women clamor for—the model you can use with no hands. With your hands free you can play with your nipples, prop yourself up in different positions, or rub your clit.

- **Prep.** This activity feels particularly great if you're nice and aroused and hungry for the dildo. Get yourself in the mood— read some steamy erotica, have phone or cybersex beforehand, watch an adult film, or just visualize a really hot fantasy. You can begin by caressing yourself all over first, touching your clit if you like, and then moving on to the dildo when you're ready.
- **Location, location, location.** Figure out where you want

to play with your dildo and get yourself ready. Suction cup dildos work best against glass or tile surfaces, so bathrooms and shower stalls are convenient and make for easy cleanup. But you can try attaching your dildo to any smooth surface; just moisten the suction cup and stick it firmly onto the surface. If you'll be kneeling on a hard surface, put a towel, bath mat, or pillow underneath you. Apply generous lubricant to your dildo before inserting it.

- **Assume the position.** You can kneel on all fours and back onto a dildo that is placed on a vertical surface, like a shower wall. Or you can remain standing, bend over, and back onto it, supporting yourself by placing your hands against the opposite wall. This is more comfortable than kneeling, and the wall offers good resistance. Alternately, you can affix your dildo to a tile floor and lower yourself onto it in a kneeling or squatting position. Both positions offer good access to the G spot.

Enjoying a hands-free dildo in the shower

- **Climb aboard.** Cover your dildo with lube, then slowly ease yourself onto it. Rest for a moment while you enjoy the feeling of fullness. Now you're free to experiment—try a gentle and slow thrusting at first while your vagina slowly envelops every inch of the dildo. Then withdraw slowly, removing yourself from the dildo entirely. Because you've got a nice erect member there, let it slide alongside your labia and rub against your clit a bit. When you're ready, climb back on the dildo and experiment with different rhythms, angles, and depths of thrusting. If you're not using your hands to support yourself, use them to play with your nipples or to rub your clit.

- **Don't forget the clit.** You can work yourself into a real frenzy from penetration, which may result in an orgasm, or you might want to add clit stimulation to the mix. If you're in a shower equipped with a shower massager, turn it on and direct it over your clit while you're humping your dildo. Try different settings (pulsating is particularly nice) and vary the water temperature. If you don't have a shower massager, use your hands or one of the many waterproof clit vibes on the market today. If you're squatting atop your dildo, try a larger vibrator like the Hitachi Wand (not in the shower, as it is electric), which you can press either against the dildo's base to add vibration internally or against your clit. For the ultimate hands-free experience, strap on one of the hands-free clit vibes before climbing on top of your dildo.

Variations

- Invite a partner to sit behind you when you're squatting on the dildo; it'll be easy for him to reach around to play with your breasts or your clitoris. Do it in front of a mirror for an added visual.
- Dildo play with a partner can be a nice alternative to intercourse. Look for longer dildos or those with a handle, so your partner can get a good grip on them while leaving plenty of room for thrusting.
- Both men and women can enjoy anally penetrating themselves with suction cup dildos in much the same way as described here. Go slow, as the dildos are fairly large! Remember, if you use a dildo for anal play, make sure it has a flared base and use lots of lubricant.

A Girl's Best Friend

by Kristina Wright

Finding a decent apartment in Manhattan is like trying to find an outfit to match a pair of shoes you bought on sale. In other words, next to impossible.

I was fresh out of college at the University of Texas–Austin and had my sights set on the publishing world in New York City. My friend Kim, who graduated the semester before me, clued me in about an apartment in her building. It was tiny and old, but in a pretty decent neighborhood with a long, but manageable, walk to my cubicle on Forty-second Street. I choked back my shock at the cost of rent and plopped down first, last, and security out of the nest egg I'd been saving from four years waiting tables. My parents had offered to help with the rent for the first year or two, but I was determined to do it on my own for as long as I could. And so on a hot day in July I moved my books, my clothes, and my cat into the cramped third-floor apartment henceforth known as Home Sweet Home.

Living in a big city was nothing like I'd imagined it would be. The noise was louder, the bugs were bigger, and the people were ruder and freakier. I loved it. I was free to be me, or at least the me I'd always imagined. I was far from small-town life in my hometown of Vicksburg, Texas. I was also far from my college friends who teased that I would be the only girl in all of New York City who had two names and was still a virgin.

First things first. Rebecca-Jane is not really two names because it's hyphenated. My parents were very forward-thinking for Vicksburg. Second, I was a virgin only in the most technical sense. I'd become well acquainted with my mama's silver-handled hairbrush at the tender age of . . . well, let's just say I finally understood why Barbie was smiling all the time. And I had my share of groping, drooling, hormone-driven boyfriends. I just had never felt an overwhelming urge to let some guy between my legs.

I was hardly home at all my first week in the city. I'd landed a job at a publishing house, sifting through manuscripts and answering correspondence for not much more money than I'd made waiting tables. A far cry from my dreams of being the next Stephen King, but still very exciting for a girl from Vicksburg whose most exciting moment to date was being nominated homecoming princess. When Kim invited me out to go clubbing on Friday night I begged off because I wanted to stay in and watch a week's worth of soaps. I know what you're thinking, but dang, it was only my first week in the city. A girl needs a chance to catch her breath!

I went all-out for my first meal in my new place, preparing a feast for one. It was only a cheap steak and baked potato broiled in my tiny oven, but it was the best meal I'd ever had because I was in my own apartment. I was heady with freedom as I sat cross-legged on the sofa with my dinner propped on a pillow. The former tenant had left the sofa. It was a ratty old thing, worn in several spots and faded in others. But I covered it with one of the quilts Mama made me bring and it looked—well, if not new, then at least homey.

I finished my dinner, put Wednesday's episode of *All My Children* on pause, and carried my plate to the little alcove that was my kitchen. I considered it quite a coup that I actually had a dishwasher. It was a cumbersome thing that had to be wheeled over to the sink, hoses and cords poking out every which way, but it beat the hell out of washing dishes myself.

I opened the dishwasher door and slid out the rack and nearly choked on my tongue. Apparently, the ratty old sofa wasn't the only thing the former tenant had bequeathed to me. I was speechless for a moment, then said the first thing that came to my mind.

"Fuck!"

What can I say? A week in the city had already taken its toll on my vocabulary. Pastor Goodwin would be appalled.

Staring up at me, or at least that's the way it appeared, was the largest, thickest, ugliest-looking dick I'd ever seen. I suppose you think that's not saying much, given that I'd only seen two for real (Jason Ritchie's in eleventh grade and Eric Linsey's during my sophomore year of college—Jason's was bigger, but Eric's was more aesthetically appealing). But I'd spent a summer working at a photo lab off-campus in addition to my waitressing job, and let me tell you, it's shocking what kinds of pictures people will take. Big dicks, short dicks, long, skinny, pale and dark. I saw an awful lot of dicks that summer and they all imprinted themselves on my brain for future reference. And this, this *thing* staring up at me from the top rack of my dishwasher was a Texas-size dick—the biggest, thickest dick I'd ever seen.

Okay, I know it's called a dildo; I'm not a complete country bumpkin. But at the moment I saw it, all I could think was "dick." It was long and thick, a fleshy-pink color complete with veins and a heavily ridged little helmet. It was wedged into one of the squares of the cutlery tray and it stared up at me with its one well-defined eye. I must have stood there for ten minutes, staring down at the monster in my dishwasher.

"What am I going to do?" I whispered to Miss Marple, my orange-and-white kitty, who was making circles around my legs. "I can't leave it in there."

Miss Marple let out a plaintive wail of agreement before stalking off to the bathroom. She knew that's where the biggest, scariest creatures hung out. After seeing the contents of my dishwasher, I wasn't so sure.

I took my fork and prodded the thing. It barely quivered when I poked it; the tines of the fork hardly made a dent in its smooth surface. I decided I was too tired to deal with the dildo in my kitchen. I pushed the rack back into the dishwasher and closed the door. I washed my plate in the sink, throwing the occasional furtive glances toward the dishwasher as if I expected its inhabitant to burst out and attack me. When I was finished, I walked quickly past the dishwasher and shut off the light. Maybe my new tenant would mysteriously vanish by morning.

My dreams that night were of previous boyfriends who had pressured me to have sex. Strangely enough, they all looked like large, pink dildos. Where was Freud when I needed him most?

I left the apartment early Saturday to meet Kim for brunch and a day of shopping the secondhand stores. I felt a twinge of guilt for leaving poor little Miss Marple alone with that enormous dildo, but I figured she was safe so long as it was in the dishwasher. When Kim asked me how I enjoyed my first dinner in my new apartment, I blushed and changed the subject.

By the time Kim tossed me out of her apartment, it was 2 A.M. and I was wired on espresso. I was relieved to see the apartment and

Miss Marple were as I'd left them. What had I expected? *Invasion of the Sex Toy Snatcher? Night of the Living Dildo?* Well, let's just say after a restless night's sleep and four hits of espresso, anything seemed possible. There are a million stories in the naked city, and one of them was living in my dishwasher.

I peeked into the dishwasher and saw my stalwart new roommate, plum-shaped head pointed to the sky (or the top of the dishwasher, rather), silent and stoic. I was starting to gain some respect for this guy. God only knew how long he'd been in there, patiently waiting for someone to take him out and—that's where my mind went dark. I couldn't imagine putting that thing inside me. It was huge! Have I mentioned that? Maybe a porn star or Becky Robinson, the cheerleading slut in my senior class, could take that thing, but a normal woman would have a hard time. A little voice inside my head asked me how I would possibly know when the only things that had ever breached my womanhood were tampons and Mama's hairbrush. I just knew, I told myself.

I shuffled off to bed and my dreams once again filled with disjointed images of giant dicks and smooth silicone. I woke up sweating and panting, still shaking from the image of the dishwasher wobbling across the floor and bursting open in a spray of semen. I was starting to think New York was too much for this Texas girl to handle.

I awoke Sunday morning to sunlight streaming through my dirty window, Miss Marple gnawing on an unidentifiable bug, and the firm conviction that the only way I was going to grow up was to experience life. I took a long, leisurely shower after cleaning the rest of the bug parts out of the shower drain and making a mental note to buy another can of bug spray at the market. The hot water felt good streaming over my body, and I toyed with my nipples and ran my hand over my tummy down to the curls on my pussy. It had been a long, long time since I'd had a boyfriend to play with me, and though I usually masturbated almost every day, I'd been too tired all week to indulge myself. I shut off the water and gave myself a quick little orgasm as I leaned up against the shower wall. It felt good, but it left me unsatisfied.

I threw on my robe and strode to the kitchen before I could change my mind. I had a moment of trepidation as I wondered if it would still be there. What if I'd just imagined it? What if, somehow, the previous owner had snuck in to reclaim her property (for, surely, it must be a her)? But no, it was still there, smooth and pink and ready to go. I hesitated a moment before adding soap to the compartment in the door and turning the dishwasher on. A girl can't be too safe these days, you know?

Two hours later, convinced that even the hardiest of bacteria couldn't have survived three hot washes, I opened the dishwasher and reached for the dildo. He was still warm, which was a bit disconcerting. I hadn't considered that he might have melted during the dry cycle, but he seemed none the worse for wear. I had to tug him a bit to get him out of the cutlery tray. He came loose and I stumbled back a step, nearly flattening Miss Marple. She darted out of the room as I stared at my prize.

"Hello, big boy," I said throatily.

Now, it may seem crazy to be talking to a dildo, but this thing had taken on a life of its own in the two days I'd known about it. It was no longer molded rubber (or whatever they make them out of); it was alive, breathing, waiting for me to be brave enough to rescue it from the dishwasher.

"It" had become "him" the moment I touched it. I hefted him in my hand before carrying him to my bedroom. His shiny, pink surface was a nice complement to my pink-and-white floral sheets. Heart hammering in my chest, I stretched out on my bed. It took me a good five minutes to spread my legs. It took a good deal longer to move Mr. Dick anywhere near my timid little pussy.

I closed my eyes and took a deep breath. A good seduction takes time, even if it's yourself you're seducing. I thought about how good this big dick was going to feel inside me. All my friends called them cocks, but "cock" sounded so nasty. Good girls didn't say "cock." Then again, good girls didn't lie in bed on a Sunday afternoon thinking about fucking themselves with someone else's dildo.

I bit back a fit of giggles and whispered, "I want this big cock inside me."

I don't know if it was the words that did the trick, or the image, but when I reached down to touch myself, my pussy was drenched. I moaned as I thumbed my clit, pushing a finger into my wetness, rubbing that delicious little spot just inside. I stroked harder, silently climbing toward that familiar feeling. I'd done this so many times with other people within earshot, I didn't know how to verbalize my passion.

Something heavy rolled against my hip and I opened my eyes. I'd forgotten all about Mr. Dick. And that's what I was here for, right? I picked him up again, studying the realistic shape and design. He really was a piece of art. One that deserved better treatment than to be left behind in the dishwasher.

"Poor thing," I whispered, kissing his plum-size knob. The next thing I knew, I was rubbing my clit and sucking Mr. Dick like a prom queen in the backseat of her boyfriend's car.

Whimpering around the dildo in my mouth, I knew I was going to come if I didn't stop. And I didn't want to come like a virgin. I wanted to come with this cock inside me. Slowly I moved it down between my legs, nudging it against my pussy lips.

"Easy," I whispered nervously, as if Mr. Dick had anything to do with it.

The head spread my pussy open and slipped inside with no resistance. I leaned up on my elbows to watch as I pushed a little harder. An inch disappeared inside my pussy, a wet, sucking sound coming from down there as Mr. Dick slid in.

"Oh, yes, mmm . . ." I moaned, throwing my head back against the pillow and pushing another little bit of him inside me.

Inch by inch, I took as much of that dildo as I could. And let me tell you, it was more than I'd imagined I could take. I winced once or twice, unused to accommodating anything so big, but I wanted to feel all of it. I was stretched open, impaled on something bigger than any of the real cocks I was likely to encounter. I wasn't interested in those real cocks, though, at the moment. I was just a small-town girl who wanted to get fucked.

And fucked I got. Mr. Dick opened up my pussy and bravery opened my mouth. I was moaning as I raised my hips to meet my downward thrusts. My clit was forgotten. This was going to be an earthshaking orgasm, the kind women whisper about but many don't believe exist. The Sasquatch of orgasms was about to overtake me and I was not going to go quietly.

"Fuck me!" I screamed. "Fuck me!"

I came so hard, I didn't think it would ever stop. My pussy clenched almost painfully around the dildo inside me. It was a good pain. The kind of pain I'd remember for a long, long time. As the ripples subsided, I eased Mr. Dick out of my well-fucked pussy and cradled him to my chest. My eyes fluttered closed and, with a satisfied smile on my face, I slept.

At first I expected my experience with Mr. Dick to be the warm-up to an experience with a flesh-and-blood lover. But Mr. Dick managed to change my mind—for the moment. I'm hanging on to my virginity, at least technically, and sticking with Mr. Dick. We both understand our relationship is based only on sex. And I treat him a heck of a lot better than his last owner did. He sleeps in my bedside table, nestled next to my journal, a dog-eared copy of *Jane Eyre,* and a bottle of pepper spray. When he needs a bath, I take him in the shower with me.

I don't have to worry about pregnancy or sexually transmitted diseases, but we did have a scare the Monday after our first adventure. I almost thought I'd lost Mr. Dick when I answered my door to see a petite blonde smiling nervously at me.

Seems she thought she might have left something in the apartment when she moved out.

I hardly paused before saying I hadn't found anything of hers. A woman like her doesn't deserve Mr. Dick. He has a better home with me and I have what every big-city girl wants—a satisfying sex life.

QUEEN BEE ABUZZ: Using a Vibrator in the Woman-on-Top Position

Toy(s) you will need: Hitachi (or favorite clit vibe)

                               Blindfold (optional)

                               Lubricant

Type of play: Partnered

If you're not already a fan of the woman-on-top position, these extra toys give you just the incentive to climb up and try it out. A woman perched on top of a lover lying on his back has complete control over the action. Not only can she control the depth and rhythm of the thrusting, she can make slight adjustments in her position to maximize G spot and clit stimulation. Men love this position because they get to relax, they have a great view of their partner's pleasure, and it's often easier to delay orgasm until both partners are ready to come.

Couples fond of gazing deeply into each other's eyes enjoy this position, but I put a new spin on it here by suggesting a blindfold. Precisely because this position does not require much activity from the man, putting a blindfold on him forces him to be completely passive, allowing him to fully indulge in his other senses (something men don't get to do enough). He can smell, hear, and feel his partner, while using his imagination to further the fantasy. By removing the mask just before they climax, she gives him a showstopping visual to remember.

Almost any vibrator will work in this position, so feel free to try whatever toy gets you off best. I recommend the Hitachi because the vibrations are strong enough for him to feel on his penis once he's inside you, which adds another layer of tactile pleasure to this exciting encounter.

Toy Testimonials

"My trick is to wear the strap-on dolphin vibe when I'm on top, then my hands are free to use the Wahl clit massager on the rest of my body, thighs, and nipples, to bring myself to an ecstatic climax. If my boyfriend's away from home, I make do with a dildo inside me."

- **Prep.** Plug in the toy and place it within arm's reach. Have your partner lie on his back, then put the blindfold on him.
- **Elevate his senses.** You want him to be good and excited before you climb on top of him, so try a mixture of favorite and unexpected moves on him. Without sight, his other senses will be keener, so play with touch, whisper in his ear, stroke parts of his body with your breasts, and tease his nipples with your tongue. Climb on top of him and rub your vulva along his penis until you're both ready for penetration. Then apply a bit of lubricant to his penis. Drip it on, then use your warm hand to

slather it up and down the shaft. Talk to him the whole time, describing what you're doing, how it feels, and what it looks like—that will keep him fully turned on.

- **Hop on.** As you're facing him, straddle his legs and slowly  lower yourself down onto his penis so that you end up in a kneeling position. You're in control, so go as slow or as deep as you like. Lean backward and his penis should hit your G spot. Lean forward and you can press your clitoris against his body. (Instead of thrusting, have him move his body in lateral jerks to stimulate your clit.) When you're upright, raise yourself up nearly off the top of his penis, then slide back down. Squeeze your PC muscle during each stroke so he can feel it press against his penis. Use your hands and breasts to keep touching your partner's body until you're ready to turn on the vibrator.

Using a vibrator in
the woman-on-top position

- **Blast off.** With the blindfold still on your partner, pick up the vibrator, turn it on low, and gently place it at the base of the penis where it emerges from your vagina. If he says this is too much, place your fingers over his penis and place the vibrator on top of them. Now remove his blindfold so he can watch you come. Then take the vibrator and turn it to your desired speed (probably low, if you're like most women). Place the side of the vibrator's head against your clitoris and resume thrusting, experimenting with a steady or a stop/start vibration against your clit. He should be able to feel the vibrations on his penis through your vaginal walls. You can also drop the vibrator down against his penis from time to time to give him a little buzz. Lean forward if you like and invite him to play with your breasts—sandwiching the vibrator between you as you lie on top of it will free your hands.

Variations

- Turn around and face his feet. This will give your partner a great view of your butt and his penis entering you. In this position you can use your vibrator on his testicles.
- If your partner wants to see all the action, forgo the blindfold.
- Consider letting your partner hold the vibrator for you. You do give up some control of your orgasm, but he gets to participate in it as well.
- Try other toys. A strap-on vibrator will free your hands to seek other pleasures, a fingertip vibrator gives you the skin-on-skin feel, and a cock ring vibrator on him offers you more control of the action. Supplement your play with a butt toy, nipple toy, cock ring, or other sex toys.

MISSIONARY ZEAL: Spicing Up the Missionary Position with a Cock Ring Vibrator

Toy(s) you will need:	Cock ring vibrator with clitoral stimulator
	Lubricant
Type of play:	Partnered

We Americans have a somewhat schizophrenic relationship to the missionary position. On one hand, we tend to view it as rather boring; on the other hand, eighty-five percent of married couples engage in it exclusively. The missionary position gets a bad rap simply because it's familiar. Once people discover there's more than one way to entwine their bodies, suddenly the missionary position goes from being old reliable to just being old hat. It's part of the American way to embrace what's new and trendy while maligning the classics, even if they remain a secret part of the bedroom repertoire.

I'm here to kick the missionary position back out of the closet.

For one thing, it's an incredibly intimate position because it offers full body contact and great eye contact. Plus, it adapts itself well to minor changes that can have major effects. Take the clitoris, for example. Picture a woman lying on her back with her lover pounding away, quietly frustrated that there's just not quite enough stimulation to the clitoris to get her off. But if they work together they can fix that. He can lie down closer to her and use friction from his penis to rub her clit, or she can put her legs up over his shoulders to find her G spot.

By adding a vibrating cock ring, the missionary position gets couples one step closer to the simultaneously orgasmic unions they see depicted in the movies. A strategically placed vibrator protrudes off the top of the cock ring, vibrating the clitoris during vaginal intercourse and giving the extra bit of stimulation some women need to have an orgasm during intercourse. Keep in mind that because everyone's anatomy is different, these toys might not hit all your parts the way they claim to. But with a little experimentation—try different positions, look for stronger vibrators, vary your rhythm—you may well meet with success.

- **Prep.** Put batteries in your toy. Apply a little lube to both your penis and the inside of the ring, then slip it on over your penis so that the vibrating Bullet is facing up (if there are two vibrating pieces, one goes faceup, the other goes down so it vibrates your testicles). Depending on how stretchy the ring is, you can strap it around the base of the penis but above the testicles (if there's not much stretch), or pull your testicles through it (if it's very stretchy).
- **Assume the position.** Your partner should be lying on her back. Kneel between her spread legs. Have her bend her knees and place her feet flat on the bed for maximum comfort. You

can also try placing a pillow underneath her hips both to alleviate strain on her back and to elevate her hips in order to accommodate your penis most comfortably, but keep in mind
that this might make contact with the vibrator more difficult.

- **Feel the buzz.** If you've got one with a battery pack, either of
  you can hold the pack and operate the controls. She might want
  to do this to better regulate the vibrations to her clitoris once
  you're inside her. Before you enter her, play with your toy a bit
  to get used to the vibrations. Vary the speed, try stroking your
  penis or pressing it against your stomach to transmit the vibrations elsewhere. Tease your partner by simulating intercourse
  without actually penetrating her. Slide your penis alongside her
  labia, gently running it up and down so that she can feel your
  slick, vibrating shaft against her vulva.
- **Go inside.** Add more lube to your penis and the toy, then
  gently insert your penis into her vagina and bend forward, very
  close to her, so that the top part of the ring vibrator is now
  pressed up against her clitoris. You may need to adjust your

Intercourse with a cock ring vibrator

position somewhat so the toy hits just the right spot—try bending far forward and having her press up against you, or wrap her legs around you. She can try draping her legs over your shoulders, which allows for deeper penetration, but she may not get enough contact with the toy in this position. It might be tempting to lie on top of her to attempt the closest contact possible, but she's not likely to enjoy bearing your weight while trying to come.

- **Experiment.** Once you've established contact, experiment with different thrusts as a way of discovering which feel best against her clitoris. Ask for her feedback along the way. If she's the kind of woman who requires more intense stimulation, she might prefer that you stay deep inside her and perform shallow thrusts (more of an up-and-down motion rather than in-and-out) so she doesn't lose contact with the vibrator. Or, if she likes to be teased into orgasm, she might want you to pump in and out because the on again–off again contact with the vibrator feels better. Whichever of you is holding the controls should remember to vary the speed as well.

- **Go with the flow.** It's not uncommon for a woman to enjoy vigorous thrusting in this position, but then as she approaches orgasm, to prefer a steady vibration. So gauge her reactions and be prepared to slow down and firmly vibrate her clitoris if needed.

Toy Testimonials

"I always thought vibes were women's toys, but the one my wife uses feels great to both of us. It's one of those penis rings with a vibrator, and it's helped her to have orgasms during sex. I love it because when I press deep inside her and she has an orgasm, I can feel the vibrations and her contractions. It is so sexy."

Variations

- Modify your position slightly: she puts her legs together, and you straddle her with your thighs on the outside of her legs. As you enter her, she'll feel your penis more directly on her clitoris, and once inside, you'll feel a tighter grip on your penis. If you switch to the woman-on-top position, she can control the pressure and pacing of the vibrator stimulation.

- Flip the toy upside down to stimulate the testicles during either solo or partner sex. Wearing the toy this way, you can also enter her doggie-style and the vibrator will feel good against her vulva.

- Try different toys. If she requires stronger, steadier vibration to orgasm during intercourse, let her hold a toy such as the Hitachi or the Fukuoku while you're penetrating her.

- Get other stimulation. Don't forget to combine this with other forms of stimulation. This position gives you good access to your partner's breasts, and either of you can comfortably wear a butt plug.

FOUR ON THE FLOOR: Doing It Doggie-Style with a Hands-free Vibrator

Toy(s) you will need: Remote Butterfly (or similar
                         hands-free clit vibe)
                         Lubricant
     Type of play: Partnered

When you invite sex toys into your bedroom, sometimes juggling them all gets to feel a bit like a circus act. Even the most agile acrobat often finds there aren't enough hands to prop oneself up comfortably and get just the right stimulation. Enter one of the industry's greatest inventions: the hands-free vibrator. These are little gems designed to do all the work for you, so your hands are free to seek other pleasures.

The hands-free clit vibe can be worn in almost all sexual positions, but women who like the rear-entry position especially appreciate it. Also known as "doing it doggie-style," this position has quickly gained in popularity, largely because it's ideal for deep penetration. The woman either kneels or bends over while the man penetrates her vaginally from behind. It's easy to work up to a rapid, deep thrusting that feels great for both partners, but it also offers her more targeted G spot stimulation. But ask anyone who's ever tried to get reliable clit stimulation during the rear-entry position and you're bound to hear tales of tired limbs, cramping hands, too much bounce, and unsteady vibrations. A woman who's propped up on all fours has to rely on a partner reaching around in order to please her clitoris. All this does is put more weight on the woman and restrict the movement of both partners. By strapping on one of these vibrators and moving the single back strap to the side, you get to enjoy the best of G spot penetration and clitoral vibrations and have full range of motion. This same routine works equally well for anal penetration.

The hands-free clitoral vibrators look a bit like thong underwear, except there's a small vibrator attached to the fabric, positioned right over the clitoris. You'll find the body of this toy comes in a veritable menagerie of animals, including butterflies, dolphins, and bunnies, so you can pick your favorite. I've chosen a remote version of this toy, because it gives you more options for partner play, but you can substitute a nonremote version (which is less expensive). Just make sure you get one with adjustable straps, rather than one-size-fits-all elastic. The adjustable straps enable you to get a snug fit, which is crucial since you don't want that vibrator straying during your climax. You should also try to find one that's powered by a microchip (as most newer models are), as these pack a more powerful vibration than the older versions. Finally, a couple of caveats about this toy: if you need a lot of focused, strong vibration, this may not be the toy for you. If you're shopping, pick them up and turn them on to determine vibration strength. You can also improve the intensity by pressing this toy against your clit with one hand, but this defeats its hands-free claim to fame.

You don't need a partner to enjoy the magic of a hands-free vibe. Don one of these toys and your masturbation play takes on new possibilities. Since your hands aren't needed to hold the vibrator, use them to explore other erogenous zones. Try playing with your breasts, pinching your nipples, or rubbing the insides of your thighs. You now have two hands free—use one to manipulate a dildo and the other to insert an anal toy. Or wear this toy under your clothes while you're tapping away at your keyboard, flying on a plane, or enjoying a night out on the town.

- **Plan some sexy foreplay.** Think about how you want to use this toy, and don't be afraid of a little adventure! If you're using the Remote Butterfly, consider going out together (dinner, a bar, club—somewhere a little noisy) with the Butterfly strapped on underneath your clothing. You can hand the remote over to your partner or use it on yourself and let him watch you turn yourself on. You can keep the vibrator on low and just enjoy a slow simmering arousal, or you can experience the thrill of a discreet orgasm in public.

- **Get into position.** When you're ready for intercourse, stand or kneel by the bed (depending on how high your bed is), and use your arms to prop yourself up while your partner stands behind you. (You can try this

The Butterfly vibe and rear penetration

with both of you kneeling on the bed, but you can get a better groove going if one of you is fairly stationary.) He can move the single strap from the vibrator over onto one of your butt cheeks. Give the remote to your partner, or hold it yourself if you want to control the vibrations. If you've got a toy with a battery pack, tuck it under one of the straps or let it rest on the bed.

- **Get rockin'.** He should apply a little lubricant to his penis and some to your vulva, then run his penis along your vulva first, caressing the clit and labia with it. Have him enter you slowly, or back onto his penis. Initially, his thrusting should be gentle, while you give him feedback about what you like. If his penis is hitting your cervix, he can place his hand around the base of his penis or attempt more shallow thrusts. You can take turns controlling the motion—he can thrust into you for a while, or you can push back onto his penis. By withholding clitoral stimulation for a bit, you can both focus on arousing your G spot.

- **Add the buzz.** When you're feeling really aroused, switch on the vibe. If you find that the vibrations aren't strong enough, hold one hand against the vibrator, or place a firm pillow between the bed and your clit, so that you press into it during thrusts. Some women find they like the intermittent stimulation this offers, while others find they prefer a steady rhythm.

- **Let go.** Let your partner know when you're ready to come so he can come with you if he likes. If he's got control of the toy, make sure he knows not to turn it off before you're through, and by all means go for another round if you like!

Variations

- You can also use this vibrator for some fun foreplay. If you're fond of frottage—rubbing your genitals against a partner's body part (like a thigh or a penis) or an inanimate object (a piece of furniture)—the hands-free vibrator gives this practice an extra little buzz. Wear the toy under some tight underwear or jeans so it stays firmly in place while you rub up against your lover's leg or crotch.
- If you aren't getting strong enough vibrations from this toy, try a different type of vibrator in this position. Prop up the Hitachi on some pillows and, when he thrusts into you, your clit will press against the vibrator.
- If you're both standing, bend over slightly and brace yourself against the wall or bed, as this will put more pressure on the G spot.
- Try gently squeezing your legs together while he's inside you, or clamping down on his penis with your pelvic muscles.
- If you like anal play, he's in a great position to play with your anus or to insert an anal toy into you.
- For extra stimulation, you can reach back and lightly stroke his testicles, or he can reach around and caress your breasts.

Toy Testimonials

"I'd been keeping my vibrator from my boyfriend, but he caught me playing with it one day and thank god! That's when we discovered that the Natural Contours vibrator is just the right shape to lie on top of while he enters me from behind. After a few more sessions we also found that it'll work in the missionary position too."

Secrets

by Julia Rebecca

Melanie surveyed the room. The setting was perfect for a romantic dinner for two. Low lights, soft jazz, and a beautifully decorated table created an exquisite arena for seduction. Melanie inhaled; the delicious aroma of the coq au vin in the oven pervaded her apartment. Since it was too cold to sit out on the terrace, she had set the small table by the window. From there, they could enjoy the last of the sunset and watch the lights of the city flicker on.

Satisfied with the room's ambiance, Melanie stepped to the mirror and checked her appearance. She wore her dark hair the way Rick liked it—loose around her shoulders. Her deep green, sueded-silk dress had a neckline that buttoned high enough to conceal, but dipped low enough to arouse interest. Its uneven, mid-calf hemline could, like its neckline, conceal or reveal, depending on her movements. Underneath, she wore the lace-trimmed ivory satin teddy that Rick had given her. She loved the feel of the cool satin sliding across her nipples when she moved. She would tease Rick with glimpses of his gift throughout the evening. Melanie's soft clothes sensuously caressed, as well as aroused, her body, which was why she had chosen to wear them.

Rick and Melanie's affair had been going on for almost a year. They both liked to design romantic evenings for each other; tonight it was her turn to set the scene. They would enjoy a delicious dinner while flirting and tantalizing each other with little kisses and touches. Every element of the evening would be a part of their subtle, drawn-out foreplay. To their mutual delight, they had discovered that they both enjoyed the dance of seduction almost as much as its culmination, which was pretty good. *Good,* Melanie thought, *but could be better.* Melanie was more adventurous than Rick, but he was loosening up. They were becoming more open with each other as they came to know and trust one another. Melanie shivered with anticipation as she glanced at the clock. She was more than ready for Rick to arrive.

Melanie smiled when she heard the phone ring. That would be Rick, calling to say he was running late. He would be a bit breathless from hurrying and apologetic as well. Rick had probably stopped for wine. He always took extra care to choose something special, which would delay him even more. Melanie's amused anticipation was reflected in her voice as she answered the phone with a sultry "Hello."

Rick spoke quickly. "Hi, sweetheart. Don't hate me."

Melanie was startled; her amusement faded. *Uh-oh. This doesn't sound good.* "Of course I don't hate you. What's wrong?"

"This damned mediation is still going. At this rate, we'll be here all night. We've got a ten-minute break, then we have to go back in." Rick sounded frustrated. "There's just no way I can make it. I'm so sorry. I was really looking forward to tonight."

Melanie sighed. "So was I. Are you sure I shouldn't wait up? The dinner and I are both simmering. We can keep warm until you get here."

Rick laughed, as she had intended. "Tempting as that offer is, I'm going to have to pass. How about tomorrow night, or will everything be cold by then?"

"Probably," Melanie teased. "I guess I could reheat it for you, but you'll have to ask nicely."

Rick's voice lowered and became seductive. "I'll ask on my knees. Will that be nice enough?" Suddenly Rick's tone changed to a more businesslike one. "Uh-oh. They're calling us back. Gotta go, sweetheart, and thanks for understanding."

Melanie heard a click, so she hung up. She was disappointed, of course, but she understood. They both had demanding careers that could, and occasionally did, get in the way of their social life. *Oh, well,* Melanie thought, *everything will keep.* At least they had made a date for tomorrow night—same time, same place; she'd even wear the same sexy clothes.

Exchanging her dress for a light robe, Melanie ate some dinner and read a while. Even though she'd had a long day, Melanie was wide awake and restless at 11 P.M. Melanie had a problem; in anticipation of her date with Rick she'd been thinking about sex all day. Those wanton thoughts had made her incredibly horny. Melanie knew herself—when she got like this she could make herself nuts; she'd be up until dawn if she didn't get relief. Melanie had some gadgets hidden away, things that could help her feel much better. Things that Rick knew nothing about. *I haven't played with my toys for a long time,* she thought. *I could take care of my needs and Rick would never find out.*

Rick wasn't a prude, exactly, but he was conservative—especially when it came to what he perceived to be kinky sex—and he had no interest in vibrators. Rick had seemed insulted when Melanie mentioned the subject, wondering why she "needed" toys. She had tried to explain that, since meeting him, it wasn't a matter of need so much as want. Prior to her involvement with Rick, Melanie had gone through a romantic dry spell—truthfully, it had been more like a drought. Because she'd had no interest in one-night stands, her toys had been her only bed companions during that time. When she and Rick became intimate, Melanie had hoped to use the toys with him, not instead of him. But Rick didn't understand, so Melanie didn't push. Nor did she get rid of her toys—she just didn't get them out when Rick was around.

Since she was alone, Melanie intended to enjoy her private playthings. She went to her bedroom, discarded her robe, and readied herself for a night of solitary pleasure. Usually she slept nude, but the teddy felt so good against her skin that she decided to keep it on. Turning on some music, she crossed the room to her night table and switched on a low-level "romantic" light. Next, Melanie went to her closet, opened the door, and retrieved her toy box from its hiding place behind her dresses. Sitting on the bed, which she had turned down in anticipation of Rick's visit, Melanie opened the box. She carefully inspected her treasures, then pulled out "Old Faithful." Melanie thought of it by that name because it was electric, not battery operated, and it never ran out of juice before she was satisfied. Faithful had a well-designed forefinger and opposing thumb attachment that was perfect for inner and outer stimulation. Plus, it had three speeds! She put Faithful on her bed next to her.

Melanie started to close the box, then paused as a flash caught her eye. It was her latest acquisition—a glittery, hot pink, vibrating butt plug. This toy was so new it was still wrapped in plastic. Melanie had bought it when she first started sleeping with Rick, thinking that it might be fun for them to experiment a little. Instead, it had languished in the drawer, forgotten until now.

Her fingers slid over the device and she pulled it out of the box. The fine print read, "two AA batteries." *No problem there; I have plenty of those.* Melanie knew she liked anal stimulation because a former lover had introduced her to that pleasure. She remembered how his finger had worked its slippery way into her ass during a shower while he was "washing" her pussy. At first, it had startled the hell out of her, but it hadn't hurt so she let him continue. After that episode, he had been smart enough to either go down on her or stroke her clit while he finger-fucked her backside, teaching her to associate his finger up her ass with pleasure and orgasm. Under his patient—and well-lubricated—tutelage, Melanie had learned to crave anal stimulation.

Unfortunately, Rick wasn't any more interested in anal experimentation than he was in sex toys, so it had been too long since Melanie had experienced that form of gratification. Even though she had gotten wet just thinking about how much she missed those intense sensations, Melanie still hesitated; she had never before used a vibrator "back there." Finally, she thought, *Why not? I'm lonely and I've been stood up; I deserve something special tonight.* Fortunately, she had some lubricant—cherry flavored—to use with her toys. She closed her special box and slid it under her bed. *What Rick doesn't know won't hurt him,* she told herself. He didn't know, either, that she liked dirty talk when she was excited. She would think dirty to herself, as she did when they made love, while she used her toys.

Melanie put batteries in the butt plug, swung her legs into bed, and lay back on her pillows. She arranged her toys within easy reach on either side of her—unwrapped plug and lube on her left, Old Faithful on her right, near the electrical outlet. Closing her eyes, she slid her hands down her body from her breasts to her thighs and back up again. She cupped her hands around her breasts, thumbing her nipples through the satin. The cool fabric warmed at her touch and her nipples hardened. Melanie pulled the top of the teddy down to her waist and then put some lubricant on her fingertips. She massaged the slippery stuff into her areolas, circling her sensitive flesh over and over. Grasping her breasts, she firmly pinched her nipples. Melanie sighed with pleasure. That wasn't as good as having them sucked, but it was close enough. Tweaking her nipples one last time, Melanie slid her hands down to her crotch. Spreading her legs, she unsnapped the dampened satin between her legs and pulled it up. Knees bent and feet flat on the mattress, Melanie stroked her thighs and lower abdomen, teasing herself by skimming her hands across her pussy.

Finally, she was too aroused to wait any longer. It was time to bring Old Faithful into play. Starting with Faithful on the lowest setting, Melanie skimmed the finger portion of the vibrator over her inner thighs and moved it across her outer lips. Taking her time, she ran the vibrator down, up, and around between her legs in an inverted U motion, slowly building up to her first orgasm. With her left hand, she squeezed a few drops of lube onto her pussy and then moved Faithful to the sensitive area between her outer and inner labia. Her skin warmed the lube, allowing Faithful to slide easily. *I love the way this feels between the lips of my cunt,* she thought. Rick would have been scandalized to hear Melanie use the *C* word; she rarely said it aloud and had never uttered it in his presence. The idea of shocking her lover and the wonderful feelings the vibrator produced combined to propel Melanie into her first orgasm.

Mmm, that was lovely. Melanie hit the switch on Faithful, increasing the intensity of its vibration. Gently she stroked its finger from the bottom of her slippery opening to her clitoris, just barely touching herself. She stroked herself over and over, resisting the urge to slide the vibrator up inside herself and come hard and fast.

Melanie didn't want to simply masturbate; at her high level of arousal she knew she'd be horny again too soon. She wanted to make love to herself and have several increasingly intense orgasms that would satisfy her for the night, making up, as much as possible, for Rick's absence.

Melanie's inner lips became swollen and slick. She shifted her hand, then used Faithful's finger to trace the outline of her vaginal opening. Around and around she moved it, slipping just the tip inside. She tantalized herself with that vibrating tip—never touching her clitoris and never putting the vibrating finger all the way inside—and slowly brought herself closer to another orgasm. When Melanie was shaking with her need for release, she resumed moving Faithful's finger lengthwise between her legs. She moved the vibrator at a steady pace, pressing firmly as she stroked upward, putting more pressure on her clitoris as it retreated into its hood. Melanie's second orgasm curled her toes.

Moving Faithful away from her quivering pussy, she switched it off and put it down. She would need it later, but just then she wanted her new toy. Melanie knew that her orgasms were just the first step in preparation for this erotic experiment. For the second step, she squirted lube onto the fingers of her left hand, rolled onto her right side, and drew up her knees. She put her lubed fingers between her butt cheeks and massaged the slick substance across her tight hole. Carefully, she inserted the tip of her middle finger into her ass. She paused, taking time to adjust to the half-remembered feel of anal penetration. Remembering her earlier lessons, she slipped her right hand between her legs and gently caressed her swollen pussy. *Oh,* she thought, *that's much better.*

Carefully, she wiggled the fingertip in her ass. The little darts of pleasure accompanying that movement encouraged her to continue.

She pushed her finger farther up her ass, then pulled it almost out again. Her past lover had done that, but Melanie had never done it to herself. She continued to finger-fuck herself in the ass while she rubbed her clitoris. Shuddering, she realized that another orgasm was almost upon her. *I'm glad Rick didn't come over tonight,* she thought guiltily. *I haven't had this for so long, I'd almost forgotten how good it feels.*

Melanie decided it was time to replace her finger with the vibrating butt plug. Removing her finger and rolling onto her back, she picked up the vibrator and the lubricant. As she spread the glistening slippery stuff on the plug, she examined it closely. The "business" end was about four inches long, tapering from half an inch at the tip to about an inch and a quarter at the base. About halfway down the shaft there was a lump; it looked as if there was a bead embedded in the plastic. At the base there was a larger bead shape that curved inward to little arms that stuck out, then came the opening for the batteries. The screw cap had a ring on it, which was presumably meant to be a handle of sorts. The cap was also the speed control; the more she twisted it, the faster it vibrated. Melanie had never taken anything that size up her ass before, but she was so turned on that she wanted to give it a try.

Melanie started the vibrator, setting it at medium, and again rolled onto her right side. Stroking her clitoris with the fingers of her right hand, she began to slowly insert the butt plug. Its vibrating tip felt marvelous. Experimentally, she moved it another inch or so in and out of her well-lubed hole; the sensation was phenomenal. *This,* Melanie thought, *is even better than I thought it would be.* Emboldened by her success, Melanie inserted more of the plug. Still fingering the soft, swollen folds of her vulva, she pushed the butt plug up to, then past, the first bead. Holding the plug in place,

Melanie paused, lost in new sensations. Her intense physical pleasure was enhanced by the thought that she was doing something forbidden, which added to her excitement.

Melanie gave the butt plug an experimental wiggle, then squirmed with pleasure at the sensations that action produced. Deciding to go for it, Melanie rubbed her clit more firmly while she pushed the vibrator up her ass to its hilt. She experienced a one-second flash of almost pain as her tight flesh expanded to accommodate the butt plug's girth, then felt pure ecstasy as her muscles clenched around the purring vibrator. She wiggled the vibrator again, reveling in the feel of its four inches moving inside her. She continued to jiggle it as she masturbated herself to another orgasm. Trembling, she decided she was ready to play with Faithful again and give herself a final, major orgasm. She wished Rick was there and that she could share this with him. *Old Faithful is great fun,* she thought, *but I really want Rick's hard cock inside my cunt while the vibrator is up my ass.* Melanie smiled at the thought. *I wonder how he would react if I said that to him?*

Keeping her left hand underneath her and on the ring of the butt plug humming in her ass, Melanie rolled onto her back. She picked up Faithful and flipped the switch to its highest setting, which was her favorite for G spot massage. Head back and eyes closed, she held Faithful over her wet, swollen flesh and prepared to bring herself to a screaming orgasm. As she lowered Faithful to her pussy, Melanie thought she heard a slight sound. Distracted, she half opened her eyes and sought its source. Seeing nothing, she touched the finger of Faithful to her slit as she jostled the butt plug. She heard the sound again; it sounded almost like a groan. Turning her head, eyes wide open this time, she spotted Rick in the darkened doorway. The sound had come from him. Rick stood there, staring at her. She couldn't tell if he was appalled or aroused or both.

Melanie was mortified at being caught masturbating, as well as somewhat amused by the thought that Rick had been watching her while she fantasized about his being there. Clicking Faithful off, she asked, "How long have you been there?"

"Long enough. What the hell are you doing?"

Melanie fought back a giggle, which was probably engendered by hysteria. She feared that the situation was potentially disastrous. "What does it look like I'm doing? I was lonely and horny and decided to play by myself. I thought you weren't coming over."

"We finished earlier than I thought we would, so I decided to surprise you. I guess I did." Rick was still standing in the doorway, as if unable to decide whether to stay or go.

"It's a good surprise. Why don't you come to bed?"

The expression on Rick's face reflected his doubt. "It doesn't look like you need me. I didn't even know you liked that sort of thing."

"I know. And I didn't know you liked to watch," Melanie remarked as she looked pointedly at the huge bulge in the front of his pants, "but it seems that you do. Apparently, we both have secrets."

"I did like watching you," Rick confessed. "It's exciting, but it's kind of over the top for me. I've never done anything like it."

And that, Melanie realized, was part of the problem. Rick didn't know how to please her with toys and was too embarrassed to ask. Melanie had to be honest with Rick, even if it meant turning him off. *I've been trying to think of a way to share my fantasies with him; I should be more careful what I wish for.* Melanie took a deep breath and then let it out. "What you see is what I like. Not all of the time, but sometimes." She repeated her invitation. "Come to bed. We can play together." She waited, and hoped that her confession had not ended their affair.

Rick met her eyes and just stared. After a few moments, he slowly entered the room. As he neared the bed, he began to pull at his clothing. Normally a tidy person, Rick dropped his clothes on the floor without a backward glance. When he was naked, he joined Melanie on the bed. His penis was rock hard.

Melanie sighed with relief. "Thank God. I thought this kind of thing turned you off."

"I thought it did too." Glancing down at his erect penis, Rick smiled. "I guess I was wrong. I have fantasized about watching you masturbate, but I was afraid to mention it." Rick kissed Melanie and ran his hands over her body. "So, is there anything I can do, or am I just supposed to watch?"

Melanie hesitated, regarding him closely. *May as well go for it,* she thought. "First I want you to watch me masturbate with the vibrator until I come. Then I want to get on my hands and knees and have you fuck me doggie-style. When you're inside me, you'll be able to feel the vibrator I have up my backside. I want you to wiggle it while you fuck me. I want you to make me scream with orgasm, then I want you to come harder than you ever have in your life."

Melanie waited for Rick's response. She had never allowed him to see this aggressive, sexually demanding side of her, and she was afraid she'd revealed too many of her secrets too quickly.

Rick kissed her. "Sounds good to me. Get started; I want to watch you come."

Giddy with relief, Melanie clicked Faithful onto high. She touched herself while Rick held her and watched. Masturbating was so much nicer with him there to kiss and hold her, plus he sucked on her nipples! *He'll probably wonder why they taste like cherries* was Melanie's last coherent thought. An intense orgasm shook her body. Instead of inserting Faithful into her vagina, as she would have done were Rick not with her, Melanie rolled to her hands and knees. "Now," she commanded Rick. "Fuck me now."

Rick willingly complied, groaning as he slid his engorged penis into her throbbing cunt. Her vaginal muscles tightened around him. Rick bumped the butt plug as he seated himself inside her and Melanie nearly fainted with pleasure. The sensation of being filled front and back was unique and powerfully erotic. Trembling with pleasure and unable to support herself on her hands any longer, Melanie lowered the front half of her body to the bed and rested on her forearms.

Rick moved slowly at first. He leaned forward and pushed all the way inside of her, bumping the vibrator with his abdomen, which made her whimper with delight. He grasped her hips and began to fuck her at a steady pace. She realized he was responding to her cries—and her request—fucking her with long, steady strokes and deliberately bumping the vibrator every time he entered her.

Melanie was in a state of orgasmic bliss. Despite his initial reluctance to experiment, Rick was making one of her wildest fantasies come true. She never thought this kind of sex would turn him on, but he certainly seemed to be. His cock felt like it was made of stone. The sound of Rick's ragged breathing, the sensation of the vibrator in her ass, and the feel of his hard penis moving inside her was an erotic sensory overload. She shuddered as another orgasm swept through her.

As Melanie's cries turned to screams of pleasure, she breathlessly commanded Rick, "Fuck me, fuck me!" He increased his pace. She no longer needed him to hold back; it was time for him to take them both over the edge. Melanie flung her head up. "Please. Oh, please."

Melanie knew that Rick would understand what she wanted. When she was this aroused she liked a rough finish—that was what pushed her to that last, highest orgasmic pinnacle. He responded to her pleas by slamming hard into her once, twice, and a third time. Melanie screamed as her body convulsed with the most powerful orgasm she'd ever had. She clamped around Rick's penis, as if trying to pull him inside her. Rick held out for two more thrusts before he, too, cried out with pleasure. She felt powerful spasms wrack his body. Just as Melanie ordered, he had come harder than he ever had in his life.

Though spent, Rick remained inside Melanie. She liked him to stay with her until the majority of her orgasmic contractions subsided. He waited for her shuddering to cease, then gently withdrew the butt plug from her body, which caused her to gasp with pleasure. He turned off the toy and tossed it to one side. Putting his arm around her and pulling her close, Rick eased them both down to the bed.

They lay quietly until Melanie broke the silence. "What did you think about that?"

Rolling onto his back, Rick sighed. "It was incredible. You looked beautiful lying there—desirable and pornographic and . . . I don't know what. The whole scene was like some letter in a men's magazine." He laughed. "And I always thought somebody made those up!"

Rick snuggled down in bed beside her, turned off the light, and held her close. After a few minutes, something occurred to him. "Uh, sweetie? You awake?"

Satiated and almost asleep, Melanie murmured, "Hmm? What is it?"

"I was just wondering. Is there anything else you haven't told me? About sex, I mean."

Melanie smiled in the dark. "Oh, nothing much. We'll talk about it later." She fell asleep, still smiling.

SIT UP AND TAKE NOTICE: Add a Vibrator to the Sitting Position

Toy(s) you will need: Pocket Rocket or Bullet vibrator
                        Lubricant
Type of play: Partnered

To the naked eye, the sitting position offers more in the way of intimacy than it does in the way of a boisterous sexual frolic. It's most often illustrated as two partners sitting entwined in the lotus position gazing lovingly into each other's eyes. Now, I don't mean to suggest that tender, quiet intercourse positions don't have their place—but this position often gets used as "foreplay" rather than the main course.

However, with the help of a vibrator, a mirror, and a taste for exhibitionism, you both can enjoy this twist (literally) on the sitting position. In this activity the woman initiates the sexual encounter with her partner, coming on to him in a deliciously premeditated and flirtatious way. She turns him on and works up his erection, then turns the tables and hands the key to her orgasm (in this case a vibrator) over to him. He gets to watch her as he makes her come, then she delivers a showstopping final performance for him.

- **Prep.** Place a sturdy, armless chair across from a full-length mirror. Put on a skirt but leave off the underwear. Wear a loose shirt and no bra.
- **Make your move.** Invite him to sit in the chair. Stash your vibrator and some lube near his chair or, better yet, slip them into his shirt pocket so he gets the message. If you want, strut your stuff for him before approaching, giving him a peek at what you've got in store for him.
- **Climb aboard.** Climb up on his lap, straddling his closed legs. Your crotch will be positioned right over his package, so

Adding a vibrator to the sitting position

he'll feel every move you make. Kiss him, stroke his hair, whisper into his ear, all while grinding away. He'll have already noticed the mirror across the way, and the sight of your lovely rear end will drive him nuts.

- **Pants off.** When he's good and hard, stand up and remove his pants, or at least unzip them so his lovely hard-on is at your service. Apply lube, turn around so you're both facing the mirror, then guide his penis into your vagina as you slide down into a sitting position.

- **Take a good look.** Enjoy the scene reflected back at you, and let your inner exhibitionist loose. Play with yourself, touching your breasts, running your hands through your hair, sucking on a finger, rubbing your clit. He'll be enjoying the show so much his hands will soon want in on the action.
- **Get your buzz on.** If he hasn't figured it out already, instruct him to take out the vibrator and help you. It's so small he can easily hold it against your clitoris or tuck it into the folds of your labia.
- **Ride him.** You can't do a lot of bouncing in this position, but you can do some really sexy grinding, with slow deep thrusts. This will feel good to you and he'll be able to focus more on the vibrations working their way through you to his penis. Clench your PC muscle and he'll be able to feel that on his penis as well.
- **Come with a bang.** Either you can let him work your clit until you come, or you can take control of the vibrator so his hands are free to play with your breasts. Now is the time to really express yourself—visually and verbally. Between the sight of you two in the mirror, your moans of pleasure, and his own excitement, you'll both be fans of this position when you're through. The image of you coming will give him something to fantasize about for a long time.
- **Blow him away.** He may come while he's inside you, or you

Toy Testimonials

"My husband and I discovered that a small vibrator like the Pocket Rocket or Lipstick vibe really perked up one of our favorite intercourse positions. It's small enough for me to hold between my lips and against my clit while we're fucking, so I get the extra buzz. When he wants to send me over the top, he holds another one against my anus and the combo is mind-blowing."

might ask him to wait. Then you can dismount, kneel before him, and give him a stupendous blow job, using the vibrator to tickle his balls while he watches you in the mirror.

Variations

- Instead of both of you facing the mirror, you can face each other. Breast and clit play are a bit more awkward, but you do get the face-to-face intimacy.
- If you're really feeling naughty, strap a cock ring on him before you mount him. When he wants it off, proceed with fellatio, which will feel especially good on his supersensitive penis.
- Add another element to your exhibitionist act by inserting a butt plug into yourself while he's watching and then sit on his lap.
- Instead of (or in addition to) a mirror, videotape this scene and you'll enjoy it for months to come!

THE SLOW SIMMER: Snuggling Up to a Vibrator in the Spoons Position

Toy(s) you will need: Fukuoku fingertip vibe
                                   Lubricant
Type of play: Partnered

How many women have woken up in the morning to a growing hard-on poking between their legs as a groggy partner spoons them from behind? A lot, I bet. Because penises often stand at attention bright and early, the spoons position (also known as the side-by-side sex position) gets used most often in the morning, before the coffee, the toothbrush, and the alarm. It's a cozy position, perfect for half-awake sex.

It's also a really intimate position because people associate spooning with the comfort and tenderness of cuddling. It allows for full body contact and gives the man easy access to his partner's breasts and genitals. When her legs are folded together, his penis gets extra friction. It's also a great position for pregnant women or anyone with a big tummy.

And since he's the one most likely to initiate this early morning encounter, he gets to bring you a gift, so you can get your rocks off too. The Fukuoku fingertip vibrator complements this position nicely because he can slip the toy over his finger and reach around easily to vibrate your clit during penetration. This simple toy is easy to whip out and slip on, and rewards you with pleasant hand-to-skin contact.

- **Prep.** Keep lube near the bed. If his penis is knocking at your door first thing in the morning, you may not be sufficiently aroused. Keep lube nearby and have him put some on his penis before penetration. Keep the Fukuoku in your bedside table with the batteries in (it runs on watch batteries).

- **Assume the position.** You can lie with your legs together on your side, or you can swing one back over his legs. This position gives him greater access to your clitoris, and having your genitals exposed can feel especially nice.

- **Breast play.** Have him play with your breasts before he slips on the vibrator. When they start to get nice and sensitive, he can slip the toy on and vibrate your nipples.

- **Open the gates.** Whenever you're ready, let him in. His need may seem urgent, but don't proceed until you feel like it. The nice thing about the spoons position is that you can enjoy a slow, simmering turn-on as you're having sex, which is a nice contrast to some of the more energetic positions. Once he's inside, you can take turns controlling the depth or rhythm of the penetration. He can thrust into you, or you can push back onto him.

- **Buzz off.** Let him know when you want the vibrator. If he's familiar with your masturbation routine, he can use the vibrator the same way. If he isn't, place his hand on top of yours and show him just how you like to be stroked.

- **Talk, or not.** You can give him feedback about whether you want to come with him inside you, or just let the action go where it wants. It's a slow and sleepy encounter, so it's fun to see where the mood takes you. Just remember, if he comes and you haven't, ask him to keep up with the vibrator stimulation. If you want more penetration, have him use a dildo on you until you climax.

Using a finger vibrator in the spoons position

Variations

- If you're awake enough, try other toys. Either of you can wear a butt plug, or he can try a cock ring.
- If you want his hands to continue playing with your breasts, you can wear the fingertip vibrator and masturbate while he's inside you. You can also use any vibrator this way—the Hitachi is another popular choice in this position because you can prop it against your clit or wedge it between your legs.
- Side-by-side is a popular position for anal sex since it's comfortable for both partners and the receptive partner can control a lot of the motion.

DOUBLE TROUBLE: The Art of Double Penetration

Toy(s) you will need: Rabbit Pearl vibrator (or any dildo)
                        Lubricant
Type of play: Partnered

You're familiar with the phrase "double your pleasure," right? Good, because it captures the reason a couple might want to try double penetration, which involves a woman being penetrated both vaginally and anally at the same time. If she's already a fan of both types of penetration, she gets to double her fun by enjoying them both at the same time. The number of couples practicing double penetration has yet to make its way into the statistics books, but there's one thing for certain—it's popular fantasy material. Women's erotica and more traditional adult films often depict double penetration by showing an insatiable woman being filled to capacity by two men.

But you needn't be part of an adventurous threesome to experience the thrill of double penetration—that's what toys are for! Using your partner's penis and the Rabbit Pearl vibrator (or any dildo substitute), you can bring your own fantasy to life.

Why do women like double penetration? It's no secret that women enjoy the feeling of fullness that a penis or dildo in the vagina offers. Fill up the anus as well, and the vagina gets more crowded, amplifying that delicious feeling of fullness throughout her entire pelvic area. What's more, the vagina and anus are separated by a thin wall that is covered with nerve endings. When both cavities are filled, there's more friction against this sensitive wall, as well as more pressure placed against her G spot. Because the openings to the vagina and the anus are rich in nerve endings, they also respond well to such abundant stimulation.

For their part, men enjoy double penetration for several reasons. Thanks again to that thin wall separating the penis from the toy, the penis will easily share any vibration from the toy. The toy and the penis will collide against each other, adding to his pleasure, as will the incredibly snug feeling of having his penis nestled in such a tight space. Visually, it's a fantastic thing to watch. And few things are as sexually intimate as being on the giving—or the receiving—end of double penetration.

Because there's a lot going on in this activity, I don't recommend you try it unless you are comfortable with anal penetration. If you are new to anal play, try masturbating with an anal plug or exploring anal penetration with your partner first, so you'll be more relaxed. (For more on anal experimentation, see "Baby's Got Back" and "Please Enter from the Rear" activities.)

In this activity, the couple lies side by side in the spoons position so he can penetrate her anally while she inserts the vibrator into her vagina. This might not be as visually arresting as the rear-entry double penetration you see in a lot of adult films, but it's an easier way for couples to try this activity for the first time. It gives the woman a lot of control over the action, it's a bit easier for her to keep the vibrator in place, and it's more comfortable for both people. Once you get a little practice, you can assume all kinds of positions to see which ones you like best. Women can also explore double penetration alone by easily modifying this activity—simply substitute a dildo where the penis is mentioned. Because things can get a bit logistically challenging, a suction cup dildo will help if you're by yourself.

I chose the Rabbit Pearl, a vibrating dildo, for this activity because it offers a lot of intriguing options. This toy has a rotating shaft meant for insertion, with plastic pearls in its midsection that move around. Whether these feel good to one or both of you is a matter of personal preference, but you do have the option of turning them off and enjoying the toy's other features. Attached to the shaft is a little bunny, whose ears flick and vibrate the clit. The dildo-with-clit-vibe combo is a truly wonderful sensation, and particularly nice when you can control the two branches separately (as you can here). Women who like more intense vibrations might find the bunny ears don't deliver enough clitoral ooomph, but pressing the ears against the clit with your hand will help a bit.

- **Prep.** Place the toy within arm's reach of the bed. A pump dispenser of lube is handy, because things might get logistically challenging later.
- **Position.** Lie on your sides in the spoons position (that is, facing the same direction). It's especially important to get good and aroused before you attempt double penetration, so turn each other on in your favorite ways. You can play with her breasts, massage her butt and body, and gently tease her vulva with your penis or the vibrator.
- **Enter by the back door.** When you're both very aroused, use your finger to gently massage her anus. If you take your time, her anal opening will begin to relax. Apply lubricant to her anus and your finger and tap at the entrance with increasingly greater pressure until you are able to insert your finger. Then apply plenty of lube to your penis, place the head at her anus, and massage her anal opening with your penis. She should exhale and push out, as if trying to have a bowel movement, while you push in gently so your penis pops past the anal sphincter. (You may want to hold your penis close to the head, which will help direct it into her anus.) Once you are inside, rest a moment until she gets used to the sensation. Let her tell you when to proceed, then go very slowly, or let her control the action by pushing back on your penis. When she's fairly relaxed and your penis is well inside the anus, begin a slow and steady thrusting. Continue as long as she wants, letting her dictate how fast or slow you should go, and adding lube as necessary.
- **Double up with the vibrator.** When she feels ready, she can cover the shaft of the Rabbit Pearl vibrator with lubricant. Stop thrusting while she inserts the toy. It will feel crowded to both of you, but she can accommodate you and the toy. She should insert the toy so the rabbit attachment is facing up

Double penetration with a dildo and a penis

toward her clitoris. If she closes her legs while lying on her side, this will help keep the toy from being pushed out. Otherwise, she'll probably have to hold it in place with one hand.

- **Play with tempo.** With the vibrator inside her vagina, take a minute to get used to the crowded environment. Now the sky's the limit. The Rabbit Pearl has separate controls for the vibrator, the rotation of the shaft, and the movement of the pearls, so you can go to town discovering which combinations you like best (see the activity "The Right Tool for the Job" for more on using the Rabbit Pearl). Both of you can try thrusting in and out of her simultaneously. Or you can thrust while she turns on the vibrator. Or you can take over the controls and surprise her.

- **Orgasms one and all.** Check in with her about whether she wants to come like this and whether she wants you to come in this position. Be prepared to withdraw if she needs you to once she's had her climax.

Variations

- If you don't care about the vibrations, you can use a dildo for vaginal or anal penetration. If she wants hands-free vibration, try a strap-on vibrator. For hands-free penetration, try a dildo with a suction cup base.
- You can switch this activity around by putting your penis in her vagina and using a toy in her anus. To accomplish this, you'll want to change positions. You could try woman-on-top while she's wearing a butt plug, then she can bounce up and down on both the toy and your penis. Or if you want to be in control of all the movement, have her get on all fours, then slip a dildo into her anus and then penetrate her vagina with your penis.
- If you want a toy that stays in place in her anus while you're inside her vagina, have her try a butt plug. Otherwise the butt toy will need to be held in place by a hand.
- I've seen another toy designed for double penetration, but you'll need to look for it by description as the name for it varies. It's a harness for a man, with a hole positioned above a flexible dildo (which is attached to the harness). The man straps on the toy, slips his penis through the top hole, and then penetrates his partner with both the dildo and the penis. In the rear-entry position, his penis would enter her anus and the dildo would go into the vagina; in the missionary position, this would be reversed.
- Use a butt plug on yourself.

BLOW HIM AWAY: Give a Blow Job with a Buzz

Toy(s) you will need:	Pocket Rocket vibrator (or other small vibrator)
	Flavored lubricant or condom (optional)
Type of play:	Partnered

Movies taught me the most important lesson I had to learn about oral sex—to shed my inhibitions and simply go for it. The image of sexy Susan Sarandon's mane of red hair bobbing up and down over Tim Robbins's cock in *Bull Durham* is forever etched in my mind, as is the surprised yet ecstatic expression on Ellen Barkin's face as Dennis Quaid explores her southern regions in *The Big Easy*. I watched these classic scenes and suddenly realized that oral sex wasn't a substitute for sex or a chore performed out of love for a partner, it was an incredibly intimate, tactile, and unscripted sex act capable of elevating both parties to new heights of pleasure. Oh, and I figured if it was that hot to watch, it ought to be that hot in real life. And hot it can be, with a little practice, a lot of enthusiasm, and a willingness to let go of your preconceptions about oral sex.

Let's start with fellatio, the blow job, giving head, whatever you want to call it. (For cunnilingus, see the "Ladies' Night" activity.) It's a given that men love blow jobs—why else would they so freely offer up the most vulnerable part of their anatomy? Having one's genitals lovingly ministered to by a delicate mouth is a feeling unlike any other. Aside from the tactile stimulation, it's a gesture of trust, intimacy, and sexual submission. It forces you to indulge in a little sexual selfishness by simply requiring you to sit back and enjoy the ride.

Learning to Love It

A lot of women enjoy fellatio—it gives them a feeling of power, it boosts their sexual self-esteem, and it expands their sexual repertoire beyond the usual sex positions. And while many women cotton to the act quite naturally, others harbor reservations or a distaste for fellatio. Here are a few of the most common concerns, along with some perspective and simple solutions:

- **I don't like the taste.** If you don't like Mother Nature's flavor, try adding some flavored lube or sucking him off while he's wearing a flavored condom. You can also try taking a sip of your favorite drink first or adding a little whipped cream to his penis and then going down on him.
- **It makes me gag.** If you're new to oral sex, pushing something to the back of your throat will trigger your gag reflex. The easiest way around this is to wrap a hand around the base of his

penis to control how much you take in your mouth—he probably won't know the difference. You can also learn to suppress the gag reflex through relaxation and breathing. Try to relax your neck and jaw muscles, and coordinate your breathing with the thrusts. Take in a deep breath and release it through your nose as you go down. Also choose a position where you can control his thrusts: with him lying on his back, you decide how much of his penis to take into your mouth, but if you're underneath him, you have little control. And by all means, let him know if you're in a position that is uncomfortable for you.

- **I don't want to swallow.** No one says you have to—the choice ultimately is yours. Some men place an unnecessary importance on this ritual, but you shouldn't feel bad if you don't want to. You can simply remove your mouth when he's about to come and finish him with your hand. Turn it into a positive experience by commenting on how far he can shoot or how exciting it is to watch. Or use a condom, so the issue is moot.

Now you're ready to adapt a few of the following suggestions to your own routine. Ask your partner for feedback, and don't be shy about expressing your reservations. You'll probably find him most receptive to compromise, if his ultimate reward will be an enthusiastic blow job from you.

This activity takes advantage of the small but powerful Pocket Rocket vibrator. It can be easily tucked underneath your hand as you run it around his penis, pressed against your cheek, or nestled

Fellatio with a vibrator

against his anus. You can make do with any similar-size toy, like the Bullet, for example, but I like the freedom from the battery pack when using this toy for oral sex.

Blow Job Finesse

- **Prep.** Put your toy within arm's reach of the bed. Bathe together if you're a bit squeamish about tasting your partner's genitals.
- **Position.** As always, your comfort is key to your enjoyment, and fellatio puts a particular strain on your neck and jaw. Kneeling before him on a pillow, while he's standing or sitting, gives you good range of motion and plenty of access. Or he can lie on his back and you can crouch in between his legs, a position that gives you lots of control. To give your neck a rest, try lying on your sides, but instead of lying head-to-toe your head should be facing his penis.
- **Get to know his sensitive spots.** Using your hands first, gently caress his inner thighs, penis, testicles, and perineum (the spot between his anus and balls), paying attention to his reactions (verbal and facial) as you touch certain spots. The most sensitive spots on a guy's penis are the glans (the head) and the frenulum (the indentation between the glans and the shaft on the underside of the penis). If you're practicing safer sex, put the condom on now.
- **Give him a lick.** Follow up with your tongue, exploring the same terrain using slow wide strokes with your tongue. Don't be afraid to use lots of saliva, as this natural lube feels great and helps create friction and suction. If you're not crazy about your lover's taste, try a flavored condom or some flavored lubricant.

- **Take him in your mouth.** When he's semierect, slowly guide your lips over the tip of his penis, making sure your lips cover your teeth as you slide gently down his shaft as far as you're comfortable. Keep your mouth taut, as the pressure from your lips will feel great as they glide down the penis. Don't worry about sucking; the seal your mouth forms on his shaft creates a natural suction as you glide up and down. If you're not adept at deep throat (taking the whole penis in your mouth), don't try it or you'll trigger the gag reflex. It's not necessary, and a similar effect can be achieved with the mouth and hand technique described below.

- **Mouth and tongue.** As your head travels up the penis, flatten your tongue so it gives his frenulum a nice wide, wet stroke. Don't be afraid to try different types of licks or kisses—the lips feel good when popped over the ridge of the penis—but perform each stroke repeatedly before changing, to give consistent pleasure. If your partner is uncircumcised, insert your tongue into the foreskin and circle around the head with it. You can also use your fingers to gently massage the head through the foreskin, alternating with deep tongue licks.

- **Mouth and hand.** A great blow job incorporates both hands and mouth. Place one hand around the shaft of his penis, and have it follow your mouth as you move up and down on the top half of his penis. If he likes this combination, bring your hand all the way up the shaft (following your mouth), remove your

---

Toy Testimonials

"My boyfriend got really aroused when I held a vibrating egg against his butt hole and then I went down on him. Between the purring toy and my warm mouth, he said it was one of the most incredible orgasms he has ever had."

mouth briefly, use your palm to slide and twist over the head, and then glide your hand back down followed by your mouth again. Repeat this stroke several times.

- **Add a vibrator.** While his penis is inside your mouth, turn on the Pocket Rocket and place it against your cheek. Hold your mouth still and use your other hand to tap the penis against the inside of your cheek next to the vibrator. Or glide your mouth up and down along the shaft with the vibrator pressed against your cheek, experimenting with a steady speed and a stop/start routine.

- **Mix it up.** Try the vibrator on different parts of his genitals while you continue fellating him. Place the vibrator in your palm and roll it around the base of the penis while using your mouth to work the head. Or place the vibrator on his stomach, press the penis on top of it, and lick alongside his shaft. You can also press it against his perineum or anus. Ask for his feedback so you know which movements to repeat and which to avoid.

- **Don't forget his balls.** Most men like having their balls handled in some way during oral sex, so try pressing the vibrator gently against them. Or, while you're going down on him, you can lightly cup his balls in one hand, or take a break from his penis to gently lick or suck on them.

- **Let him come.** When he's ready to orgasm, keep your movements consistent and firm—don't slack off. Once he starts ejaculating, see him through with a few strokes and then stop, as most men don't want continued stimulation once they've come.

Variations

- Complement or alternate your oral play with other stimulation (if you have a free hand!). Nipples, thighs, stomach all feel great when touched or kissed.

- Try other toys. He can wear a butt plug. You can tie a cock ring around the base of his penis. Even nipple clamps can enhance your blow job.

- Another toy that's great for blow jobs is a stretchy tube normally used as a penis sleeve for masturbation. It's open at both ends, so during oral sex, put his penis all the way through and slide it down toward the base. Work the head of the penis with your mouth, and use your other hand to stroke his penis through the sleeve.

- Your hand work can be just as important as your mouth work. Apply pressure or light massage to the perineum, gently massage his testicles, or run a finger lightly around his anus while you're going down on him.

- Experiment with temperature—suck on an ice cube before taking his penis in your mouth. Or place a breath mint or cough drop in your mouth and then fellate him.

Ixchel Does It All

by Sage Vivant

The small awning hung from a second-story window and he might have missed it if not for one word: *sexo.* The somewhat familiar word in the longer *La Tienda del Sexo* intrigued Mason enough to seek out the staircase in the building's atrium so he could pay a visit.

Upon entering the tiny shop, he silently confirmed that *sexo* did indeed mean "sex." Vibrators and dildos in vibrant hues and wild patterns hung from the ceiling and walls like the festive piñatas and chili peppers on the street below, as colorful and abundant as any display he and Elizabeth had seen in Cozumel since their arrival three days earlier. He wished she was here with him now to see this outrageous presentation, but today, she'd wanted to shop for Yucatán-inspired fashion, so they'd separated for a few hours. He'd wanted to find, well, something exactly like what he'd just walked into. Elizabeth might have dubbed it "Penis Paradise," he thought, grinning inwardly.

"You are looking for something special?" Mason turned to see a round, cheerful man smoking a cigar behind the scratched glass counter. The man addressed him in English, understanding immediately that Mason was a tourist.

The dazed and overwhelmed expression on Mason's face brought a bemused smile to the shopkeeper's. "So much to look at, eh?" He chuckled.

"Almost too much, I'm afraid." How on earth did one begin to choose? The assortment was both robust and inaccessible. Amid the plentiful selection of phallic toys, he could not focus on even one that he thought might appeal to Elizabeth, either aesthetically or sexually.

"They're all so . . . bright," he commented, getting ready to leave.

"You want something different?"

Mason looked at him, uncertain what "different" might mean in a shop like this one.

"Something *elegante, sí*?"

Mason's eyebrows shot up with interest.

The man motioned for him to step toward the counter. Meanwhile, he reached into a bottom drawer and eventually withdrew a small item wrapped in deep purple felt. Mason had once visited the papal gift shop at the Vatican, and the sales help there had handled their merchandise with the same level of quiet respect.

"This is not for everybody. I don't show it to most people because they are only looking for cheap fun. But I see in your eyes that you love your special lady, *sí*?"

Interesting sales pitch, Mason thought. *Where was he going with it?*

The man extracted an intricately carved figure, no bigger than a lipstick. Its small face beamed benevolently from its ornate setting of flourishes and designs.

"The Mayan goddess Ixchel. She will bring you many children." He flicked the switch at the bottom and a steady hum emanated from the ivory deity. Mason stifled a laugh, sensing the man would take offense.

"Yes," Mason said. "I think that's perfect. I'll take it."

The man nodded, as if he knew all along that Mason would find the vibrator irresistible. Just as he began to wrap Ixchel in her purple vestments, Mason interrupted.

"I won't need all that. I need it to fit in my pocket."

The man looked disappointed, even slightly perturbed, but complied with his customer's wishes. He handed the purchase to Mason, who slipped it into his pocket, paid the shopkeeper, and headed for the corner where he and Elizabeth had agreed to meet.

As she approached, he chuckled at her three bulging shopping bags but was struck by how sexy she looked in her short white skirt. Those long legs always took his breath away.

"Let's go back to the hotel," he said into her hair as he slipped an arm around her. His response to that skirt was always the same—he couldn't wait to explore what was under it. Though he'd had twelve years of becoming intimately familiar with the treasures between her legs, the Pavlovian response to that white skirt was as reliable as the sweltering humidity in Cozumel that summer.

"It *is* pretty warm," she replied, pretending not to understand the real reason for his request. "And since this is your birthday, your wish is my command. Besides, I'm dying for a cold drink."

They walked to the hotel in minutes. The large balcony, shaded by the thatched roof, was considerably cooler than the hot cobblestone streets where they'd spent the last few hours. He sat down in one of the upholstered patio chairs and unzipped his fly. Elizabeth joined him moments later with two cold bottles of water from the small fridge.

Upon seeing his very rigid, very large cock sticking out of his shorts, she grinned and put the bottles on the nearby table.

"That looks like a much better thirst-quencher than water," she purred.

He spread his legs and she stood between them, bending from the waist to put her lips to his rock-hardness. Her breath warmed his tip, which was already leaking pre-cum. She licked it reverently and explored the remainder of his mushroom head slowly, dragging her tongue over the top and under the ridge.

He decided to tease her too. He could smell her arousal, even amid the lush tropical foliage that shielded their balcony from others. And that skirt . . . He helped himself to her wet muff, burrowing between her soft, dripping folds to find her most sensitive spot.

She took all of him into her mouth and squirmed seductively as his fingers explored her pussy. He slipped the day's purchase inside her and flipped the small button at its base. The instant buzz was audible but muffled by her moist cunt. As he slid it in and out of her, she moaned, sending gentle reverberations from her throat to his cock.

The faster he pumped the small vibrator into her juicy hole, the harder she sucked him. Her beautiful, big tits brushed against his thighs as she moved. Soon he could hold back no more and dumped a thick load into her hot mouth. She swallowed and took hold of his wrist between her legs.

"What is that, anyway?" she asked, referring to the vibrator. "It feels funny."

He turned it off, extracted it, and let her see what had been fucking her. The five-inch molded replica of the Mayan goddess Ixchel glistened with Elizabeth's juices.

"Fertility goddess," he smirked. "Hope she doesn't make you pregnant."

LADIES' NIGHT: Performing Creative Cunnilingus

Toy(s) you will need:	G spot vibrator or dildo
	Lubricant
Type of play:	Partnered

To be a truly great lover, you must be able to give good head. Sure, you can enjoy a thousand and one intercourse positions and be an ace masturbator, but until you can get your partner off with your lovely mouth, there will always be something special missing from your sexual repertoire. There you are, up close and personal with your lover's genitals—inhaling the scent and tasting the juices. No wonder this sex act inspires such profound gratitude and desire. It's intimate, it's vulnerable, and it's a wee bit naughty.

Just as plenty of men love fellatio, legions of women love cunnilingus. Call it what you will—giving head, muff diving, eating her out—cunnilingus performed enthusiastically and with skill will endear you to her forever.

If you are already an oral enthusiast, good for you! I hope this activity will give you a few fresh ideas to try the next time you're both in the mood. If you or your partner is new to oral sex, the most important advice I can give you is to be patient. If your wife or girlfriend has never tried oral sex, she may have mixed feelings about it. She may also feel some performance anxiety that may inhibit her enjoyment of oral sex. Make sure she knows you're in it for the long haul—and follow through.

Learning to Love It

You may harbor a few reservations about cunnilingus yourself, which probably can be alleviated with a little information and a simple change of attitude. Here are the most common concerns:

- **I don't like the taste.** Enjoying a lover's juices can be an acquired taste; you may just need practice and some perspective in order to come around. If you've ever expected her to take your penis in her mouth, then you've got some reciprocating to do. If you really do have a difficult time with the taste, try bathing together, putting some flavored lubricant on her genitals, or putting a dental dam or cut-open condom between your tongue and her vulva.
- **What if I can't find her clit?** You will, it may just take some inspection and a little trial and error. The clitoris is a small but pleasure-packed little button that gets bigger when aroused. If you can't find it with your tongue, use your finger to locate it, or have her show you where it is.

- **I'm afraid my tongue will get tired before she comes.** Alternate your tongue strokes with kissing and sucking so your tongue gets a break. You can also incorporate manual or vibrator stimulation into your act. Whatever you do, find a way to stick with it. If she feels like she's taking too long, she'll start worrying about it and the orgasm may elude her forever.

Creative Cunnilingus

Hopefully you're now ready to dive in. This activity begins with some basic cunnilingus tips, then incorporates a G spot vibrator into the play. This can be a powerful combination for many women, but be sure to listen to her feedback since the multiple stimulation can be just right one minute and too much the next.

- **Prep.** Make sure you've got batteries in your toy. Shower together to alleviate any anxieties about taste or smell. Make sure your hands are clean and your nails trimmed. Shave—nothing kills the mood quite like sandpaper on her sensitive parts.
- **Get excited.** A lot of women prefer to be pretty excited in order to enjoy oral sex. Take your time turning her on. Use your mouth all over her body—this will send her a message about what will follow. When she's good and excited—her hips are thrusting and the moans pretty regular—head south.
- **Position.** She should lie on her back or sit back in a reclined position with her knees bent and her legs spread. You should be lying on your stomach with your head poised over her vulva, your arms hooked underneath her thighs. You may both find it more comfortable to prop her pelvis up on a pillow or two.
- **Get the lay of the land.** Take a good look at her genitals so you know what you're doing. If you need a refresher course on

female anatomy, see the chapter "A Pleasure Primer." Your goal during cunnilingus is to stimulate her clitoris, but not to the exclusion of the rest of her genital anatomy. Use your fingers to spread her labia and take a good look at her clitoris, her inner and outer lips, her mons, her vagina, her perineum, and her anus.

- **Ease into it.** A lot of women have very sensitive clits, so don't attack her vulva as if it were a juicy ripe peach. Instead, imagine licking an ice cream cone. Flatten your tongue and use wide slow strokes to explore her inner and outer lips, her vagina, and her clitoris. And when it comes to oral sex, the more saliva you generate the better it feels, so don't worry about the mess.

- **Love her clit.** If you know what kind of manual stimulation she likes, you have some idea how to approach her clitoris with your tongue. Does she like a circular motion, a side-to-side, or an up-and-down motion on her clitoris? In general, women tend to like firm pressure and repetitive motion. Quick tongue flicks against the clitoris can be irritating. If you're not sure, ask her to give you feedback while you try different kinds of stimulation. Don't take it personally if she flinches—discovering what pleases is often a process of trial and error—just stop and try something else. Alternately, you can offer to place your hand on hers as she demonstrates the kind of stroking she prefers (this can be great foreplay!).

- **Use all of your mouth.** Take her clit in your mouth and gently suck on it. Use your mouth to suck on or nibble her labia.

> ### Toy Testimonials
>
> "Explore that threesome fantasy in a nonthreatening way—have your boyfriend penetrate you with your favorite insertable vibe while he pleasures your clit with his tongue. He'll enjoy the view and how much it excites you. Ramp it up a notch by talking out the fantasy."

Use your lips to kiss her clit and to glide over her labia. Run your tongue down to her vagina periodically and slip it inside; this will give her a taste of what's to come.

- **Fill her up!** When she's good and excited, stop and get your toy. Add some lubricant and gently insert it into her vagina, with the curve of the toy pointing up toward her belly. Turn the vibrator on, but if she finds it too annoying, turn it off and just use the toy as a dildo. Move the toy inside of her using short but firm strokes. Once you've got a good rhythm going, put your mouth back on her clitoris and lick her while you penetrate her with the G spot toy. If your tongue gets tired, switch to using your mouth and the vibrator on her clitoris. This gives you a break but keeps the stimulation constant for

Cunnilingus combined with a G spot toy

her. You can also use the vibrator on her clitoris to get her aroused, then slip the toy inside her and finish her off with your tongue.

- **Don't stop.** Women like steady stimulation, so don't stop unless you need to come up for air. You'll see the signs when she's ready to go over the top—her moans, her thighs pressing against your head, her body arching, her hands tightening on your head! When the orgasm washes over her, she'll let you know when to stop. She'll probably move your head away and her pelvic muscles will try to expel the dildo. If you're up to the task, you might want to ask her if she wants more, as some women can move into another orgasm pretty quickly with steady stimulation.

Variations

- Try other positions. She can squat over your face while you're lying on your back, though she's not quite as relaxed in this position, which can be important if she has a hard time coming from oral sex. In the much-touted sixty-nine position you're lying head to toe, each pleasing the other's genitals. Again, unless you're pretty comfortable with oral sex, simultaneous orgasms from oral sex in the sixty-nine position is a pretty tall order to fill.
- Experiment with temperature and sensation. Suck on an ice cube or a cough drop before or while you're licking her, or try spreading some warming gel on her genitals.
- Try different toys. For vibrator variations, try tucking a small egg-shaped vibrator between her labia while going down on her or using a Fukuoku finger vibe to accompany your mouth

maneuvers. Or for a different G spot toy, use a dildo with a bend toward the tip or an S-shaped toy.

- Don't forget other body parts. You can leave the vibrator in place and use your hands to play with her breasts, or try nipple clamps that she can pull on herself. If she's fond of anal play, use a butt plug on her while going down on her.

BOTTOMS UP: Massaging the Prostate with Anal Beads

Toy(s) you will need:	Anal beads (or a butt plug)
	Lubricant
Type of play:	Solo or partnered

Men's penises typically get all the attention; they're just so prominently placed and easy to please. But if your erotic exploration stops there you're missing out on a fantastic erogenous zone that's not visible to the naked eye: the prostate. Located behind the pubic bone and just below the bladder, the prostate gland is analogous to the G spot in women—think of it as your "P" spot. The big difference, of course, is that access to it is through the anus rather than the vagina. If you've been reluctant to try anal play because you regard the anus as dirty, try some of the basic hygiene tips below, and you may soon count yourself among the many men who find the prostate an exquisite source of sexual pleasure. Some men can have an orgasm through prostate stimulation alone, while others find it enhances other types of sexual activity. A lot of men report that prostate massage prolongs or intensifies their orgasms.

While it's certainly possible for you to find your own prostate, it's often easier with a toy and/or a partner. In this activity, your partner will first locate your prostate with a finger and then stimulate it manually using anal beads. Since anal play requires a good amount of focus and relaxation, you might prefer trying this activity alone. In that case, consider substituting a butt plug or curved dildo for the anal beads, as these can be a little easier to insert by yourself.

Anticipate how you want to introduce your partner to anal play if it's new for both of you. Many women are tickled to learn that men have a spot that's similar to their G spot, so sometimes that's motivation enough! Make sure you share your expectations and concerns with each other, especially since anal play can be a rather charged subject for people at first. You may want to do some reading together on the subject—modern sex manuals encourage anal exploration, with a few devoted exclusively to the subject (see Resources). These can be particularly helpful in dispelling many of the myths associated with anal sex (that it's dirty, that it means you're gay if you like it, that it hurts) and can help normalize the subject for both of you. And if you keep in mind the three requirements for good anal sex—communication, relaxation, and lubrication— you'll be good to go.

Anal beads look a lot like a strand of pearls: a series of beads are connected by a cord with a ring at one end, which is used to pull them out. They lend an interesting twist to prostate play because they're designed to stimulate many parts of the sensitive anal anatomy. The anal sphincter contracts each time a bead passes through the anus, which many find arousing. Others find that as several beads are pushed through, the prostate receives a "rolling" massage. And others discover the ultimate rush comes from having the beads "popped" out during orgasm.

- **Practice good hygiene.** Most newcomers to anal play are understandably squeamish about poking around the same orifice they use to go to the bathroom. Fear of coming into contact with feces and worrying about having to defecate are very real concerns. Showering first will leave you both clean feeling and is also great foreplay. Bear in mind that since feces travel through the rectum on the way out of the body, you're likely to encounter only a tiny amount of feces. If you want to avoid even that much contact, don a latex glove and apply lube. This is a great safer sex option and can lend a slippery feel to your play. Finally, if you have a bowel movement before you begin, this shouldn't be an issue during your anal play.

- **Make it smooth.** Your partner should trim her nails as you don't want anything that can nick or scratch coming into contact with the sensitive lining of your anus. Again, a latex glove is a great option if she's got hangnails. As for your anal beads, make sure there are no abrasive edges (sometimes the plastic ones have seams that need to be filed down with an emery board) and that the cord is strong.

- **Get hot.** Because the prostate swells when aroused, it's easier to locate when you're turned on. Engage in some of your favorite foreplay to get yourself in the mood.

- **Assume the position.** Lie on your back, knees bent, with

> ## Toy Testimonials
>
> "My wife really takes her time while she's inserting the beads, so the anticipation nearly kills me. When that little bead finally 'pops' in, I get this surge of pleasure through my groin."

Anal stimulation with anal beads

your partner sitting in between your legs. It might help to prop your butt up on a pillow.

- **Massage the perineum and anus.** This is the area between the testicles and the anus. It's very sensitive and feels good when gently stroked with the pads of the fingertips. With a well-lubricated finger, she can work her way down to your anus and slowly circle the rim of the anus. She can push rhythmically on your anus, as if she's ringing a doorbell. It's loaded with sensitive nerve endings, and stimulating this area will help relax the anal sphincter.

- **Breathe out as she pushes in.** When you're ready for her to come inside, have her position her lubed finger at the entrance to your anus so that her palm is faceup and her index or middle finger is ready to enter. Breathe deeply, and as you exhale, push out (as if you're trying to go to the bathroom) while she pushes in. It may take a few tries, but she should be able to get a finger in eventually. You may want her finger to remain still for a moment while you get used to the sensation of having something in your anus. Remember, if you experience pain, stop. Try to relax, have her add more lubrication, then start again.

- **Locate the prostate.** About two inches in she should be able to feel a walnut-shape bump. Ask her to try touching it in different ways, beginning first by stroking her finger forward in a "come hither" motion. A firm pressure might feel best, or you might like more of a thrusting motion. It may feel like you have to go the bathroom, but that's a natural sensation (the rectum is accustomed to trying to expel what's inside it) that diminishes as you relax.

- **Pop in the anal beads.** After you've had some fun with your partner's finger, have her withdraw it. Now you're ready for the anal beads. She can dip the anal beads in lubricant and begin by inserting the smallest one gently into your anus. When you're ready, give her the go-ahead to insert another, and another, until you've had enough. She can tug gently on them or pull hard enough to remove one or more, and then reinsert it.

- **Stroke your penis.** Play with your penis and experiment with the timing of your strokes as she pushes the beads inside. When you're ready to orgasm, let her know so that she can pull the beads out while you're coming. She should pull them toward her in a straight line (rather than off to one side). Experiment, because you may find that you prefer to have the beads remain inside you during orgasm, rather than being pulled out.

Variations

- The side-by-side position is also great for beginners because it's comfortable for both of you. She has good access to your anus and you're in a good position to relax.
- As you get comfortable with anal play, experiment with different types and sizes of toys. Butt plugs are designed to be left in place, which can feel great all by themselves or while you're focusing on other kinds of sex play. Dildos double nicely as anal toys, especially if you enjoy the in-and-out movement. Vibrators also add a unique sensation to anal play. Whatever toy you choose, *always* make sure the toy has a flared base, to prevent it from slipping into the rectum.
- Although women don't have a prostate, they too can enjoy anal penetration (see the "Baby's Got Back" activity) with beads, plugs, and dildos.
- Anal beads come in different sizes and textures, and some are attached to a dildo rather than a cord (nice if you prefer a "handle" rather than a string). If you can find them, try the silicone beads, as they are the most comfortable and easiest to clean.

The Meeting

by G. Merlin Beck

I've learned my lesson, all right . . . never bring your laptop to a meeting!

But I'm jumping the gun. Let me start at the beginning. It was the weekly strategy meeting, otherwise known as Big Benny's Blah Blah Session. At least, that's what we called it behind his back; none of us would dare say it to Ben's face. He may smile a lot, but he takes himself pretty seriously. And he expects us to do likewise.

The meeting started as usual, with Ben breezing in late. He seemed pretty cheerful, chatting and joking with us while he booted up his laptop. I could see the hope in everyone's eyes. Maybe today would be one of those rare, bloodless meetings. Ben tossed his network cable at me; I plugged it into the hub for him. That way, he would be connected to the network like the rest of us, able to check his e-mail (or surf the web) during the meeting.

John from Quality Assurance was scheduled to talk first. He

collected his transparencies and walked to the front of the room. Ben smiled. His curly hair and boyish smile made his wolflike expression all the more alarming. I knew what was coming—and I was right. It took Ben about three slides to tear John apart. By slide six, John had become the stammering, blushing straight man for Ben's one-liners. Everyone around the table was laughing that sick, "Oh god, I'm next!" laugh. I decided to tune out and check my e-mail.

I started my e-mail program and clicked the "get messages" button. I had mail. It was from my Mistress. Anxiety made my face and neck prickle with heat. The subject header said: "Immediate!" Oh shit, I thought. I opened the message. Here's what it said.

My dearest duane,

Wherever you happen to be, you will immediately insert your butt plug. The second to largest one. Oh, and you may not go to the restroom or to any private place to do it.

I look forward to hearing about your experience,

Mistress Ana

Shit. Double shit! I quickly crafted a reply, typing quietly to avoid attracting Ben's attention:

Dear Beloved Mistress:

Please, my exalted Goddess! Not now. I'm in a meeting . . . with Ben! Remember, Benjamin the Hun? Ben the Impaler? Benny the Terrible? There's no way for me to do it!

Have mercy, my most desirable, my most delicious!! I will do anything you wish tonight, anything. Hurt me extravagantly, humili-ate me. Anything!!

With all my love,

Your devoted slave

I clicked send and crossed my fingers. Every once in a while, a few heartfelt pleas for mercy would soften my Mistress's edicts. That is, if she was in the mood. I tried to control my breathing. Her reply was almost immediate.

My "dearest" duane,
　I'm sorry, but your mail program must not be working right. I believe I ordered you to insert your butt plug . . . but I just received an e-mail questioning my orders. Since I know this would never happen, I can only assume you are experiencing some sort of soft-ware problem.
　Proceed immediately.
　Mistress Ana

I looked down at my backpack, where the butt plug (and several other toys) were hidden. I uttered a silent prayer and reached for the black canvas bag.

"Duane!"

I jumped and looked up. Ben was staring at me, smiling.

"What's wrong? You look kind of queasy."

"It's . . . uh, I guess I was up late working last night."

"Working, huh? Hey, what a great idea." Ben looked up at John. "Say, John—maybe you should try that next time."

John's face burned red. He opened his mouth. Ben cut him off midstammer with a wave of his hand.

"Well, I don't know about you guys, but it's time for a break. Sorry, folks, but I just can't compete with the Olympic-size bladders in this crowd."

Ben closed his laptop, got up, and walked out. A stampede of people followed him. John grabbed his slides off the projector and sat down heavily in his chair.

Ben stuck his head back in the room. "John! Would you come with me, please?"

I bent over my keyboard, pretending to type a reply message. Out of the corner of my eye I saw John turn pale and get up. He walked out of the room, leaving me alone. The door shut behind him.

I sighed with relief and then pulled open my backpack. The butt plug was hidden in a zippered pocket. I unzipped the pocket, took out the plug, and found a tube of lubricant. My hands shook as I smeared shiny goop all over the cold silicone. I stood up. Fortunately, I was wearing a baggy suit. I unzipped my fly and thrust the plug in, maneuvering it between my legs. Underwear was no problem: I was never allowed to wear it. I slid the butt plug between my cheeks until I could feel the tip touch my asshole. Gingerly I sat down, making sure that the plug's base rested flat on the chair. I pulled out my hand, zipped my pants back up, and quickly wiped my fingers on a tissue.

Now came the tricky part. I relaxed my leg muscles, slowly putting more and more weight on the plug. There was a tingling, burning sensation as my asshole fought back. My heart pounded. I silently commanded the balky ring of muscle to relax. If the plug didn't get inside me soon, it might slip. Then I'd be in trouble—I had visions of standing up, the butt plug sliding down my pants leg, then landing with a plop on the floor. I took a deep breath and exhaled.

My asshole relaxed a little bit. The silicone tip pushed in, dilating me. It hurt—sharp little jabs of pain that made me feel like I was being scraped and abraded. And as usual, the pain went right to my cock. It stretched and yawned. I could feel it pressing against my trousers. The plug slid in farther. It was all I could do to keep from groaning aloud. I felt like I desperately had to shit. There were voices outside the door. I let more weight onto the plug. It was at the widest point. I grimaced. The doorknob turned. Now or never!

I relaxed and let my full weight drive the plug deep into my body. I gave a little shriek just as John and Ben walked in the door. They looked at me funny; I covered it up by pretending to cough. People streamed in after them. My asshole closed around the neck of the plug, gripping it tight, holding it inside me.

I sat there, trying to act normal, feeling this large, hard lump stretch my bowels. My cock was standing up straight. What a cruel Mistress I had! She knew that this would happen. I sat very still and tried to breathe quietly.

"Okay!" Ben's voice startled me back to earth. He sat down in his chair and reopened his laptop. "Let's get going. I believe Kim is up next; she's going to explain the principles of TMF."

Kim's face fell. She gathered her slides and walked slowly to the front of the room.

"TMF?" someone asked.

"Total Market Failure," Ben said. "She's going to tell us how she managed both a twenty percent marketing cost overrun and a six percent slip in market share."

Kim swallowed hard and put her intro slide on the projector. In spite of my discomfort and embarrassment, I felt sorry for her. I shifted in my seat. The plug swiveled around inside of me, sending a jolt of pleasure through my cock. I couldn't help myself; I wriggled around in the chair. My cock swelled and burned—I could feel the head pressing against my belt. A couple more minutes of this and I would come. I looked up and saw Ben staring at me. He grinned a predator's grin.

"Don't get too comfortable, Little Bunky. You're next."

Everyone stared at me. I sat as still as I could, hoping not to catch

Ben's attention again. And then I saw that I had another e-mail message. It was from Mistress Ana.

> *My dearest duane,*
>   *I imagine that by now the plug is firmly ensconced in your body and that you are experiencing some most interesting sensations. Since I am in a generous mood today, I give you permission to cli-max. In fact, you are ordered to climax within one half hour. Of course, you may not leave the room that you are currently in.*
>   *Mistress Ana*

Fear churned around in my stomach and then ran, ice cold, into my bowels. I quickly typed a reply.

> *My Most Beloved, Adorable Mistress:*
>   *Please do not make me do this. I'm in a meeting. Everyone will see! I'll make a mess. I'll get fired!*
>   *Please, please, please. I'm begging you!!*
>   *With my undying love,*
>   *Your devoted slave*

I clicked send and clenched my teeth. I could see Mistress Ana's face in my mind's eye, her pale cheeks flushing scarlet with fury, her fingers twining through her red hair. Nothing to do but wait, and hope for mercy. I looked up. Kim was stumbling through her presentation. She was on slide three, and Ben hadn't said a word. Kim was getting more and more nervous. Ben just sat there smiling. I shifted in my seat, making the butt plug rotate inside me. Pleasure shot up my spine like a jolt of electric current. Another message arrived.

My most disobedient duane:

Your manners have become dismal and your obedience has become shockingly lax. I suppose I share some of the blame for letting you get into this sorry state. But worry not; I intend to rectify things. Today you're going to be taught a little lesson. The first part will be administered before you leave this meeting. The second part will be administered when I decide to let you see me again. As for making a mess, let's not forget that little technique I taught you for holding it in when you climax.

Now do it. And do not make me repeat an order again. Ever.

Mistress Ana

My heart pounded so loudly I was sure everyone at the table could hear it. I looked up at Ben; he was still just sitting there, smiling at Kim. Kim was talking fast. She had this wide-eyed look that was equal parts hunted and hopeful, a look that said, "Maybe I'll survive this. Maybe it'll be okay." She finished her last slide and looked around the room.

"Any questions?"

There was a long silence. The tension in the room was like a high-pitched, barely audible whine.

Ben grinned. "No questions, Kim. No questions at all. But thanks so much for sharing."

The tension broke and dissolved into a flood of mean-spirited laughter. Kim looked like she was going to cry. She quickly scooped up her slides and sat down, staring at her laptop screen.

Ben talked for a few moments. I was up next. I adjusted my waistband so that it trapped the head of my erect cock. The last thing I needed was to stand up in front of everyone with a huge erection! I checked my laptop screen one last time. No more messages.

"You're up, Duane."

I stood up, still adjusting my pants. The butt plug moved inside me; my belt pressed deep into the head of my cock. I stood there, trying to get myself under control. All of a sudden, the ten steps to the projector looked like a vast distance.

"Need some help, Duane?" Ben smirked up at me.

"Uh, no thanks. I just . . . it was just some postural hypotension."

"Try getting more exercise, old fellow. Now let's hear what you've got to say. You've got ten minutes."

I looked at my watch. There were ten minutes left out of the half hour that Mistress Ana had granted me. So in ten minutes I had to get through all these slides and climax! I buttoned my jacket and strode carefully to the front of the room. I put down the first slide and started talking. My words spilled out fast; with luck, I'd get through all my slides and still have time to sit back down and climax. Although how I was supposed to do that, unnoticed, I still didn't know. I had an image of everyone staring at me as my face turned red and I groaned aloud with ecstasy, grinding my filled ass against the seat.

I talked faster. Ben grinned. I realized my mistake: he had smelled blood.

"Whoa! Slow down, Duane. We can hardly follow you. You're starting to sound like The Chipmunks at a poetry slam."

Everyone laughed.

"Well, I only have ten minutes, and fifteen more slides to cover—"

"Eight minutes, to be precise. Now relax and finish."

Forcing a grin, I took a deep breath and leaned against the whiteboard. It was a mistake. The base of the butt plug bumped against the metal tray that held the colored markers. The plug pressed hard against something inside me, something very sensitive. I gasped out loud; my cock, which had been wilting a bit, stood at attention again. Everyone stared at me. I coughed, trying to cover up the gasp.

Next slide: a competitive analysis of our products against our biggest rival's. I talked through feature lists quickly, trying to will my ass to move away from that metal tray. But it would not. My every movement caused the plug to wriggle around inside of me, sending shock after shock of excruciating pleasure up my spine. The head of my cock pressed against the hard leather belt. I felt like my awareness was slowly checking out, becoming an observer of what was happening rather than a controller. All of a sudden, I very much wanted to see what would happen if I did come in front of all these people.

The last slide. I was teetering, teetering, swaying from side to side, making the butt plug swivel around inside me. At that moment, Ben chose to launch into one of his little tirades.

"Guys, I look at this slide, and I just can't believe it."

Rotating hips, burst of pleasure. I know I'm blazing red now, but everyone thinks it's Ben's onrushing assault.

"A year. It's been a year, and we've only achieved parity on one feature. And it's not even our most competitive one."

Cock pressing into leather and fabric. Arms in front of me, hands clasped together, covering my burning cock.

"This is not an organization in recovery; it's an organization hoping that the rigor mortis will go away soon."

Hands press cock. The butt plug churns pleasure deep in my bowels. There's a knot of fire inside me. All eyes are now on Ben as he rants.

"If I let this product release in this condition, I'm going down. I'm taking the fall. And you know what? I'm taking you all with me."

He nodded! He looked at me and nodded. For a second I had the insane thought that he knew what I was doing, what was going on.

And the thought pushed me over the edge. The orgasm built and then exploded with a rush of fury. It took all my strength to keep from screaming as a firehose of pleasure blasted through my brain. Every muscle in my pelvis was clenched in a desperate attempt to keep come from shooting, fountainlike, from behind my waistband. Ben's rant went on and on; the orgasm slowed down into great rolling waves of ecstasy that made me want to collapse weeping to the floor. Ben's eyes were fastened to mine. Even though I was sure my expression had never changed, I knew that he suspected something. My knees shook, and I leaned against the board for support. Finally, the tirade ceased. Eyes turned back to me.

"Duane, I want you to revise the product plan and have the new version on my desk in the morning. Okay, folks, meeting's over. I've got someplace else to be."

I teetered back to my seat, hoping that I didn't look as disoriented as I felt. But there was no need to worry. Nobody noticed me; they were fairly running for the door, relieved at getting to miss the last half hour of the meeting. That was when Ben typically grilled everyone on their weekly accomplishments.

I was about to shut down my laptop when I got an e-mail message. It was, of course, from my Mistress. And here is what it said:

My now-on-probation duane:
Excellent job! You will still suffer the first part of your punishment . . . but I may be a bit more lenient about the second one.
You have permission to see me tonight.
Mistress Ana

I sighed and shut down my laptop. I'd made it! And then it hit me—how did she know I had done it? How?

"Show!"

Ben's voice boomed inside the empty room. I jumped and looked around. We were the only ones left.

"Huh?"

Ben closed his laptop's cover. "I said show. Drop your drawers so that I can be sure the plug is in."

Raw terror squeezed the blood from my face and made me feel faint.

"I don't know what you're talking about!" My voice was a high-pitched squeal.

"Yes you do. You're supposed to have a butt plug in your ass. And I've been told to verify it. That's installment number one of your punishment. I hear you'll get the rest tonight."

The blood rushed back to my face as I slowly stood up, turned around, and unfastened my belt.

Like I said, I've learned my lesson!

PLEASE ENTER FROM THE REAR:

Anal Intercourse with a Dildo

Toy(s) you will need:	Bobbi Sue (or long dildo or anal toy with flared base)
	Harness
	Bullet vibrator
	Lubricant
Type of play:	Partnered

Most people think of strap-on sex—having penetrative sex using a dildo and harness—as an exclusively lesbian sex activity, but that's about as true as the notion that heterosexual couples only have sex in the missionary position. It is true that dildos and harnesses were designed originally so that lesbians could simulate vaginal intercourse, but like all truly great sex toys, dildos are an equal opportunity pleaser. In fact, dildos have gained a tremendous following among heterosexual couples in the last decade, as women strap them on in order to anally penetrate their husbands and boyfriends. One of the best-selling vidoes in recent years is the woman-produced *Bend Over Boyfriend,* a show-and-tell guide to strap-on anal penetration.

What's the appeal? Men have discovered that it feels great to be anally penetrated by a lover wearing a dildo because (a) it's an incredibly intimate act, (b) it provides exquisite prostate stimulation, and (c) it lets them experience the thrill of penetration. For their part, women enjoy turning the tables on their male partners, donning faux phalluses and running the show for a change.

If either of you is new to anal play, review some of the suggestions in the "Bottoms Up" and "Baby's Got Back" activities for overcoming common reservations. Those activities will also teach you about anal masturbation, which can be a great way to ease into partner penetration. When you do get together for a round of eagerly awaited strap-on sex, review the basic rules of anal sex together: communication, lubrication, and relaxation. As the receptive partner, you are actually in the driver's seat: it's up to you to communicate your desires to her, so she can adjust her movements accordingly. She should check in with you regularly, to make sure you're enjoying her handiwork. As for lubrication, remember that the anus does not self-lubricate, so apply and reapply often. And the more you are able to relax your sphincter muscles, the easier it will be for her to penetrate you with the dildo. Finally, it helps if you're patient and have a good sense of

Toy Testimonials

"It took awhile for me to get comfortable with the harness that lets you wear a dildo in yourself too. It was frustrating at first because I'm smaller than average and the whole thing kept sliding off my hips. We had a good laugh and I finally got it adjusted just right, and now my husband can't wait for me to strap on our his-and-hers dildos."

humor—as with any new sex technique you're in for some trial and error, but you will eventually get the hang of it.

For this activity she will get to use a silicone dildo that was designed with boys' back ends in mind. The Bobbi Sue silicone dildo (by Vixen Creations) has got a smaller head, to facilitate entry into the anus, but the shaft widens toward the base. Its hollow core accommodates a Bullet vibrator, allowing the two of you to share vibrations: you'll feel them internally, and she'll feel them as the base of the dildo presses up against her clit. Feel free to choose another dildo or anal toy for this activity; just make sure it has a flared base, that it's fairly long (over six inches), and that it's pretty firm. (There's nothing quite so disappointing as tapping on his backside with a flimsy rubber toy only to have it bend in two when it meets resistance.) The Bobbi Sue gets pretty fat as it tapers down; if you're worried about size, choose a slimmer dildo to start. As for the harness, your main concern is comfort and a snug fit, so see the chapter "Toys for All Seasons" for advice on choosing among the styles.

And now, since your partner will be running most of the show, I'm going to switch gears and address her as the active partner.

- **Prep.** Make sure you have plenty of water-based lube on hand, particularly a thick lube. (One caveat: don't use silicone-based lubes with silicone toys, as they can cause some dildos to break down.) Shower together first as part of your foreplay.
- **Get into the gear.** Insert the Bullet vibrator into the Bobbi Sue, then thread the dildo through the harness hole, with the dildo pointing away from you, and step into it. Position the dildo over your pubic area, then adjust the straps so it doesn't move around. Give it a couple tugs to make sure your dildo won't pop through and to ensure the harness fits snugly. Secure

the battery pack underneath one of the harness straps (or purchase a Bullet vibe without the battery pack).

- **Get into the role.** Once you're rigged up, step back and take a moment to admire yourself in the mirror. If you feel the urge to laugh, go for it! It's not every day you get to see yourself with a penis. I don't know of anyone who didn't feel a bit silly, or least very odd, the first time they strapped on a dildo. But you can play with that—ham it up by admiring and stroking your penis. Ask your partner to get in on the fantasy—have him compliment, touch, even taste your new friend. You might be surprised at how thrilling this role reversal can be. Engage in your favorite kinds of foreplay to get really turned on.

- **Assume the position.** When you're ready to move into anal penetration, have your partner bend over the bed with his legs spread slightly, with you standing behind him. This position is comfortable for him and minimizes the moving-target effect of a bouncy bed! Apply an abundant amount of lube to your finger, the toy, and his anus.

- **Fingers first.** Use your finger to gently massage his anus and perineum. Slip a finger into his rectum to help him practice relaxing for your dildo. Have him push out (as if he were trying to have a bowel movement) as you enter, which will relax the anal sphincter enough for you to insert your finger.

- **Try the toy.** Once you've gotten a finger in, pull it out and give your toy a turn. Grasp your well-lubed dildo near the top and guide the tip into his rectum. Have him push out again as you push in from behind. Push very gently, just enough to pass the sphincter. Then stop and let him get used to the sensation. Turn the vibrator on, and let him feel the vibrations.

- **Get rockin'.** When he's ready, ask him whether he'd prefer

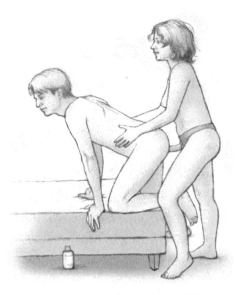
Anal intercourse with a strap-on dildo

that you or he control the thrusting motion. He may be more comfortable easing back onto your dildo, until he's ready for more active thrusting from you. Even though the dildo is attached to your body, you can't feel it, so in the beginning it might help to put one hand around the base of the penis and guide your toy in and out for a while until you get comfortable with the rhythm. Make sure your partner lets you know what angle and depth of penetration, as well as speed and pacing, feel good. Don't withdraw completely (unless your partner requests it), as getting past the anal sphincter is probably the most challenging part for beginners. Should you find you need more lube (and you can never have enough during anal play!), withdraw your dildo about two-thirds of the way, apply fresh lube to the shaft, and reinsert.

- **Don't forget the penis.** As the anal penetration increasingly turns on your partner, invite him to play with his penis. He may find that your movements create pleasant friction between his penis and the bed, or he may want to back up a bit and masturbate with his hand.
- **Let him come.** When he's ready to come, keep up your thrusting unless he asks you to change. Don't stop until he's finished coming, and check in with him after he's come as he may want you to remove the dildo quickly.

Variations

- Experiment with different positions. Instead of the rear-entry position, try the missionary position, with him on his back and his legs up over your shoulders. This position and the side-by-side position are great beginner's positions, because it's easier for him to fully relax his anus.

- If you want more focused stimulation on your clit, you can slip a small cock ring vibrator under the harness and around the base of the dildo, so the Bullet part vibrates your clit.

- Of course, if you crave penetration of your own during this activity, you have a couple of choices. You can try a double dildo like the Nexus, which bends at a ninety-degree angle. One end is inside you, the other pokes through the harness (or some tight jeans) and is ready for your partner's butt. And of course, if it's anal penetration you seek, you can always insert an anal plug in yourself.

- A man can also strap on a dildo and experiment with double penetration on a lover or to prolong intercourse after an erection has subsided. For double penetration, look for a harness with two holes, one for your dildo and one for your erect penis. If you'll be wearing the harness without being erect, you can wear a two-strap harness with one hole for the dildo and position it over your penis.

BABY'S GOT BACK: Masturbating with a Butt Plug

Toy(s) you will need: Anal plug (or dildo with flared base)

Lubricant

Clit vibe and/or dildo (optional)

Type of play: Solo

Most discussions of anal play focus on male pleasure—the lure of the prostate, the excitement of male penetration—so women are often left wondering it there's anything in it for them. And the answer is a resounding yes. If you recall from the anatomy lesson earlier, the anus is full of sensitive nerve endings that feel great when stimulated. And just as women enjoy the feeling of fullness in their vaginas, so too can they experience this sensation anally, whether it's delivered by a finger, a toy, or a partner's penis. The wall between the vagina and the anus is thin and sensitive, so a butt plug, especially when used in conjunction with a dildo for double penetration, can offer amazing G spot stimulation.

Anal masturbation is a prerequisite to enjoying anal penetration by a partner. Unfortunately, some women have had bad anal sex experiences, usually the result of insensitive partners who think they'll just "slip in through the back door" without first informing their partners. Good anal sex requires both partners' willing participation, a high degree of arousal, good communication skills, and lots of lubrication. Anal masturbation will teach you why and how these skills come in to play, so you'll be better able to enjoy anal penetration with your lover later on. Anal intercourse is an incredibly intimate act, capable of sparking a whole new level of emotional excitement in your relationship.

If you're new to anal play, refer to the "Bottoms Up" activity if you have concerns about cleanliness. A lot of women also equate anal sex with pain, which discourages them from trying it. So let me be clear: anal sex should not be painful. If you're experiencing pain, you or your partner are doing something wrong, and you should stop. People tend to feel pain for two main reasons: there's not enough lubrication, or entrance into the anus is forced (rather than welcomed). If you're sufficiently turned on, you're relaxed and in control of the activity, and have plenty of lubrication on hand, you shouldn't experience any pain. Unlike the vagina, the anus does not produce its own lubrication, so it's essential to keep your toy and your anus well lubed during play.

For this activity, you want a butt plug (also known as an anal plug). These are usually short, diamond-shape toys that bulge in the middle, but have a narrow neck at the base. Once the widest part is inside of you, your sphincter muscle contracts around the narrow neck, lodging the toy in place. The toy must have a flared base, which prevents it from slipping up inside you. Choose one with a modest bulge for starters. You can always work your way up to something larger.

Finally, although this activity is addressed toward women, men can follow the same instructions for inserting and playing with plugs. Anal toys can stimulate the prostate and lead to more intense orgasms.

- **Prep.** Make sure your fingernails are trimmed and clean. Keep a bottle of lube nearby (the pump style is most convenient). Make sure your toy is clean and has a flared base.
- **Get in the mood.** Listen to sexy music, read or watch erotica, play with yourself in the mirror—do what you usually do to get yourself excited.
- **Get comfortable.** Experiment with a couple different positions to find the one that is most comfortable and gives you access to your butt. Lying on your side leaves one hand free for your clit while another reaches back to your anus. You might try lying on your stomach with a vibrator strapped on or propped underneath you and one hand reaching back between your legs. Or you might prefer to squat—a great position for getting a good look at your anus in the mirror and for easing down gently onto a toy. You can also try this in the shower and enjoy the combination of warmth, water, and cleanliness.
- **Have a look around.** If you've never seen your anus, get out the mirror and have a look. Apply some lubricant to your fingertips and explore the skin all around the anus. Then gently tap on the anus, watching how it reacts as you do, noting any special sensitivity as well. Breathe deeply, focusing your mind on relaxing your butt muscles (unclench them if you've tightened up).
- **Fingers first.** As you exhale, gently insert your fingertip in

past the anal sphincter, which has a tendency to contract when it meets resistance. If you have difficulty, massage the anus and try pushing out (as if you were going to the bathroom) as you push your finger in. Once inside, hold still while you get used to the sensation. When you're ready, move your finger around as much as you feel comfortable—many people enjoy a gentle circular motion; do this as long as it's pleasurable.

- **Slip in the toy.** Withdraw your finger, add lubricant to your butt plug, and then try to insert the toy. If your toy is long or a bit soft, it might help to hold the toy near the top and guide it in. If you have trouble, stop for a bit, massage your anus, relax your muscles, and try again. It might help to change positions too. Once inside, hold still with just a bit of the toy inside you, rather than pushing it in to the hilt, as your rectum will need a minute to get used to the object coming up (rather than going out). If you feel the urge to push out, that's natural, since your anus is used to expelling objects. Try to relax your muscles and this feeling should diminish somewhat.

- **Nice and easy wins the race.** Once inside, slowly push the toy farther in if it feels good. Keep adding lubricant, because slipperier is better. Your butt plug should get smaller at the base, and when it's inserted as far as it will go, it'll stay lodged in your rectum. At this point, you can leave the toy in place and go on to stimulate other pleasure points, or you can explore subtle variations in movement— try turning it slowly, gently push-

Masturbation with an anal plug

ing or tapping on it, or turning on/up the vibration if you've got a vibrating plug. (Some women find the vibration distracting, but I think it's nice to have the option—you don't have to have it on if it bugs you!) If you've chosen a butt plug with a gentle curve, make sure you insert it so that when it's inside your anus, the curve points toward your stomach. This position may indirectly stimulate your G spot.

- **Get a move on.** Because the plug is designed to be "worn," you are free to get up and go about whatever business you like. I suggest spending some time exploring different possibilities— walking around the house, taking a stroll outside, cybering someone on your computer—anything that'll keep you tuned in to the sensations in your butt. Chances are, the longer you go at it, the more turned on you'll get. As you get more practiced with the toy, this can be just the thing to get you "in the mood" for an adventure with a partner later on.

- **Finish yourself off.** You can enjoy your anal plug and then remove it when it loses its thrill, or you can take your play to the next level and try to reach orgasm with the plug in place. Get in a position that is both comfortable and gives you access to your clit. Use your favorite vibrator or your hand to masturbate until you come. You may want to remove the plug quickly after you come, but remember to do so gently.

Variations

- If you find you like movement in and out of your anus, try a slim dildo rather than a plug. To get a better grip, use a dildo with a long handle on one end or one of the bent double dildos.
- If you get one with a suction cup on the base, you can attach it

to a wall, back yourself up against it, and penetrate yourself without having to use your hands.

- Use a dildo in your vagina and a vibrator on your clit while you have the butt plug in place for intense stimulation.
- Your partner can insert your plug or dildo, if you want to try this activity together. Just make sure it's well lubed and that you're in control of the action—that is, you say when to stop, go, speed up, or pull out.
- Anal beads are another great toy for exploring anal play, as the sphincter muscles contract around each bead as it is inserted, which many find pleasurable.
- If you don't want to worry about toy cleanliness, invest in a silicone plug or dildo. These are nonporous so you can wash them off easily with soap and water. Porous toys (those made out of rubber and cyberskin) can also be used with condoms.

Toy Testimonials

"I put a vibrating Bullet in my pussy and a plug vibrator in my butt, and then I go make cookies!"

A String of Pearls

by Madeleine Oh

"For you."

When Robert speaks, in his slow, deep, "I've got a surprise for you" voice, he gets my undivided attention. Chicken with holy basil can't compete.

This was our wedding anniversary and I expected a surprise. But what? A bright red butt plug with a green ribbon round the base? A pale-as-the-inside-of-an-oyster-shell vibrating egg? Quilted purple silk restraints? That had covered Christmas and Easter and my birthday.

Our first wedding anniversary could be anything.

He set a black velvet jeweler's box on the table. Had Robert turned conventional? Buying me a string of pearls or perhaps an add-a-bead necklace? Possible, but highly improbable.

He nudged the box closer to my wineglass. "Open it."

I had it opened just enough to glimpse the white satin lining in the lid, when our waiter reappeared. All he wanted was reassurance that our meal was perfect, but I almost slammed the lid on my finger.

Maybe it was matinee-length pearls, but you can't be too cautious in public. Not when you're married to Robert Kelly.

Checking first to make sure no solicitous waiter or maitre d' loitered, I snapped open the velvet lid. It was pearls, all right, but I'd never wear these to the opera—I hoped.

Nestling against the velvet padding and almost reflected in the gleaming satin lining of the lid were six large pearls strung on a fine twisted cord, one end sporting a polished metal ring, plenty big enough for hooking and tugging with a strong middle finger.

I did an involuntary Kegel exercise, imagining how they'd feel pushed one by one up my asshole. Knowing how the butt plug stretched and stimulated as Robert pulled it out, my stomach churned jasmine rice and holy basil imagining six round beads exiting my tight opening one by painful one.

I was so wet thinking about it, I was scared I'd leave a damp patch on the upholstered seat. Wearing no panties didn't help in the least. I should be used to that by now, but I wasn't. I never crossed the street without thinking about my mother's warnings in case I got run over.

Sitting in the Thai Pavilion, smelling my own arousal while Robert smiled promises at me across the pink linen tablecloth, I wanted to shove back my chair, grab my husband's hand, and drag him home to bed. But Robert ordered mango mousse, which I ate, one tiny bronze spoonful at a time, and never tasted a thing.

By the time he'd sipped the last of his decaffeinated espresso and finished signing the credit card slip, I could feel myself soaking though my skirt. I was the next best thing to panting as I settled into the leather upholstery of Robert's Merc. Only a ten-minute drive— fifteen max if every light was against us—and we'd be home.

I was ready and willing for whatever Robert had in mind, even six gleaming pearls up my asshole.

What Robert had in mind was having me strip in the garage. I half expected him to fuck me over the hood of the car, but no, while I was stepping out of my shoes and getting ready to roll down my lace-top stockings, he grabbed me by the waist and tossed me over his shoulder.

Head hanging halfway down his back, face rubbing against his silk jacket, Robert held my ankles in one hand and stroked my butt with the other. I was tempted to wriggle and complain, but with my ass literally under his hand, I decided against it. That part of me was going to get enough attention tonight; no point in getting it reddened as well.

Besides, I was more worried about one of the neighbors seeing as Robert carried me across the breezeway into the house.

Once inside, Robert eased me down his body. Every inch, from my shins and knees to my boobs and face, rubbed the warm, rough surface of his jacket as he lowered me down until my feet touched the cool, tiled kitchen floor.

"Happy anniversary," he said, and kissed me.

Lord! This guy of mine can kiss! Slow and sure, with the unhurried confidence of an expert, he pressed my lips apart and caressed them with his tongue until I let out a little sigh. He delved right in. His tongue poked, pushed, stroked, pressed, and teased until I tried to push away. He's made me come with just kissing before, but I didn't want to give in yet.

"No," Robert muttered into my mouth and set to with enthusiasm. I wrapped my arms around his neck, mashed my body against his, and gave as good as I got. Now he was the one moaning. He'd been hard when we started; now his cock felt like an iron pipe inside his wool slacks.

"I'm almost coming," I managed to get out between groans.

"Good," Robert replied, bringing his hand to my breast.

I gave up thinking, forgot speech. His fingers tweaked and pulled and rolled one nipple then the other until he whipped me into a frenzy of need and wanting. His mouth clamped down on mine as he gave my nipple one hard twist and I came with a shout that resounded in my head, echoing like the spasms of heat that radiated from my cunt. I'd have collapsed on the Mexican tile floor if his two strong arms hadn't held me. As it was, my cries sent the dog off in a yapping frenzy.

"He's upset because he isn't getting any," Robert said, holding me with one arm, as he reached for a doggie treat to keep the mutt quiet. While Hercules chewed on his biscuit, Robert dipped into his pocket and brought out my anniversary pearls, holding them by the loop and dangling them right in my line of vision. "Hold them," he said, and dropped them in my hand. "While I carry you." He scooped me up in his arms—head against his chest instead of down his back this time—and carried me across the house to our bedroom.

"Don't go anywhere," he said as he plopped me on the bed.

As if I would when I had the chance to watch the best striptease in town. Robert played soccer in college, and he still moves with the grace of a world-class player. He performs even mundane things like hanging his jacket up or unbuttoning his shirt with grace, and I am riveted as he unbuckles his belt and slides down his zip with a slow scritch. But the ultimate exhibition is what I wait for, the moment when his wonderful, hard cock juts out for me to hang my hopes on. Looks are great but taste is better, and I was licking my lips as Robert came toward me. I needed to taste that beautiful cock, my beautiful cock, and feel it between my lips.

Robert paused by the nightstand for a tube of jelly (which I should have expected, given what I was still clutching in my hot little hand) and a bottle of massage oil. "You're looking tense," he said. "Roll over and I'll help you relax."

After that climax I was about as tense as a marshmallow. But who'd turn down an offer like that? I rolled onto my belly and closed my eyes as Robert poured warm oil between my shoulder blades.

It trickled down my spine in a slow stream. It ran down the side of my waist and pooled in the hollow of my back. Then my husband got busy. Using a firm touch he spread that spicy scented oil all over me, anointing me from my shoulders to my thighs. His practiced fingers found tension in my shoulders and the place where my neck meets my skull. He gently stroked and smoothed until all I wanted was to spend the rest of my life in bed under Robert's expert hands.

Then he blew on me. He'd used the Kama Sutra oil! Heated trails flowed over my skin in the wake of his breath. Was it possible to be utterly relaxed and aroused? You bet! I swear he huffed and puffed over every square centimeter from the back of my knees to the nape of my neck, and, while my skin still glowed, his hands began again.

Fingertips at first, five on each butt cheek, tracing ever-widening circles on my ass. Soothing and stimulating at the same time. His hands gently flattened, pressing and opening my cheeks. His fingers stroked my crack and then dipped between my legs.

"You're sopping wet," he whispered against my skin, starting another warm shiver with his breath. "Now, what am I going to do about that?"

"You could fuck me," I suggested. "Fill me up with your lovely, hard cock." Just saying it aloud had me soaking.

"Oh, I will, my love, later. Right now . . ." He paused and I gave a little gasp as cool lubricant oozed between my ass cheeks.

He held my cheeks apart, opening me wider. The metal tip of the tube kissed my opening as a rush of gel surged inside. Robert's finger followed, gently pushing, circling, stretching, and opening until my sphincter relaxed. I was passive, anticipating the intrusion, while my mind whirled. Would it hurt? How tight would it feel? Would the beads stretch me more than the butt plug or Robert's cock? Would it . . .

One soft gasp as my butt hole stretched and I felt—not much different—as one pearl nestled inside me. I exhaled.

"How's that feel?" Robert asked.

"Okay." I'd barely spoken when the second slipped inside.

I hardly felt it once it was in but the sensations as the beads pushed past muscle drove me wild. The third seemed bigger, tighter. They were nestling inside me, and the fourth nudged them deeper. How big was I in there? How far would they go? What if they got stuck?

"Easy, easy." Robert's free hand stroked my head and shoulders. "It's okay. We're halfway. I wish I had a camera handy. If you could see these beads disappearing up your ass." With that another popped inside.

Robert ran kisses up and down my spine, awakening the last traces of heat in the oil drying on my skin. As I murmured my contentment, the last two pushed inside. I knew they were there. Stretching, filling, pushing . . . warming. The cool of the gel faded and all I felt was the heat. It set my cunt flowing and caused little soft groans to rise from deep in my belly.

Robert rolled me on my back and reminded me what a great mouth he had. He licked from fore to aft with tantalizing slowness until my hips moved of their own accord and little groans became big ones.

He stopped, damn him! He sat back on his heels and grinned. "Okay, love, now it's my turn to lie back and enjoy it."

Turnabout is fair play, and heck, sucking Robert's cock isn't my idea of hardship. Hardness maybe, but not hardship. He leaned back, a pillow behind his back, and I went to it between his legs, softly circling the smooth head of his cock with the tip of my tongue. Taking him between my lips, fluttering his hard muscle with my tongue until he ran his hands through my hair, pushing me lower. I took most of him in, running my tongue up and down the warm skin at the side of his cock. Lifting back a little to flicker round his ridge again and again until he groaned. I let up a little—but not much. Down and up I went in a smooth rhythm, enjoying the taste of him and the magnificent scent of male arousal. Nothing like knowing your own power.

"Easy!" he said at last, and pulled my head away. "Let's fuck!'

I grinned up at him. "Brilliant idea." I didn't wait to be asked twice. I scooted up the bed until I was squatting over his thighs. As Robert's hands on my waist steadied me, I impaled myself on his wondrous erection.

And gasped. I'd married a big cock but not this big! I was stuffed, packed tight with solid erection and hard round beads. As I rocked gently, I felt Robert press inside until he rubbed the beads through my cunt walls. I took a deep breath and rocked again . . . and again . . . Incredible! Wonderful! I gave up thinking adjectives and concentrated on the sensations as I worked my cunt up and down Robert's cock.

I watched him. Saw the pleasure soften his face and the heat glimmering deep in his eyes. I wasn't the only one spiraling to the outer galaxy. I leaned forward so my clit felt more of the pressure and rocked up and down until Robert moaned. I was close to coming now, breathing hard as sensation built and grew.

"Nearly there?" Robert gasped.

I nodded. I let out a long, slow moan as the nerve endings in my cunt drew up for the leap into joy. The first waves of orgasm rippled through me as Robert pulled out the first bead. A wild yell of delight burst in my chest. My whole body roared and the next one came, and the next. My body awash, my mind drowning, I shouted and groaned and sang the wildness that flooded me. I lost balance, collapsing on

Robert just as he came, his heated spunk bursting into me as my last vibrations slowed and calmed.

I lay on top of him, as his warm jism oozed out of my cunt and the last sweet spasms of pleasure faded to gentle ripples. I rolled off him, nestling beside him, my head on his chest. The beads in his hand glistened with lubricant and I still throbbed deep inside.

Robert opened his eyes and grinned. "Happy anniversary."

I can't wait for Halloween.

THE TOUCH OF LOVE: Erotic Massage for Beginners

Toy(s) you will need: Massage oil
                               Water-based lubricant
Type of play: Partnered

Few things are as sensually pleasing as a slow, lovingly administered erotic massage. As a lover's hands travel along your body delivering exquisite tactile pleasure, you find yourself simultaneously relaxed and aroused. You abandon yourself totally to a lover's care, which feels both indulgent and freeing. As the giver you are the master of ceremonies—running the show, reveling in the spectacle, and turning yourself on in the process.

Erotic massage differs from regular massage in that it is designed primarily to excite the recipient. Whereas the breasts and genitals are usually ignored in most therapeutic massages, they are hot spots in an erotic massage, which contributes to a full-body sensuality.

Make sure your partner is aware that erotic massage is on the menu. There's a big difference between a massage that can put you to sleep and one that can wake up your sex drive.

Some folks are intimidated at the prospect of giving a massage, but if you stick to a few of the basic techniques listed here, I promise your partner will not kick you out of bed. In general, the most important things to remember in massage are: keep warm, go slowly, repeat strokes, don't break contact with the skin, and pay attention to your partner's reactions. Encourage your partner to offer verbal feedback—even if it's an occasional moan of pleasure—so you can learn as you go. Remember, you can't go wrong with erotic massage. There are just too many things right about it.

- **Prep.** Warmth is the key to a good massage, so make sure the room you will be using is well heated. Warm up towels in the dryer and drape them over your partner. Heat up your massage oil in the microwave or a bowl of hot water. Your lover might want to bathe first (why not bathe together?), which will both relax and warm her or him up. Turn off the phone and put on some relaxing music if you like.

- **Position.** Choose a space that will give you good access to all sides of your partner's body. Massage tables are nice, but a bed that is big enough for you to kneel on either side of your partner will do just fine. Have your lover strip and lie facedown on the table. If you are naked as well, your partner will get a nice visual as you work your way around, and you can deliver some skin-to-skin contact when the spirit moves you.

- **Plan your moves.** Before you get started, map out your moves in your head. I suggest starting with your lover facedown and massaging the back, shoulders, arms, hands, butt, legs, and feet. Then turn her or him over and begin with a face and scalp rub, then do the legs, feet, abdomen, chest, and genitals. It's fine to improvise, just make sure you don't neglect body parts.

- **Apply the oil.** Pour about a tablespoon of oil into one of your hands, rub them together, and place them on your partner. Skin soaks up the oil quickly, so replenish as often as necessary, taking care to keep one hand in contact with the skin at all times (a pump facilitates this, or turn the hand that's resting on the body over and pour the oil into it).

- **Stroke all over.** Begin by placing both of your hands on your partner's hands and traveling with one long firm stroke up the arms, across the shoulders, down the back, butt, and legs, and all the way to the toes. Keep your hands on the toes and reverse the stroke. Repeat this several times. When your partner turns over, make sure to repeat this stroke on the front side.

- **Use thumbs, palms, fingers.** Your thumbs and palms are capable of delivering focused pressure, while your fingers add spot pressure or a feather-light touch. Whatever stroke you use, modify it periodically to apply more or less pressure with the different parts of your hands. Or focus on one part of your hand and use it all over your partner's body. For example, take your thumbs and place them at the base of the spine. Slowly move up the spine, the arms, or the legs, applying firm, smooth pressure.

- **Fanning up the spine.** Place your hands palms down at the base of your partner's spine, with thumbs next to each other and fingers pointing toward the head. Now fan out your hands at a ninety-degree angle so that they massage the sides, then bring your hands back together. Inch your way up the spine while repeating this stroke, pressing down with your palms to apply pressure to the spine.

- **Pulling along the sides.** Place your hands next to each other along one side of your partner. Both sets of fingers should be pointing toward the bed, with the heels of your hands near the spine. Now, using an alternating motion, pull up with one hand toward the spine, while sliding down with the other toward the bed. You can travel all over the body with this motion, but it feels particularly good on the sides, thighs, and breasts. On the breasts, pull your palm up and around the breast, grazing the nipple along the way.

- **Kneading all over.** A good stroke for applying firm pressure, move your hands in unison as if you were kneading bread. Use this when you're traveling over a large expanse of skin, like the back, or around the tense shoulders and neck area.

- **Attending to the butt.** Standing or sitting at your partner's feet, place one hand on each butt cheek and move them in opposite directions. Or squat over your partner's butt, facing the feet, and massage the inner thigh, ending with a luxurious upward pull on the butt cheek. Or place both hands on the butt cheeks and pull upward and outward in unison. These moves tug on the genitals and can be particularly arousing.

- **Pampering the breasts.** Breasts are an integral part of your erotic massage, so don't skip them (unless your partner has asked you to). Sitting or standing over your partner's head, reach over with your palms and place them on her stomach. Slide up the stomach in between the breasts and glide around the outside in a circular motion. You can cup them gently, then slide back down around. Another pleasant sensation on the breasts involves spreading your fingers and placing them on the outside of the breasts, gently bringing your fingers together as you move up toward the nipple, and finishing with a slight nipple pinch. Men's nipples are often overlooked as an erogenous zone, so try these moves on him too.

- **Arousing the genitals.** If you've ever watched your lover masturbate, you've received the best instruction in how to massage his or her genitals. Whether you want to masturbate your lover to orgasm is up to the two of you, but you'll still want to explore every part of the genital anatomy. You may want to switch to water-based lubricant instead of oil, especially if you'll be inserting any fingers into your partner's vagina (or if you'll be having intercourse later), since the oils take longer to wash out.

- **On women:** Place a well-oiled hand over her vulva with the fingers pointing toward the anus, and pull up so that your palm grazes the clitoris on the way. Follow this motion with your other hand and repeat it several times. Use your fingers to explore her labia, running a smooth finger alongside them or tugging gently on them. Stroke the entire vulva in a circular motion by starting with two fingers on the perineum and traveling clockwise up and around the clitoris, then back to the perineum. If you plan to focus on the clitoris, try several fingers and experiment with different directions and pressure.

Using your thumb or forefinger, apply pressure as you trace circles around the vagina and anus. Pop a finger into the vagina and massage the inside of her vaginal walls.

- **On men:** Cradle your partner's testicles with your well-oiled hand and hold them for a few seconds. Use the other hand to form a ring around the base of the penis, and slide up and down the shaft several times. Lay his penis against his stomach and use your palm to apply pressure as your stroke the underside of his penis. Or use one hand to stroke the shaft while you use the fingers of your other hand in a twisting motion on the head, just as if you were juicing an orange. To massage the sensitive frenulum (the indentation on the underside where the ridge of the glans meets the shaft), interlock your fingers with his penis in between, bringing your thumbs together to gently rub this spot. Use your fingers or thumb to lightly circle his anus, and apply pressure to the perineum.

- **To come or not to come.** Whether you've brought your partner to an orgasm or not, it's nice to complete your massage with a few full-body strokes. This will help her or him relax if a climax has already occurred, or it will prolong the excitement until you move on to something else. After you've finished with the hand strokes, climb up alongside your partner and press your fully naked body against hers or his for a delicious ending to an incredible experience.

Variations

- Use body parts other than your hands to tease a partner—hair, breasts, lips, and tongue all can elevate the massage to a new level of tactile delight.

- Introduce other sensual toys—a feather, fur, silk, body paints, or edible gels.
- Some massage oils or gels will warm up when you rub them or blow on them, lending an extra bit of heat to your massage.
- Put a blindfold on your partner to add an element of excitement and anticipation to the massage.
- Give your partner a vibrator and let him or her control the vibrations while you're busy with the massage.

WHAT'S THE BUZZ?

Hot Talk Meets High Tech

Toy(s) you will need: Audi-Oh vibrator
                        Erotica on tape or CD (optional)
         Type of play: Partnered or solo

Some folks call it "talking dirty"; others call it "hot talk." Whatever your preference, the art of turning your lover on by words
alone is an erotic art form lost on most people. Which is unfortu-
nate, because sound can be a key arousal trigger. Given that our
ears are often assaulted by unpleasant sounds—traffic, crying kids,
power tools—it can be especially pleasant to soothe them with sexy
sounds, words, or music.

I once heard from a man who discovered that *p* words whispered
into his ear turned him on. He didn't go in for elaborate scenarios
or fancy word play, he just wanted a little alliteration and the bursts

of warm breath that phrases like "pretty pussy" and "pounding penis" sent into his ear. His experience exemplifies what makes dirty talk so rewarding—it appeals to several of our senses and involves one of our most powerful sex organs, the brain. Your brain creates the mood or scene, your voice triggers the erotic awakening, and your breath can put the finishing touches on your literary web of seduction.

There's a pretty obvious reason most of don't talk the talk—we're afraid of making fools of ourselves. The idea of using words we've been taught to avoid our whole lives just feels embarrassing, silly, or uncomfortable. But it's precisely the forbidden quality of these words that infuses them with an erotic charge (just as the taboo nature of some fantasies makes them more potent), so if you can muster up the nerve to flex your vocal chords, you just might be rewarded with a particularly explosive sexual encounter.

Many people are intimidated by the idea of talking dirty to a partner because they're afraid they don't know what to say or how to say it. In reality, all it takes is a little practice and a mischievous attitude. In this activity, I've included suggestions for practicing alone, for picking up explicit vocabulary, and for topics that lend themselves well to aural encounters. In order to find out what kind of language turns your partner on, do a bit of sleuthing first. Read some erotica together and sample different writing styles—including some that's very euphemistic (Victorian erotica) and some that is very explicit (contemporary erotica). Talk about which scenes you each found arousing and why. This will give you a feel for the speaking style and the subject matter your partner prefers. You can also ask your partner a few open-ended sex questions, such as "Tell me how you like oral sex." This will give you an idea as to whether he or she is comfortable with words like "pussy" and "cunt" or would prefer something else (bearing in mind, however, that someone who's not comfortable using them still might get turned on hearing them).

If you've never talked about trying this activity with a partner, you might be afraid of rejection. But isn't this the case with just about anything new you try? Take the risk, and either talk to your partner beforehand or dive straight in and see how it goes. When it comes to performing, you'll be most successful if you just go for it. Be brave and confident. My high school debate coach used to say, "If you can't dazzle them with brilliance, baffle them with bullshit." Which is just another way of saying it doesn't matter so much *what* you say as *how* you say it. Remember, you needn't be a prize-winning author or an adult film star to incite your partner's lust, as the *P*-man reminded us. All you need is willingness, an adventurous spirit, and a good sense of humor.

When you're ready to take it to the bed-room (or boardroom or bathroom, depending on your fantasy), add this innovative toy and your sex play will take on an even more thrilling dimension. The Audi-Oh is a Bullet vibrator that responds to sound, so that any words you utter into its microphone are transmitted as vibrations to your partner's genitals. With this toy your words will literally turn your partner on.

> ## Toy Testimonials
>
> "I turned this toy on and walked around the room— every time I moved, my shirt would rub against the black box and the vibe would work its magic. I tried standing near the stereo to see what would happen. It was like having Aerosmith's amp attached to my waist and connected to my clit. It was my idea of heaven."

- **Practice your technique alone.** If you need help learning to express yourself, practice alone for a while until you've gained enough confidence to try it with a partner. You might feel foolish, but it also might be exciting. Here are a few starters:

- Get vocal while you masturbate. Try out a few sentences, describe your fantasy, or imagine your partner is stroking you and you're talking to him or her.
- Read some erotica out loud.
- Try phone sex. Why not learn from the pros? This is a great way of finding out how voice intonation, detail, and fantasy can build toward a great climax. Those phone sex operators are paid to drag out your fantasy, so you can learn how to tease your partner indefinitely.
- Pen a sexy story, an erotic e-mail, or try cybersex. These can help develop your vocabulary and give your some confidence.
- Find a website or sexual slang dictionary. Pick up a how-to-talk-dirty book for more explicit scenarios, or read a book of fantasies to get an idea of how people use explicit language.
- Try the Audi-Oh alone. Hold the vibrator against your genitals and play with it (see tips below) alone first. If you're aware of how it feels, you'll be better able to use it with a partner.

- **Set the scene.** Decide where you want to try your toy. You might want to have your partner put it on underneath his or her clothes and try to go about "business as usual" around the house first, with just the subtle sounds of everyday life contributing to his or her low-grade eroticism.
- **Suit up.** The Audi-Oh is a Bullet vibrator attached to a battery pack, but the pack has a microphone in it. It also has a jack so you can hook up the toy directly to a stereo. There's an (optional) strap-on butterfly sleeve for the Bullet, so women can wear the vibrator hands-free over their clits (just add plenty of lube first as the Bullet can be difficult to extract later). Men will

probably want to hold the Bullet against the penis, testicles, or anus. There are two vibration options—one will transmit vibrations according to the sound input, the other will allow for a continuous vibration. If you have them both on at once, you'll get a steady vibration that increases in response to the sound. In general, it works best to hold the vibrator in place against your desired body part, rather than move it around.

- **Woo with words.** When you're ready to seduce your partner with your naughty tongue, try some of these subjects:
  - Tell your partner in explicit detail what you want to do to him or her. Or turn the tables and describe how you'd like to be made love to.
  - Comment on the activity as it is occurring, describing how it feels, what you're fantasizing about, what you're planning to do next.
  - Describe your favorite sexual encounter.
  - Relay a favorite sexual fantasy. Be as creative and as outlandish as you like. You can cast yourselves in some role-playing.
  - Recount your favorite sex scene from a racy movie. Recast yourself and your partner in the lead roles.

  Vary your voice intonation and experiment with words that emit stronger or weaker vibrations, so you can bring your partner to the brink of climax and then taper off again. You can sing, recite poetry, rap, whisper, or shout your affection into the mike.

- **Utilize home entertainment.** Give yourself a break and pop an erotic CD or tape into the stereo, then hook it up to the Audi-Oh. Now you can both relax and enjoy the story. If you want to add another aural element, put some sexy music on the stereo. Choose something with a nice strong beat and either use this as background music while you talk or plug it directly into the box for stronger vibrations. Find out in advance what your partner's favorite sexy songs are and play them, or choose some of your own. I can promise that the irony will not be lost on your lover (nor will the pounding bass) if you choose classics like "Feel Like Making Love" or "Tell Me Something Good." While your sweetie is writhing to the music, you can concentrate on using your mouth on other parts of his or her body.

Variations

- You won't get the sound vibrations, but you can do a version of the activity with a remote-control vibrator or any vibrator with a battery pack. Just hand the controls over to your partner, and let him or her control the vibrations on your clit or penis while turning you on verbally.
- Dirty talk can be accessorized even further if you combine it with role-playing. You add a visual element when you introduce a few props and assume the roles of some classic sex games (schoolgirl/teacher, celebrity/groupie, boss/employee).

At Home with the Vibrapen

by Joy VanNuys

I found it hard to resist the idea of the Vibrapen. It's a vibrator attached to a pen. Or a pen attached to a vibrator, depending on how you look at it. As a writer who works at home, I thought this might be the perfect sex toy to add a little zip to my lonely desk-bound existence while increasing my time-on-task ratio.

I donned my writer outfit (long T-shirt, no bra, panties, socks) and sat down at the kitchen table that serves as my desk. I pulled out a note pad, some stationery, index cards. And I went to work.

To Whom It May Concern:

I was interested to learn that you're looking for a developer of training materials for your new software. I am a freelance writer with a strong background in technical training, and I'd like to learn more about this potential project.

Well, the ink part works just fine. The barrel is smooth, doesn't cramp up my fingers. Let's check out the business end, shall we?

The vibrator tip of the Vibrapen is tiny, just the right size for a quick nipple buzz. But how does it work? Maybe you just press in this doohickey at the end and *mmmm.* That feels nice. Even through the T-shirt. Oops, I guess you have to keep pressing down for it to keep buzzing. But now I've lost that cover-letter feeling. What's the next item on my to-do list?

Dear Aunt Mildred,

It was such a treat to see you on Sunday afternoon. Darjeeling is my favorite, too, and you were so sweet to . . .

How would it be under the T-shirt? See, there are those little nubbly spots on the end that might feel nice on my skin. Wow. There's no way to get this thing to give you a feathery light touch, is there? It's grind away or nothing. Okay, you've got my nipples' attention. Look, it's just about the right size for my clit too! I can take turns using one end of the pen to write, then the other to vibe.

paper towels
kitty food
(buzz)
pussy—wet pussy
cock
pussy
skim milk
cheddar
(buzz)
zucchini carrots eggplant
suck it

take it in you

harder

harder

tissues

coffee

Fuck this. If there's one thing the Internet has taught me, it's how to type with one hand. Pens are obsolete. And maybe if I kind of slide it between my legs and press down against the chair . . .

Dear Mr. Edwards,

I enjoyed your panel discussion so much that I had to write and let you know what a naughty girl I am and how I thought the whole time about how those big ham hands of yours would feel coming down hard on my ass.

Your anecdote about the figs was so amusing. The inside of a fig is soft and ripe and wet, Mr. Edwards. So am I.

Your years of experience as an editor were evident as you shared your words of wisdom and I would like to fuck you fuck you fuck you fuck you.

Sincerely yours,

Joy VanNuys

LOG ON AND GET OFF: Cybersex
with a Sex Toy

Toy(s) you will need: Hands-free clitoral vibrator

Cock ring vibrator

Type of play: Solo or partnered

"You husband-stealing harlot! Cybersex is adultery." This was what
the woman shouted at me when I appeared on a call-in radio show
in the Bible Belt while promoting my book, *The Woman's Guide to
Sex on the Web*. Despite my patient attempts to explain that (1) I
didn't know her husband, and (2) cybersex could be a liberating and
sexually fulfilling experience, especially for women, I was having a
hard time being heard over her diatribe.

What is cybersex? It's when two or more people hook up online
for a mutually arousing, but virtual, sexual escapade. No bodies
come into contact, just brains. Unfortunately, when it comes to sex
and the Internet, tales of sex addiction, sexual betrayals, and cheat-

ing husbands scare off most people. These are the stories that make the headlines, not the ones about the newlyweds who met in a chat room, the single mom who's having great virtual sex while the kids are asleep, or the women who are learning how to express themselves sexually through their chat experiences. The good experiences vastly outnumber the bad ones, and I invite you to look beyond the negative stereotyping and just consider the possibility that cybersex could be a whole new milestone in your sexual path. Sure, it's not for everyone, but as with anything in this book, you won't know whether you like it unless you try it first. And I've made it easy for you to try, but suggest that you and your partner explore cybersex *together* in this activity. If you're single, you can still apply most of the suggestions for chat and masturbation to a "virtual" partner.

What's so great about cybersex? There's no question that our ability to express ourselves sexually is improving thanks to cybersex. The anonymity of the chat experience emboldens people to express themselves in ways they might not be able to with a partner. On the Internet, if you don't explicitly ask for something, you won't get it. Being able to articulate your desires and negotiate them with a

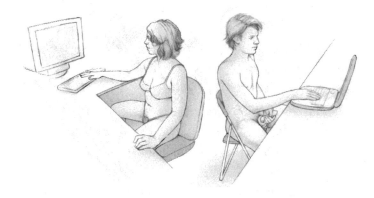

Cybersex with sex toys

virtual partner is excellent practice for doing this in your real life. It's great for your self-confidence and self-esteem. What's more, because your connection is generated solely by words, you flex your imagination in new ways.

Online sex experiences also contribute to a richer, more varied sexuality. Because the action remains in the fantasy realm, people are more willing to explore sexual activities they might be intimidated by in their normal lives. Dressing up in dominatrix gear is easy enough online; should you find the experience thrilling, the practice may eventually make its way into your real-life sexual repertoire.

Cybersex also makes us a bit more sexually adventurous. Because we don't have to make commitments, fret over appearances, or worry about safer sex, we're free to take chances on people or scenes we might normally shy away from. And if you're new to sex or have had only one or two lovers, cybersex is a great way to do research on the sexual likes and dislikes of the opposite sex.

Enough about why you might try it, let's talk about how. I've included his-and-hers hands-free vibrators for this activity, so you can add a little buzz to your banter.

- **Prep.** You and your partner agree to meet as strangers in your chosen chat room. You should decide on a time where you will meet and exchange usernames in advance (or agree on a verbal cue of some kind) so you don't end up picking up the wrong person! You each need to have access to a computer and an Internet connection. Whether you try this activity from your offices or separate rooms in your home is up to you.
- **Strap yourself in.** At the designated time, put batteries in your toy and strap it on before you sit down. The hands-free or panty-style vibrators are great for women, and the cock ring vi-

brators or vibrating sleeves are ideal for men. Wait to turn the toy on, but enjoy how it feels.

- **Get the lay of the land.** When you first enter a chat room, simply "lurk" for a bit to get a feel for the conversation. Chat rooms are public, meaning a whole bunch of you are present at once, and your comments are visible to everyone. When you want some private time, you and your virtual partner can go off into a private chat room, which is visible only to the two of you. Public sex chat rooms are great for exploring your voyeuristic and exhibitionist sides, so spend some time flirting with strangers or each other before you excuse yourselves to a private room. It can be exciting for your partner to watch you work a crowd, or vice versa.

- **Get private.** When you and your partner are finally alone, you can really let your imagination run wild. Remember that you're pretending to be strangers, so use this opportunity to act as if you've just met at a party and are intent on seducing this wonderful new person: lay on the compliments, the double entendres, the wit, the charm, and the humor. Since you're not able to actually see your partner, let your imagination fill in the blanks—compliment her dress (describing the one in your fantasy), ask him where he got that rugged scar, offer to mix her a cocktail (Sex on the Beach?), comment on the sexy celebrities at your party.

- **Get nasty.** How much verbal foreplay you desire is a matter of

Toy Testimonials

"I had the most sensational orgasm when I used the Fleshlight while I was cybering. I wedged it between my desk and my lap and slid it right in. It was great because I was describing to my virtual partner just what it would feel like if I was doing her, and the toy helped make the fantasy so real!"

personal preference, but at some point the chat will turn naughty. If you haven't had any practice with the language of sex, don't worry, it's awkward for most people at first. You can practice ahead of time by reading some erotica, studying a sexual lexicon, or reading a book on how to talk dirty. In the chat itself, you can always ply your partner with probing questions about favorite body parts or fantasies, but at some point be prepared to respond with your own story. You can lead the conversation to areas you're most comfortable with at first—perhaps describing your coming-of-age experience, your most erotic sexual encounter, or a sexy scene from a movie (with you and your partner cast as the leads). You can speak in the first person, or you can weave a narrative in the third person. As with any story, detail is key—when you describe the way your nipples felt through the silk blouse, it will add to the sexual tension. After a while, and depending on the expertise of your partner, you will learn how to engage in sexual repartee that can prolong the foreplay, playing off of each other until you're ready to come.

- **Rev it up.** By all means turn your vibrator on at any point. Put your arousal in your virtual partner's hands. Tell him or her you'll wait to be instructed on when to the turn the vibrator on, how high, and whether you should be doing anything else with your hands besides typing. (Or you can keep your toy a secret, and use it to get you off on your own terms.)

- **The logistics of coming.** At some point, you may want to come. (You might not—plenty of cybersex is about charging your engine.) The hands-free vibrator makes it easier for you to come and type at the same time (since you don't need to use one hand for masturbation). Even so, it's pretty hard to type while you're coming, and plenty of onscreen encounters climax with a series of "ooooooooohhhhhs" and "xx!!!xxs." If you take turns coming, one of you can script right through the dialogue to make sure your partner feels your presence all the way through your orgasm.

Variations

- No need to stop at one toy. Butt plugs and nipple clamps are also great cybertoys.
- As technology advances, expect to see vibrators that plug in to your computer. Some do exist now, but they merely draw power from your computer (great for cybersex on business trips). The real revolution will come when the person on the other side of the computer can control your vibrator speed and motion, or speak and have the vibrator respond to words or vibrations.
- *Note:* If you are single and meet someone online, if your relationship progresses to the point that you want to meet in real life, take a few precautions first: consider exchanging photos if you haven't yet to avoid any surprises, arrange to meet in a public place, and bring cab fare, a cell phone, and safer sex gear. Make sure you tell someone where you're going.

WET AND WILD: Underwater Sex Adventures

Toy(s) you will need: Waterproof vibrator
Silicone-based lubricant
Rubber or latex cock ring
(optional)
Type of play: Partnered or solo

What did toga-clad Romans and leisure suit–wearing swingers have in common? They both understood the erotic appeal of water. Whether it was an orgy in an ornately tiled bath or a dalliance in a swirling Jacuzzi, they reveled in the sensual decadence that warm water and nudity inspire. And while these practices may have been a product of the times, pursuing a few aquatic adventures of your own can be just the thing to spice up your sex life.

Plenty of women have already discovered the orgasmic pleasures of water, thanks to masturbatory encounters with shower massagers, tub faucets, and hot tub jets. But if your wife or girlfriend is spending more time in the bath than in your bed, it's time you got your feet wet and joined her. Fortunately, adult toy makers have invented some waterproof toys that are guaranteed to make bath time much more fun. Most vibrators today come in waterproof versions, including one that looks just like a rubber duck, so none of your guests will be the wiser! Most dildos or cock rings, particularly those made out of latex, rubber, or silicone, can be played with safely in water. Add to that a silicone-based lubricant that won't wash off underwater and you're all set to slip and slide to your heart's content. Of course, you needn't have a partner handy to enjoy the pleasures of underwater sex. All of these toys can be enjoyed with a partner or alone.

Toy Testimonials

"I love my waterproof vibrator and have the prune fingers to prove it! If I close my eyes and let the water and the vibrations work together, I can imagine my lover's tongue is doing the work."

A Few Tips

- **Wear clothes that are easy to remove.** It's much easier to slip off the panties of your two-piece bathing suit than it is to peel yourself out of a wet one-piece. And you can still be clothed from the waist up!
- **Find warm water.** The mountain stream may be picturesque, but chilly waters will make it hard for him to get a hard-on.
- **Look for still waters.** The only waves you want around are the ones you're making; otherwise you'll find it difficult to stay together.
- **Keep it private.** Exhibitionism can be thrilling, but not if

you're spoiling someone else's view. Respect other people's right not to be voyeurs, and try to keep your trysts discreet.

- **Be cautious.** Water can contain microorganisms or bacteria that can cause vaginal infections. Showers are the safest place, if you're prone to yeast infections. Also, underwater sex tends to be unsafe sex because condoms feel rather painful when used underwater (the water washes away a woman's natural lubricant, so the friction during penetration hurts). But add some silicone-based lube and that condom will stay wet while you get wild.

Underwater Sex Games

- **Go for a midnight swim in the hotel pool after hours.** Play your own version of Marco Polo—when you get "caught," your partner gets to please you with whatever waterproof toy you brought along. He can play with a vibrator on you, you can put that latex cock ring on him.
- **Apply lube to his penis, then jump in the hot tub.** Position your clit in front of the Jacuzzi jet by putting your legs up over the edge of the spa. Have him enter you from behind, so you're basically sitting on his lap. Now you can bounce freely up and down on his penis with little effort while getting your clit stimulated by the Jacuzzi jet.
- **Take a tub for two.** Get in the bath together so that you're facing each other and you can easily reach his penis. Place a waterproof Bullet vibe or Pocket Rocket in the palm of your hand and roll it around his penis, while gently tickling his testicles with the other. Or sit facing the same direction with the woman in front and the man behind. He can reach around and play with her breasts while she uses a vibrator on herself.

- **Let the shower massager work its magic fingers on you.** Shower massagers have sent many a woman into rhapsodic orgasms, so play with one together. What's so great about a shower massager? Its long arm will accommodate a variety of positions, its adjustable settings allow you to change the intensity of the jet spray, and you can experiment with the temperature at the same time. So get in the shower together and experiment with the shower massager on the clit, breasts, penis, testicles, and anal area. You'll be awash in pleasure and squeaky clean when you're done.

Bathtime with a
waterproof vibrator

- **Consider a tropical getaway.** On your next tropical vacation, snorkel in a secluded spot. Strip down to your birthday suit, but don your mask and snorkel. Have your partner stand, sit, or float in waist-deep water while you use the waterproof toy on him or her. With your mask on you'll get a clear picture of the action, and your snorkel will help you stay under for a while. And for once, the fish get to watch the show instead of being the main attraction!

Variations

- Bring along a book. Books like *Aqua Erotica* and *Wet* were printed on waterproof paper, and can help get you hot and steamy while you're in the bath.
- Most dildos and anal toys can be used in the water, so add those to your bath or swim. Silicone is especially easy to clean up.

EXERCISING RESTRAINT: Playing with Light Bondage

Toy(s) you will need:	Wrist and/or ankle restraints
	Blindfold
	Vibrator (optional)
	Nipple clamps (optional)
	Feather and other tactile toys (optional)
	Paddle (optional)
Type of play:	Partnered

One of my favorite sex toys is a pair of wrist restraints called Jane's Bonds. I imagine a scene in which a woman ultimately bests the elusive 007. She's pinned him to the bed with her wide hips, muscular thighs, and, of course, ample chest. She whips out the wrist restraints and says, "James Bond, meet Jane's Bonds." Then she ties him up and proceeds to shake his martini just the way *she* likes it.

If you have ever fantasized about being tied up (or tying some-one up), you're a good candidate for bondage play. Quite simply, bondage is the act of restricting someone's movements, usually through restraints of some kind. The person running the show is referred to as a dominant or "top," while the person tied up is called the submissive or "bottom." You don't need to identify with or use these terms, but for the purposes of explanation, I'll use them. Bondage play is consensual, meaning both partners are willing participants (even in my fantasy James Bond begs for it).

What a lot of people find exciting about bondage play is the freedom it gives them from certain performance expectations. In contrast to a sexual encounter where there is a high degree of sexual give-and-take, this activity requires one partner to assume complete control of the activity, while the other lies back and just experiences the thrill of being "done to." This can be pretty liberating if you get tired of the my turn/your turn sequence of events in your everyday sex life.

Bondage play offers a unique opportunity to focus on the entire body, something that is rarely a priority in our genitally focused sex play. When your lover is tied up and lying prone before you, his or her body becomes a canvas awaiting your paintbrush. As the dominant partner, you get to use your hands, tongue, hair, body, or toys as your tools, teasing out delicious sensations as you go about painting your elaborate picture. Since your goal is to make your partner squirm with delight, to moan with ecstasy, and to crave your next move, you become really attuned to your partner's hot spots and sexual responses. As the submissive partner, you get to focus solely on the sensations you are experiencing, anticipate what will come next, using all of your senses to push to new levels of sexual nirvana. As you can see, bondage play offers a potent combination of both the psychological and physical aspects of sex.

Playing with light bondage

Your bondage play can take many forms—you can use different toys, assume different positions, even trade places. For the purposes of this activity, the partners will stick to their assigned roles, and the focus will be on enhancing the senses, achieved largely through the use of a blindfold and a host of different tactile toys. I've listed several different optional toys so you can experiment with more intense sensations if you choose to go in that direction. You may have noticed that when you're highly aroused, a nipple pinch feels more pleasant than it does when you're not. Since you have a higher tolerance for pain when aroused, toys like nipple clamps and paddles can help you reach that point of heightened sensation.

For bondage play to be successful, you need trust and good communication. If you're tied up, you need to trust that the person doing the tying has your best interests at heart. As the dominant, you need to stay tuned in to your partner's experience. You'll want to establish some verbal and nonverbal ways to communicate during your play. Agree on some signals or signs that allow the submissive to give feedback to the dominant, especially a "safe word" that will immediately bring play to an end. Here are some basic safety precautions you should keep in mind:

- Make sure the restraints fit properly. You should always be able to slip a finger between the restraint and your partner's skin.
- Make sure you can easily remove the restraints.

- Don't leave your partner unattended. You can pretend to disappear, but don't leave your lover alone for any length of time.
- Make sure his or her limbs don't fall asleep. Feel the appendages periodically to make sure they're not cold; release them immediately if they're turning blue.

Still not sure if bondage play is for you? Ask yourself whether you're turned on by images of dominance or submission, whether your fantasies ever stray to power play, whether you enjoyed any childhood games involving this type of play (evil villain ties you to a railroad track), or whether you could just use a break from the roles expected of you in your daily life. If you answered yes to any of the questions, you'll probably enjoy a little restraint in the bedroom.

- **Decisions.** First agree on who wants to be tied up. If you both do, then you'll have to take turns, but I suggest waiting for another day before you swap. That way, you can each focus on your own roles, without planning what you'll be doing when you've traded places. Second, talk about what kinds of activities you're both comfortable with. Maybe you want to tie up just the wrists first and leave the ankles free, and forgo the blindfold. Maybe you're fine with the light toys, but want to save the paddle for another day. Or you might decide to wait and see how things are going, and the submissive will decide when to add another toy.
- **Prep.** Make sure you've got the appropriate rigging before your partner is splayed before you on the bed. Do your homework by affixing the bonds to the bed in advance to determine if the tethers are long enough to reach the bedposts or if adjustments need to be made. When choosing restraints, go with wrist or

ankle restraints that are lined and have easy-to-remove binding. These are more comfortable than using rope or silk scarves, as the latter can too easily cut off your circulation. If you do use rope, make sure you can quickly undo any knot you tie or have some blunt scissors nearby just in case.

- **Position.** Blindfold your partner and have him or her lie back on the bed. Gather any toys you'll be using and put them within easy reach. If you're anticipating sexual intercourse as part of your play, make sure you've got lube on hand.

- **Tie me up, tie me down.** Secure the restraints to your partner's ankles and wrists (or just the wrists if that's what you've decided). Make sure they are neither too tight nor too loose by slipping a finger between the cuff and your partner's skin. Tight cuffs will cut off circulation, and loose binding can come free or cause chafing.

- **Talk it up.** If you're up to the task, keep up a steady stream of hot talk as you work over your partner's body. Describe what you see, what you're doing, what you have in store, or what you're fantasizing about. Without benefit of sight, your words will have a tremendous impact on your partner's sexual experience. Play with sound as well: you can shift from sultry commands to whispered seductions. Even shifting your proximity can have a certain effect—one minute you're absolutely quiet and the next your mouth is right up against his or her ear.

- **Tactile explorations.** Experiment with different body parts and toys to awaken your partner's erogenous zones and to gradually build excitement. Use hair, breasts, or your genitals to tease, but in such a way as to leave your partner wanting more. You may want to suck on her breasts until she's writhing, then replace your mouth with a feather-light touch. You can play with the inside of his legs and tickle his balls with a vibrator, but hold off touching his penis until you want to move to the next level. Use lots of lubricant when you want to keep things slippery.

- **Love's lovely aroma.** Since you're appealing to all the senses, don't forget the often-overlooked sense of smell. If you know what scents turn your partner on, things like vanilla-scented candles or fragrant massage oil, make them available. Remember, the smell of your own arousal is a potent aphrodisiac, so dip a finger into your vagina or get a dab of pre-come and give your partner a whiff.

- **Temperature play.** Alternating between warm and cool sensations on the body and the genitals can be an incredible turn-on. I heard from one man who kept a bowl of warm water and one of cold, each with a glass dildo immersed in it. His girlfriend went nuts when he switched from the cold to the hot dildo, and vice versa. Freezing a waterproof dildo or microwaving a silicone dildo can achieve a similar effect. Warming gels feel great when they are dabbed on genitals or nipples and blown on or licked off. And oral sex gets a new twist when you suck on an ice cube or a breath mint before placing your mouth on that penis or clit.

- **Play with intense sensations.** If your partner is really turned on and you've agreed that it's okay to explore more intense sensations, consider introducing nipple

Toy Testimonials

"I tied my girlfriend spread-eagled to the bed and took her vibrator, turned it on, and rested it between her legs, so that the business end was resting on her clitoris. While I played with her breast (alternating the use of ice cube and a fur-covered mitt), she writhed her hips around, trying to get the vibrator to touch exactly where she needed it. It's possibly the most exciting thing I have ever seen."

clamps. Nipples fill with blood as you get aroused and become increasingly more sensitive to stimulation. Some folks like having them massaged, pinched, and bitten. Nipple clamps resemble clothespins that can be placed over erect nipples—good ones will let you adjust the amount of pressure they place on your nipples. Once they're on, you can tug on them for intermittent thrills, or find ones that vibrate for an extra buzz. Or roll your partner on to his or her stomach if you want to experiment with spanking. Whether you spank with your hand or a paddle, focus on the well-padded butt and thighs and stay away from bones. Spanking holds an erotic charge for many, because it lends itself well to fantasy play (you naughty boy!). If you're intrigued by intense sensation, find a good book or website on the subject to learn more about role-playing, props, technique, and safety.

• **Go for the climax.** At some point you'll probably want your partner to climax, so decide whether you'll be providing an enjoyable hand job (see the "All Hands on Deck" activity) or having intercourse. Either way, you may want to remove your partner's blindfold so he or she can enjoy the visual, or leave it on so all the attention stays focused on the experience. When your partner has come, and your fun is over, lie down on top of your lover for an intimate finale.

Variations

• Skip the blindfold and your bondage takes on an extra dimension of exhibitionism and voyeurism.
• Consider performing erotic massage on your restrained partner if you want a slow, sensual buildup of sexual excitement.
• If you want to add more toys, try whips or floggers for one ex-

treme and soft fur mitts for the other. Websites and books are a great resource for more toy information.

- You can role-play as part of this activity. Just assume the guise of your favorite pair of power duos (celebrity/groupie, superhero/villain, headmaster/student), and get into your part verbally and/or with props.

Jane's Bonds

by Shanna Germain

Jane's Bonds Martini

- 1.5 ounces gin
- 1.5 ounces vodka
- 1 dash dry vermouth

Mix all ingredients together in a glass with half a dozen ice cubes. Stir and strain into a cocktail glass with olive. Put drink aside while you find alternative uses for leftover ice cubes.

It comes to her by mistake. Although it's her address on the plain brown envelope, it is someone else's name; perhaps the house's previous owner. She and Derek have lived here for almost five years, but they still get mail for the people who owned the house before them, people they've never met. She's about to stick the envelope back in the mailbox with a *please forward* notice on it when something below the name catches her eye: "Or current resident." Oh, that's me, she thinks. It looks like junk mail of some sort, but she opens it anyway.

Inside the envelope is a purple catalog, offering "sexual satisfaction for women." She lies down on the bed and starts flipping through it—she's never seen so many sex toys in her life. Sure, she's been to Fanta-Shes-R-Us downtown (once even with Derek), but it always seemed like all the products were geared toward men—videos that offered nothing more than fake boobs and ugly men grunting, those ridiculous-looking blow-up dolls, and row upon row of cock rings.

But in this catalog (which, she realizes with little surprise, is from a woman-owned company), there are tons of toys for women—cool tie-dyed dildos in pink and purple, lipstick-shape vibrators, even videos directed by women. She flips toward the back and there, tucked away on the last page, is a toy that catches her eye: two purple cuffs lined with fake fur.

She traces her hand along the page, imagining the cuffs' fur-lined softness against her skin. She's never been tied up before, but she's thought of it often, when Derek sometimes takes her hands and presses them to the bed during sex. She wonders if he'd go for it.

She reads the description: "Soft and delicate, yet tough in all the right ways, these fur- and silk-lined bonds are sure to please." And there's even a matching blindfold. She wonders if she should just buy them, let Derek find them somewhere in the house, and act surprised. Or maybe she should put them on her wish list—her thirtieth birthday is coming up.

An image pops into her head of opening a gift like this, late at night, after a good meal and a glass of wine. Perhaps she's already opened her other gifts, and they're cuddled up in bed when Derek reaches beneath the pillow and pulls out the blindfold and cuffs.

They're not gift-wrapped, but it doesn't matter because they're so soft and silky and festive already. She's about to say thank you and wrap her arms around his neck when he grins sheepishly and says, "Shhhh . . . I'm afraid I'll change my mind."

So she lies back and closes her eyes. He fits the blindfold over her eyes a little clumsily, his big fingers fumbling through her hair. She's tingling down to her toes in anticipation—it's all she can do to lie still and let him work. But she doesn't want to scare him, so she stays still, focuses on her breathing—in, out, relax—and enjoys the waves of excitement running through her body. When she opens her eyes, she can't see anything—a little aura of pink light through the fabric, but that's all.

He presses his lips to hers, and she realizes she's never kissed him before without watching him lean closer and closer in anticipation of the impending kiss. But now she doesn't know what to expect, his lips are there and then they are elsewhere, and she doesn't know how to react, how to plan. Instead, his lips light unexpected little fires wherever they land, as though he's pressing fireflies to her skin. He is kissing the curve of her neck when he whispers, "Undress for me."

She feels a jolt of panic. Get undressed? How? She can't see anything. How will she know what she looks like? What if she does something stupid? But he is kissing her along the back of her ear, across the front of her shoulder blade, and she realizes it doesn't matter, that she'll do as he asks because she wants to, because he wants her to.

He helps her to stand, and then she hears him lie back down on the bed. The room around her feels too large, too empty, too alone, even though she knows it isn't. She fights the urge to reach out for something, anything—the dresser, the edge of the bed, the closet door—and instead reaches down to find the tie of her robe. She unties it slowly, then slides it off her shoulders and lets it fall to the ground. Then she takes a deep breath and pulls her tank top slowly over her head and throws it over her shoulder. Her nipples are erect from the excitement and the cold air makes them pucker even more. Then she leans down, and drops her panties down over her feet, and stands back up.

She hears Derek sigh, and tries to imagine where he is in the room, what's he's doing. Then his hands are on her, trailing down her hips and across her thighs, and she realizes he's sitting on the bed and she must be standing right in front of him. He takes her ass in his hands and pulls her toward him, then runs his tongue across her belly button, down her thighs.

"Lie down," he says, and it doesn't even sound like his voice. It's gruffer somehow, more forceful. "Put your arms up," he says, and she does, feeling his strength as he holds both her hands above her with one of his own. Then she feels him slide the cuffs around her wrists, their furry softness caressing her skin, and then tightening and pulling just enough so that she can't slide out. He hooks them to something—she's not sure what—and suddenly she can't move.

"Okay?" he asks tenderly, and she can't do anything but nod. She's not sure what she feels—excitement, anticipation, fear, desire; she wants him to do whatever he wants to her. She would say yes to anything he asked.

Suddenly she realizes there is silence all around her. She can't hear or feel Derek anywhere. Her skin comes alive, and she imagines this is what it's like to be in a horror movie, where you know something's coming for you, but you don't know what it is or where it's going to come from. Or like being prey—every nerve, every muscle twitching, ready to react with a flight-or-fight response. "Derek?" she whispers. She's afraid to break the silence, but she feels like she has to do something. "Derek?"

She doesn't hear anything. A pull on the cuffs only seems to draw them tighter around her wrists. Is he sitting there watching her? Did he leave her here? What if he's taping her? She knows, of course, that he would never do any of these things, but the longer she waits the more the fear creeps in.

Then, finally, she hears a noise. She pricks her ears in that direction, feeling like a wild animal. Is that him? Is it the cat? She can't tell. She feels like her senses are deceiving her. Something cold brushes against her stomach, and she has a moment of near panic—she's ready to rip the cuffs right off—but then she feels Derek's tongue too, next to the coldness, and hears him crunching something in his teeth.

He runs his tongue, along with the ice, up her stomach, leaving a tingling trail of heat and cold, until he reaches her chest and the ice melts. Her stomach does somersaults as he winds his cool tongue around one nipple and presses his palm firmly between her legs. She presses against the flat of his hand, willing him to touch her, stroke her, enter her. She has forgotten she is handcuffed to the bed, that she cannot see. All of her senses are focused on just one spot—she feels that if he doesn't split her open soon, she will explode.

"Please . . ." she whispers. "Please . . ."

"Please what?" Derek asks as he enters the bedroom. She realizes she didn't even hear him come in, and her face flushes with embarrassment. She thinks about pretending she was asleep, then thinks better of it and hands the catalog over to him.

"Please . . . please buy me these," she says softly, pointing to the silk bonds with one tired, trembling finger.

Shop

GETTING THE GOODS: Where to Shop for Sex Toys

Until recently, purchasing a sex toy involved sneaking into a XXX bookstore and choosing from a display of plastic penises while the salesclerk winked from behind the counter. If you were a woman, you could expect a come-on or two from the other patrons and a staff who knew as much about female sexuality as the latest porn flick could teach them. I remember getting up the nerve to shop in one of these stores when I was younger. The small line of vibrators, all kept under a counter, disappointed me, but the clerk noticed my curiosity and directed me to the hottest new item—a talking vibrator. He handed it to me and I turned it on, only to recoil in horror as the thing cackled, "Hey, baby, let me come inside that hot pussy of yours." The clerk seemed genuinely surprised when I exclaimed "Wow, that's obnoxious" and hightailed it out of the store.

Fortunately, today's sex toy shoppers have a lot more options.

Retail boutiques that cater to women and couples have sprouted up in major cities, and most department and drugstores carry at least a vibrator or two. But the real revolution in sex toy shopping came via the Internet, which now offers people the chance to buy adult products anonymously, conveniently, and privately. I'll address the advantages of shopping in person versus online or from catalogs, then you can decide for yourself what works best for you. You can consult the Resources section for individual store listings.

HOW DO YOU LIKE TO SHOP?

In-Store Shopping

Nothing compares to shopping for sex toys in person, from a store you like. You can pick them up, turn them on, touch the material, and get a much better sense of the product than you would from a catalog or website. But notice I said "from a store you like." If the store intimidates you, offends you, or just makes you uncomfortable, you won't want to linger long enough to make an informed decision. But if you're lucky enough to live near one of the retail boutiques that cater to women and couples, you're way ahead of the game. You're more likely to get a quality selection of toys, staff who are knowledgeable about human sexuality, and a more relaxed, non-threatening atmosphere. Most of these retailers have paper catalogs and websites, so you can always look first and buy later.

Even under ideal conditions, it takes some courage to walk into a sex toy store for the first time. During my days as a salesclerk I lost track of the number of times people told me, "I was so scared the first time I came in!" Exhale, take a look around, distract yourself with a book, and just take a moment or two to relax. Try to let go of your preconceived notions about sex and just take in the various products as you encounter them. If you have specific questions, don't hesitate to ask a clerk. If you're unsure what to get, ask what toys are most popular or which ones the staff recommends.

Online Shopping

The Internet and mail order catalogs cater to the large number of people who don't live near a nice toy store or who prefer to do their sex toy shopping in private. Because websites do not have the same economic restrictions as paper catalogs, they are able to devote more space to information, which in turn breeds more informed consumers. By doing a few targeted searches you can find out just exactly how to put on a cock ring, why you'd want to wear a leather corset, or what the Centers for Disease Control has to say about condom elasticity. The savvy consumer can compare prices, track down brand names, read consumer product reviews, or get help with product selection—all without ever talking to a human being. Be sure to read the next chapter, "The Art of the Deal," for useful consumer tips.

The downside to the Internet is that sex toy retailers are a dime a dozen, and separating the wheat from the chaff can take some time if you don't know where to start. The tips at the end of this chapter are intended to help you find better companies or verify the legitimacy of those that are unknown to you. The other perceived drawback to online ordering has to do with concern about the safety of online ordering. Many people are afraid their credit card information might be stolen, but the likelihood of this happening is pretty small, as most companies use encryption software that is difficult to hack. Also, it might ease your mind to know that credit card companies typically won't hold you responsible for fraudulent charges over fifty dollars.

Catalog Shopping

If you don't have Internet access, then what? Fortunately, mail order catalogs, while becoming increasingly overshadowed by the Internet, still represent a thriving part of the sex toy business. You get the same anonymity and convenience the Internet provides, but from a catalog that is mailed to your door. You won't get the same abundance of sex information you'll find online, and it's not terribly easy to compare prices—but if you find a company you like, this option may suit you just fine.

WHERE DO YOU WANT TO SHOP?

Once you've decided whether you want to shop in person or through the mail, you get to decide what type of store you'd like to patronize.

Stores and Sites that Cater to Women and Couples

These get my vote as the best places to shop, because you get good service and quality toys in one place. They prioritize female sexuality, so many of the products are chosen, tested, and reviewed with the woman's experience of sex in mind. That doesn't mean men are absent from the scene—on the contrary, most men enjoy the low-key atmosphere, the sound advice, and the honest product reviews characteristic of these stores. These shops have had a positive impact on the sex toy industry. Since women now comprise a larger percentage of sex toy shoppers, retailers who serve them can effect change behind the scenes, by demanding product designs that reflect customers' specific sexual needs and requesting packaging that's not plastered with porn stars' private parts. Check the Resources section for some notables in this field.

Drugstores and Department Stores

Sex toys are not in huge supply at drugstores, but you can usually pick up a reliable electric (plug-in) vibrator or a name-brand battery vibrator. They won't be advertised as sex toys, so look for them in the health section sold as "massagers." Don't expect the clerk to know much about the sexual uses of the toy, unless of course you get a knowing smile when he or she's ringing you up. A couple of online drugstores now offer sex toys, and they are marketed as such, so perhaps the retail chains will one day follow suit.

Adult Bookstores

These are the traditional venues for sex products, but you can expect the adult videos to far outweigh the toy selection. You can pick up a functional, inexpensive battery vibrator, but there's no vouching for quality, unless you recognize a name brand. The patrons and staff are usually men, so women often find they stick out uncomfortably in these places. Interestingly, Penthouse and Adam and Eve, two large adult video retailers, have launched large retail stores with an eye toward the women and couple's market. You'll find plenty of toys, books, and videos, all presented without quite as much T&A as more hard-core stores, and a youthful staff designed to disarm (but not necessarily to educate).

Specialty Stores

Many stores that cater to the leather or BDSM community carry some basic sex toys. These stores can be a bit sophisticated for the sexual novice, but they do offer good one-stop shopping if you enjoy a little kink with your toys.

HOW DO YOU KNOW IT'S A DECENT STORE?

If you've never shopped in a toy store, or don't like the ones you've seen, these suggestions will help you sift out the better ones.

Finding a Store You Like

- Rely on name recognition. If you remember reading favorable comments about certain companies in a newspaper or magazine, or if you've seen their advertising in reputable publications, chances are good that they're not fly-by-night operations. If it's a retail store and you don't live nearby, find out if they have a catalog or website.
- Get recommendations from friends. Friends who share your tastes can be an excellent source of leads. If you participate in any online discussion groups, ask for referrals. If you've read any sex books (like this one!), see what companies the author recommends in the Resources section.
- Use links from your favorite sex information sites. In other words, if you trust a site, trust its links. Links can be as help-

ful as personal referrals in helping you zero in on specialized resources. For example, BDSM sites will refer you to manufacturers of bondage gear, safer sex sites will refer you to condom shops, and so on.

- Look for a mission statement in catalogs and websites. To distinguish themselves from the masses of carbon-copy adult sites, many companies post a personal introduction or mission statement, which gives you a sense of who's behind the site.

Verifying a Company's Legitimacy

The flip side to the abundance of sex toy venues on the Internet is that some can appear more reputable than they actually are. Check for these basic indications of a company's validity, but a good rule of thumb is to follow your instincts.

- A toll-free number is a good (but not foolproof) indication that a company is at least established enough to foot the bill for your call.
- Order copies of any catalogs or brochures before placing an online order or, if the company doesn't offer any print materials, ask for additional references. How well a company responds to individual requests is a good indication of its commitment to customer service.
- Check to see if the company employs encryption before you order (you'll often see a pop-up window announcing this). If it's not obvious, call or e-mail to find out.
- Check the company's privacy policy. Confirm that the company will not sell, rent, or trade your street or e-mail address to other companies.
- Scratch the surface. Because the women and couples' market for

sex toys has expanded, I've noticed adult companies trying to pass themselves off as tasteful women-run stores without putting much substance behind them. For example, a company might say it's woman-owned, but you can't find or prove there are two X chromosomes anywhere but in the porn videos. Or they claim all toys are individually tested and reviewed, but the reviews are all glowing—and sound suspiciously like the product copy on the back of the box. Peek around a bit, and trust your instincts.

- If you're really dubious about a particular company, check with the Better Business Bureau to see if any complaints have been filed against it. If you're still suspicious, shop somewhere else.

WHAT ARE YOU WAITING FOR?

Exciting sex toys are only a step, a click, or a postage stamp away—so bring one home today!

THE ART OF THE DEAL: Shopping Tips for the Savvy Consumer

There's nothing like expecting a night of fireworks from a sexy new toy only to find out it's got more fizzle than bang. Sometimes this is the fault of the toy, and sometimes this is the fault of the toy buyer. How do you make sure you've chosen the right toy for you? Once you decide, how do you find the quality toys? And is there anything you can do to ensure a good shopping experience? I'll answer these questions and more in an effort to help you become a more confident sex toy consumer.

NARROWING YOUR CHOICES

As often as not, a disappointing toy experience is the result of a toy bought for the wrong reasons—it can't make someone go out with you, it can't fix a broken relationship, it can't express your feelings for you, and it usually won't turn you and your lover into multiply orgasmic sex fiends. Yes, you will always encounter toys that are more hype than help, but if you're clear on what you want from the toy before you go shopping, you're much more likely to meet with success. Where to begin?

Work with What You Know

Plenty of people are interested in sex toys, but they stop short because of that little voice in their head saying, "What in the world would I buy?" That's kind of like looking at a menu and asking, "What would I ever order?" Think about what you like to do in bed, what you've always wanted to try, or what your partner might like to try. Maybe you like massage, so a warming oil would be a nice way to explore erotic massage. Maybe your best friend says her best orgasms come from a vibrator, so you want to try one of those. Maybe you like to watch your partner masturbate, so you'll get him a penis sleeve. Adult videos can be a great way to rev up your imagination and your libido, so consider renting or buying one to see if any of the activities depicted intrigue you. I'll bet a few of the activities in the Play section sparked your interest, so you can start with those toys.

Know Yourself!

I mean this in the biblical sense. Believe it or not, many people buy toys without really thinking about where or how they want to use them. What you need to think about is what you want your toy to do—do you want to stimulate your clitoris or penis to orgasm? Then you're in the market for a vibrator or a penis sleeve. Do you want to find your G spot? You could be looking for a curved dildo or an insertable vibrator. Do you want a toy that'll fit on the penis and vibrate the clitoris during intercourse? Then it's a vibrating cock ring with a clitoral attachment you're after.

If you're not sure what body part you want to stimulate, masturbate. This will help you discover what kind of stimulation you like (hard, soft, slow, fast) so you can choose a toy with a similar intensity or texture. Lots of people share stories of experimenting with things they find around the house as a way of discovering what feels good: a candle might help gauge dildo size, an electric toothbrush might clue you into vibrator intensity, a cardboard toilet roll might turn you on to a penis sleeve.

Know Your Toys

Once you've figured out what body parts you want your toy to stimulate, you'll want to choose a toy that will get the job done just the way you like it. In general, if you can answer the questions on this short checklist, you'll have narrowed down your toy criteria immensely.

- **Purpose.** Do you want a toy that does one thing well or one that stimulates multiple pleasure points?
- **Material.** Do you want a toy that's pliable or one that's firm? Rubber products are the most flexible; silicone and acrylic are the most firm.
- **Shape and size.** Do you want a toy that's anatomically correct or something more whimsical or discreet? If inserting, figure out the length and width you'll want. If you plan to use it anally, make sure it has a flared base.
- **Vibrator intensity.** Electric vibes tend to be stronger than

battery vibes. Look for "intensity" ratings in some catalogs and websites.

- **Vibrator sound.** Coil vibes are the quietest, hard plastic battery vibrators the loudest. Look for "noise" ratings from some catalogs and websites
- **Cleanup.** Nonporous surfaces like silicone, hard plastic, latex, and acrylic are easiest to clean.

Now you can start shopping, or you can review "Toys for All Seasons" if you want more advice on choosing between styles.

FINDING THE GOOD TOYS

Your shopping expedition will be much more successful if you keep one simple maxim in mind: all sex toys are *not* created equal. For decades sex toy manufacturers exploited people's ignorance around sex and sold mediocre toys at inflated prices. Quality sex toys were the exception, not the norm, which no doubt resulted in many disappointing toy experiences. While it's true that there are still a lot of lousy toys being sold today, advancements in technology have resulted in some across-the-board improvements. In addition, increasingly savvy consumers and better access have made it easier for consumers to track down the quality toys.

How can you tell a quality toy from a lousy one? It certainly isn't always visible to the naked eye, but there are a few tricks:

- **Look for name brands.** Some appliance companies like Hitachi and Wahl have long produced quality electric toys. Increasingly, sex toy makers are building reputations for better-made gadgets, so take a quick look at some of the trusted names in the business. Refer to "Toys for all Seasons" for some of the brand names mentioned in this book.

- **Search.** Unless you recognize the brand name, prepare to search for the toy based on its description. Adult retailers often make up their own names for toys, so even if all your friends are raving about the G-Spot Divining Rod, don't restrict yourself to searching for it by this name unless you know exactly where they got it. If you have a physical description, you improve your chances of locating the right toy, especially because common names like Classic Vibe can be used on any number of dissimilar products.

- **Look for reviews.** Some websites will post customers' reviews of their products, giving you a firsthand look at individual experience. Keep in mind, though, that any number of things (unrelated to the toy) can affect a person's sex toy experience, so it pays to be dubious unless there are numerous reviews confirming the toy's strengths or weaknesses.

- **Look for best-sellers.** A lot of companies post best-seller lists, which genuinely reflect the cream of the crop, particularly if you're dealing with a company you trust.

- **Give the toy a quick workout.** If you're shopping in person, by all means pick up the toy and put it through its paces. Turn it on and leave it on to see if it gets hot. Turn the dial on and off quickly to see if it functions smoothly. Give it a gentle shake to see if can withstand a bit of turbulence. Pull on it, twist it, or grip it as hard as you would if you were coming.

- **Be a skeptic.** If the sales hype on a toy sounds too good to be true, it probably is. Once in a while something really exciting comes along that's worthy of the praise. There's usually a groundswell of interest, so try to find supporting customer reviews if you can.

Of course, you can also trust someone else to do the work for you. Plenty of quality sex toy shops have earned a loyal customer base by carrying a higher caliber of product. Check out "Getting the Goods" and Resources for more on this.

BEFORE YOU BUY

No matter what you're buying, being a good consumer requires a little homework. If you put just a fraction of the amount of time you'd spend shopping for a new car into your toy research, particularly if you go online, you're bound to find a selection of quality toys at reasonable prices, along with suggestions for how best to use them. You should also expect the same quality of service you would get from any mainstream retailer.

- **Price compare.** If you're willing to put in some time, you can surf the web and compare prices from dozens of retailers. Two caveats: your lowest price may come from a company you know nothing about, and sex toy retailers don't always use the same name for products. Search on brand names or try to locate a toy by its description if it's got a generic name.
- **Pay attention to shipping charges.** You may find a good price on a product only to see the savings eaten up by excessive freight charges.

- **Research customer service policies before you place your order.** What is the company's return policy on unwanted items and defective items? When can you expect to receive your order? If this information isn't clearly available, call or e-mail the company for an answer. Contrary to what you might expect, most sex toy companies will take returns and exchanges within a reasonable amount of time, so don't settle for less.
- **Check the privacy policy.** Unless you want your e-mail inbox overtaken by spam ads for penis enlargement pills, make sure the company does not sell, rent, or trade your name.
- **Make copies.** When placing a mail order (either online or through a paper catalog), always make or print a copy of the order. This will come in handy should you have problems with your order or need to file a complaint.
- **If you're not satisfied, take action.** Unfortunately, there's not much regulation in the sex toy industry, but you can stop payment on a check, ask your credit card company to refund your money, or complain about the toy store at every opportunity.

KEEP SOME PERSPECTIVE

If you're hesitant to experiment with toys because you're not sure the risk is worth the payoff, here's a little perspective: think of a disappointing sex toy experience as somewhat akin to a disappointing meal out. You might pay sixty dollars at a fancy restaurant for a meal that didn't thrill you, but it wouldn't stop you from trying another new restaurant. When you do stumble on a great restaurant, you've just improved the quality of your life. Accept the fact that not all sex toy experiences will be great ones, but that the more you explore, the more likely you are to end up with the orgasmic equivalent of culinary bliss. And remember, most toys are returnable, so take the risk!

Finally, when you do have a good sex toy shopping experience, spread the word. Because most people imagine sex toy businesses are run by drug lords or corrupt businessmen, it's important to let the world know that's not the case. Tell your friends, your chat buddies, and the toy company. They can't hear it enough. I'll never forget the woman who came back to my store after buying a vibrator to tell me she had dedicated her first vibrator orgasm to me!

Resources

Recommended Toy Stores

(some of these are Internet or mail order only)

My Alma Maters

Good Vibrations
San Francisco, CA
800-289-8423
www.goodvibes.com

Libida
San Francisco, CA
415-822-3035
www.libida.com
Internet only

Toys in Babeland
Seattle, WA, and
New York, NY
800-658-9119
www.babeland.com

Other Good Stores

A Woman's Touch
Madison, WI 53703
888-621-8880
www.a-womans-touch.com

Adam and Eve
Carrboro, NC
800-274-0333
www.adameve.com

Ann Summers
Surrey, Great Britain
0845-456-2320
www.annsummers.com

Blowfish
San Francisco, CA
800-325-2569
www.blowfish.com
Internet only

Come as You Are
Toronto, Ontario
877-858-3160
www.comeasyouare.com

Condomania
Los Angeles, CA, and New York, NY
800-926-6366
www.condomania.com

Eve's Garden
New York, NY
800-848-3837
www.evesgarden.com

Extra Curious
Torrance, CA
866-437-2639
www.extracurious.com
Internet only

Grand Opening!
Los Angeles, CA,
and Brookline, MA
877-731-2626
www.grandopening.com

My Pleasure
San Francisco, CA
866-697-5327
www.mypleasure.com
Internet only

The Pleasure Chest
West Hollywood, CA; Chicago, IL;
New York, NY
800-753-4536
www.thepleasurechest.com

Vixen Creations
San Francisco, CA
415-822-0403
www.vixencreations.com
Internet only

Xandria Collection
Brisbane, CA
800-242-2823
www.xandria.com
Internet only

Womyn's Ware
Vancouver, British Columbia
888-996-9273
www.womynsware.com

Sex Information Hotlines

- American Social Health Association hotline 800-971-8500
- Centers for Disease Control national AIDS hotline 800-342-AIDS
    Spanish 800-344-7432
    Hearing impaired 800-243-7889
- Centers for Disease Control national STD hotline 800-227-8922
- Emergency Contraception hotline 800-584-9911
- National Abortion Federation hotline 800-772-9100
- National Herpes hotline 919-361-8488
- San Francisco Sex Information 415-989-7374
- Seattle Sex Information 206-328-7711

Favorite Sex Sites

Betty Dodson
Sex instruction from one of the pioneers in the sex field
www.bettydodson.com

Clitical
Great resource for female sexuality, with fun product reviews
www.clitical.com

Erotica Readers and Writers Association
Great erotica resource with active community
www.erotica-readers.com

Go Ask Alice
Great Q&A on all matters sexual
www.goaskalice.columbia.edu

Hoot Island
When you need a break from the serious side of sex
www.hootisland.com

Isadora Alman's Sexuality Forum
Intelligent online forum
www.askisadora.com

Jackinworld
The ultimate masturbation resource for men
www.jackinworld.com

Sexuality.About.com
Information and links about sexuality prepared by yours truly
www.sexuality.about.com

Sexy Toy Tales
Sexy erotica starring sex toys
www.sextoytales.com

Society for Human Sexuality
Good how-tos and sexuality resources
www.sexuality.org

The Clitoris
All about that unique spot
www.the-clitoris.com

Vulva University
Free classes in female sexuality
www.vulvauniversity.com

WebMD
Great sexual health resource
www.webMD.com

Recommended Books

Books by Anne Semans

Sexy Mamas: Keeping Your Sex Life Alive While Raising Kids, by Anne Semans
 and Cathy Winks (Inner Ocean, 2004).
The Good Vibrations Guide to Sex, by Cathy Winks and Anne Semans (Cleis
 Press, 2002).
Sex Toy Tales, edited by Anne Semans and Cathy Winks (Down There Press,
 1998).
The Woman's Guide to Sex on the Web, by Anne Semans and Cathy Winks
 (HarperSanFrancisco, 1999).

Other Books

Anal Pleasure and Health, by Jack Morin (Down There Press, 1998).
The Big O, by Lou Paget (Broadway Books, 2001).
The Big Bang, by Emma Taylor and Lorelei Sharkey (Plume, 2003).
The Big Book of Masturbation, by Martha Cornog (Down There Press, 2003).
The Clitoral Truth, by Rebecca Chalker (Seven Stories Press, 2000).
Exhibitionism for the Shy, by Carol Queen (Down There Press, 1995).

Female Ejaculation and the G Spot, by Deborah Sundahl (Hunter House, 2003).

Femalia, edited by Joani Blank (Down There Press, 1993).

The Good Vibrations Guide to the G Spot, by Cathy Winks (Down There Press, 1997).

Good Vibrations: The New Complete Guide to Vibrators, by Joani Blank and Ann Whidden (Down There Press, 2000).

Great Sex: A Man's Guide to Total Body Sensuality, by Michael Castleman (Rodale Press, 2003).

The Guide to Getting It On: A New and Mostly Wonderful Book About Sex, by Goofy Foot Press (Goofy Foot Press, 2000).

The Multi-Orgasmic Couple, by Mantak Chia, Maneewan Chia, Douglas Abrams, and Rachel Carlton Abrams, MD (HarperSanFrancisco, 2000).

Orgasms for Two: The Joy of Partnersex, by Betty Dodson (Harmony Books, 2002).

Sensuous Magic: A Guide to SM for Adventurous Couples, by Patrick Califia (Cleis Press, 2001).

Sex for One: The Joy of Selfloving, by Betty Dodson (Crown Publishers/Harmony Press, 1987).

Sex Toys 101, by Rachel Venning and Claire Cavenaugh (Simon & Schuster, 2003).

The Ultimate Guide to Anal Sex for Men, by Bill Brent (Cleis Press, 2001).

The Ultimate Guide to Anal Sex for Women, by Tristan Taormino (Cleis Press, 1997).

The Ultimate Guide to Strap-on Sex, by Karlyn Lotney (Cleis Press, 2000).

Recommended Videos

Bend Over Boyfriend, Volumes 1–2 (Fatale and SIR Videos, 1998, 1999).

Celebrating Orgasm (Betty Dodson, 1996).

G Marks the Spot (Sex Positive Productions, 2003).

How to Female Ejaculate (Fatale, 1992).

The Joy of Erotic Massage (Sinclair, 2001).

Nina Hartley's Guides

    ... *to Anal Sex* (Adam & Eve, 1996).

    ... *to Cunnilingus* (Adam & Eve, 1994).

    ... *to Fellatio* (Adam & Eve, 1994).

Selfloving (Betty Dodson, 1991).

The Ultimate Guide to Anal Sex for Women, Volumes 1–2 (Evil Angel Productions, 1999, 2001).

Unlocking the Secrets of the G Spot (Sinclair, 1999).

Whipsmart (Sex Positive Productions, 2002).

About the Author

ANNE SEMANS is an author, sex toy fan, and single mom living in San Francisco with her two daughters. She and Cathy Winks have written three other sex books: *Sexy Mamas, The Good Vibrations Guide to Sex,* and *The Woman's Guide to Sex on the Web.* They also edited the popular anthology of sex toy erotica, *Sex Toy Tales.* She owes her interest in sex education to the nun in her eighth-grade English class who instructed her students to "think of a hamburger when your thoughts stray to the impure—it will distract you." Visit her online at www.anneandcathy.com or www.sextoytales.com.

About the Authors of the Steamy Toy Tales

G. Merlin Beck is a San Francisco resident who works in Silicon Valley during the day and writes erotica at night. Beck's short stories appear in several anthologies, including *Erotic Travel Tales II* and *Roughed Up: More Tales of Gay Men, Sex, and Power.*

Kate Dominic is the author of *Any 2 People, Kissing* (Down There Press, 2003). Her erotic short stories have appeared in dozens of publications, including *Herotica 6* and several volumes of *Best Women's* and *Best Lesbian Erotica.* She and her husband are exceptionally fond of the Good Vibrations toy catalog.

Shanna Germain splits her time between writing articles, drinking mochas, and doing "research" for her newest erotic stories. Her work has been published in *Clean Sheets, Good Vibes Magazine, The Sun,* and *Salon.com.* Learn all about her at www.shannagermain.com.

Colin Ladd is a writer specializing in various genres, including occasional forays into erotica. He's part of the lively web discussion group at Erotic Writers and Readers Association (www.erotica-readers.com), and hopes to write a longer work of erotica, encompassing his broader interests, ranging from archaeology to wine. He lives in Europe with his girlfriend and cat.

Lauren Mills began writing erotica several years ago as a creative outlet from an oftentimes stressful day job. She is a sales manager for a conservative computer company. She's been happily married for twenty-one years and has two teenage daughters. She loves reading, writing, golfing, chocolate, and red meat.

MADELEINE OH is a transplanted Brit, retired teacher, and grandmother now living in Ohio with her husband of thirty-three years. She has erotic short stories in several anthologies, a full-length novel, and several novellas published by Elloras Cave, available at www.ellorascave.com.

JULIA REBECCA is a writer, artist, and sailor who lives in the Caribbean. Her stories have been accepted for publication in *Closet Desire IV, Swing: Third Party Sex,* and an *Erotic Women* anthology. Forthcoming erotic works include stories, poetry, and a sexually oriented board game.

JOY VANNUYS is a chef and a writer who lives in Brooklyn, New York. Her work has recently appeared in *On Our Backs, Nervy Girl, Grunt and Groan* (Boheme Press), *Best Bisexual Women's Erotica* (Cleis Press), and *Best American Erotica 2004*. Visit Joy on the web at www.JoyVanNuys.com.

SAGE VIVANT operates Custom Erotica Source (www.customeroticasource. com), the home of tailor-made erotic fiction for individual clients since 1998. Her work appears in numerous anthologies. She is the author of *29 Ways to Write Great Erotica* (www.29eroticways.com), editor of *Swing: Third Party Sex,* and coeditor of two books with M. Christian.

KRISTINA WRIGHT lives in Virginia with her amazing husband, a menagerie of pets, and an impressive collection of sex toys. Her erotic fiction has appeared in numerous anthologies, including *Best Lesbian Erotica 2004, Sweet Life: Stories of Sexual Fantasy & Adventure,* and *Ripe Fruit: Well Seasoned Erotica*. Contact her at KristinaCW@aol.com.